*The Love-Letters of Robert Browning and
    Elizabeth Barrett*

A Selection

*The Love-Letters of Robert Browning
and Elizabeth Barrett*

---

*Selected and with an Introduction
by V. E. Stack*

HEINEMANN : LONDON

William Heinemann Ltd
LONDON   MELBOURNE   TORONTO
JOHANNESBURG   AUCKLAND

First published 1969

Selection and Introduction © V. E. Stack 1969
434 73490 X

Printed in Great Britain by Cox & Wyman Ltd
London, Fakenham and Reading

To the memory of my sister

God be thanked, the meanest of his creatures

Boasts two soul-sides, one to face the world with,

One to show a woman when he loves her!

ROBERT BROWNING, 'ONE WORD MORE'.

Contents

Illustrations

Preface

These letters were first published in 1899, ten years after Robert Browning's death, by Smith, Elder in London and by Harper Brothers in America. In 1913, a new edition of them was published by John Murray Ltd, to whom I am much indebted for their generous permission to make this selection. I am also grateful to Miss Hannah D. French, Research Librarian at Wellesley College Library, for her help and for permission to reproduce two facsimiles of the letters; to Miss Moira Lynd of Messrs. Heinemann's for her invaluable advice and encouragement; and to my friend Helen Liddell for her help in the preparation of the Index.

Browning's son, in his original introductory 'Note' to the letters, wrote:

'. . Ever since my mother's death these letters were kept by my father in a certain inlaid box, into which they exactly fitted, and where they have always rested, letter beside letter, each in its consecutive order and numbered on the envelope by his own hand.

'My father destroyed all the rest of his correspondence, and not long before his death he said, referring to these letters: "There they are, do with them as you please when I am dead and gone!" '

His son interpreted these words as sanction for the publication of this intimate correspondence, and posterity has been grateful to him. It has, however, for long been out of print as a self-contained collection, although constantly referred to in critical and biographical work on the Brownings. In its entirety it is of great importance and interest to scholars; the present selection is intended to introduce these splendid letters to a wider public.

In this edition, as in the previous ones, the writers' original punctuation has for the most part been preserved, including

Elizabeth's very individual use of dots and dashes in mid-sentence. A few errors of transcription have been corrected. To avoid confusion, omissions made by the editor are indicated by a row of small dashes (- - -). (Postscripts, however, are omitted without this sign.) The addresses on the envelopes of the letters, which all passed through the post, are not reproduced, since they did not vary: Browning's were all sent to 50 Wimpole Street, and Elizabeth's to New Cross, Hatcham, Surrey.

Sonnets from the Portuguese are printed as an appendix to the letters. Although they were first shown to her husband three years after their marriage, and not published until 1850 (under a fanciful title intended to make them seem less intimately personal), Elizabeth almost certainly composed them during the months covered by her correspondence with Browning. This is suggested by the references on pp. 98 and 150, and still more strongly by the close relationship in thought and feeling between the sonnets and her letters. Two short poems by Browning which also seem especially relevant to this period have been added.

V.E.S.

Introduction

The Browning–Barrett love-story has always had a very obvious popular appeal. It is dramatic, unusual, highly charged with personal feeling; the 'happy ending' completes it to everyone's satisfaction. Two stage versions of it have attracted romance-loving theatre-goers: Rudolf Besier's play, 'The Barretts of Wimpole Street', first produced in 1930, and 'Robert and Elizabeth', a fantasy version in the form of a musical, current in London during the 1960s. It is only when one reads the letters exchanged by Browning and Elizabeth during the months between their first acquaintance and their marriage that one realizes how hopelessly over-simplified and foreshortened any stage presentation of their story must be. These letters give us the reality, of which 'The Barretts of Wimpole Street' and 'Robert and Elizabeth' are the merest shadows. Both writers were exceedingly fluent, and they needed, and rejoiced in, an almost daily exchange of letters, which continued even when they were meeting two or three times a week at Elizabeth's home. Nearly six hundred letters passed between them, and these give us an extraordinarily vivid impression not only of the depth of feeling between two completely articulate lovers, but of the close sympathy between two creative minds.

Browning wrote his first letter to Elizabeth in January 1845, when he was thirty-two and she was thirty-eight. They knew each other's poetry, and had friends and acquaintances in common, but their lives up to this point had not touched.

Elizabeth Barrett Moulton Barrett, the eldest child of Edward and Mary Moulton Barrett, was born on March 6th, 1806, at Coxhoe Hall, Co. Durham. Eight sons and three more daughters (one of whom died in infancy) were to follow, and it is against the background of this very large family, whose members continued to live under the same roof long after they were all grown up, that we must see Elizabeth's early life. Of her mother, who died in 1828, we know little; Elizabeth wrote of her later as 'very tender - - - and of a nature harrowed up into some furrows by the pressure of circumstances . . . A sweet, gentle nature, which the thunder a little turned from its sweetness.'[1] Her two surviving sisters, Henrietta and Arabel, were very dear to her, and figure constantly in her letters; but the member of the family most closely linked to her in an intimate affection was the brother next to her in age – Edward, two years younger than herself.

In 1809, the family moved to Hope End, Mr. Barrett's newly-built house in Herefordshire. In one of her letters to Browning,[2] Elizabeth writes of these childhood years in the country: 'it was a lonely life, growing green as the grass round it' – made happy by the companionship of her dearly-loved brother, and above all by her books, her poetry – ('I used to make rhymes over my bread and milk when I was nearly a baby')[3] – and that sense of dedication to the poetic life which developed in her very early and was to remain a passion with her throughout life. She had no formal education; Browning tells us in his Prefatory Note to her Collected Poems (1887) that she was 'self-taught in almost every respect', and acquired her knowledge and love of Greek through sharing in her brother Edward's lessons. She was reading and studying over an immensely wide field while she was still a child, and her long Preface to 'The Battle of Marathon', written in imitation of Pope's 'Iliad' when she was thirteen, is strikingly mature in expression, recondite in its allusions, and convinced in its ideas, for a child of that age. Its Preface opens in fine style: 'That Poetry is the first, and most celebrated of all the fine arts, has not been denied in any age, or by any philosopher. The culture of the soul, which Sallust so nobly describes, is necessary to those refined pleasures and elegant enjoyments, in which man

[1] Letter to R.B., Aug. 27th, 1846.
[2] Letter to R.B., March 20th, 1845.
[3] Letter to R.B., Jan. 17th, 1846.

xiv

displays his superiority to brutes.' References to Sappho, Homer, Virgil, Cicero, Horace, Montesquieu and many other writers, together with a considerable sprinkling of classical quotations, must have convinced her readers – (her father had the poems privately printed for her) – that here was a remarkably learned little girl. Six years later she published, together with some shorter poems, 'An Essay on Mind' (whose plan, she writes in the Preface, embraces 'the sublime circuit of intellect'), and in 1833 a translation of Aeschylus' 'Prometheus Bound' (afterwards rewritten).

The Barrett family had meanwhile, in 1832, left Hope End and gone to live in Sidmouth, Devon; thence, in 1835 they moved to London. It was three years, however, before Mr. Barrett found a house to his permanent liking – 50 Wimpole Street; here they all settled in 1838, and in this year Elizabeth published 'The Seraphim, and other poems'. It was at this time that she suffered a serious breakdown in health. She had already had one alarming illness, in 1821, and now an affection of the lungs (whose exact nature remains conjectural) made her for several years an almost complete invalid. She was sent out of London, to Torquay, accompanied by her brother Edward; and here in 1840 occurred the overwhelming tragedy of his death by drowning – a loss which for a time completely prostrated her, and which for the rest of her life she could never bear to speak of. She went back to London in 1841, and her family gradually came to regard her as a permanent invalid. She lay on her sofa, as she says herself, 'all day, and day after day'; she seldom left her room, received few visitors, and could see no happier future for herself. Nevertheless, she lived with intensity the life of the mind. She read ceaselessly; she was a brilliant and copious letter-writer, and corresponded eagerly with her friends; she was in touch with some of the writers and scholars of the day, and was vividly aware of what was going on in the world of letters. Especially interesting to us are her comments on Browning's poetry, to which she often refers in her letters to Miss Mitford,[1] an intimate friend; she is critical of his 'want of harmony' – ('what I miss most in Mr. Browning, is *music*')[2] – but

[1] Mary Russell Mitford (1787–1855), author of *Our Village* and other works.
[2] Letter to Miss Mitford, July 17th, 1841.

recognizes in his work 'the palpable presence of poetic genius everywhere';[1] in another letter[2] she calls him 'a true soul-piercing poet'. She wrote critiques and reviews, and in 1842 contributed to the *Athenaeum* a series of articles on 'The Greek Christian Poets'; she was becoming, indeed, a well-known figure in the literary world. But above all she was a poet, wholly devoted to her calling; and during these invalid years she was composing her new *Poems*, published in 1844. They made a substantial volume, which included the long poem 'A Drama of Exile' (the exile of Adam and Eve from Paradise), twenty-eight sonnets, and a number of romantic ballads and miscellaneous poems. She wrote of them in her Preface: '- - - While my poems are full of faults, – as I go forward to my critics and confess, – they have my heart and life in them - - - Poetry has been as serious a thing to me as life itself; and life has been a very serious thing; there has been no playing at skittles for me in either. I never mistook pleasure for the final cause of poetry; nor leisure, for the hour of the poet. I have done my work, so far, as work, .. as the completest expression of that being to which I could attain, – and as work I offer it to the public - - -'

These were the poems which were to bring her not only critical renown but the admiration and love of a fellow-poet.

Robert Browning, the only son of his parents, was born at Camberwell on May 7th, 1812; his only sister, two years later. His father was a clerk in the Bank of England who, in early manhood, had worked in the West Indies, in charge of slave labour on a plantation owned by his mother, a Creole, but had abandoned all his prospects there, and returned to comparatively pedestrian employment in England, owing to his hatred of the slave-system. (His son was later to write with admiration of his action – 'If we are poor, it is to my father's infinite glory'.)[3] Mr. Browning was a bibliophile and a scholar; Robert grew up in a house overflowing with thousands of books, and imbibed class-ical learning from his father almost from babyhood – in this way:

[1] Ditto, October 14th, 1842.

[2] Ditto, May 4th, 1843.

[3] Letter to E.B.B., August 26th, 1846.

My Father was a scholar and knew Greek.
When I was five years old, I asked him once
'What do you read about?' 'The siege of Troy.'
'What is a siege and what is Troy?' Whereat
He piled up chairs and tables for a town,
Set me a-top for Priam, called our cat
– Helen, enticed away from home (he said)
By wicked Paris, who couched somewhere close
Under the footstool ..[1]

and so on. His scholarly father was evidently no pedant. He was
also gentle, generous and kind, and his son's references to
him in later life are full of affection; he speaks of him as 'chivalrous', and 'tender-hearted to a fault'.[2] With his mother, Browning
had an especially close relationship; it has indeed been suggested[3]
that he was too much dominated and influenced by her in youth.
We know from his letters that he recognized a link of exceptional
strength between them; when they are both ill, he writes: 'The
connection between our ailings is no fanciful one', and quotes his
doctor as saying: 'Why, has anybody to search far for a cause of
whatever nervous disorder you may suffer from, when *there* sits
your mother .. whom you so absolutely resemble - - - I can
trace every feature'[4] - - - Mrs. Miller speaks of his childhood as
'sheltered, enclosed, dependent', and this it certainly was; securely
founded, too, on the love and sympathy of his parents. Of them
both, he writes: 'Since I was a child I never worked for the least or
greatest thing within the compass of their means to give, but given
it was, – nor for liberty but it was conceded, nor confidence but
it was bestowed.'[5] He was not an easy-tempered child – (he
describes himself as 'born supremely passionate')[6] – and his
aggressive, turbulent nature must have made exceptional demands
on their tolerance and understanding.

To all intents and purposes, he was educated at home. As child

[1] 'Development' (from R.B.'s 'Asolando', pub. 1889).
[2] Letter to E.B.B., August 27th, 1846.
[3] e.g. by Betty Miller in 'Robert Browning, a portrait'.
[4] Letter to E.B.B., August 22nd, 1846.
[5] Letter to E.B.B., June 12th, 1846.
[6] Letter to E.B.B., December 22nd, 1845.

and boy, he attended private schools in the neighbourhood of his home, but they made no lasting impression on him, and as a pupil he did not especially distinguish himself. He left school at fourteen, and for the next three years was taught by tutors at home. The bias of this education was almost wholly literary and musical, and included, according to his biographer Mrs. Orr, none of 'those subjects which train, even coerce, the thinking powers, and which were doubly requisite for a nature in which the creative imagination was predominant over all the other mental faculties'. When he was sixteen, he attended some classes in Greek at London University, but gave them up after not much more than a term. He had decided to be a poet – and a poet he became. Financial struggles and anxieties played little part in his life, either now or later, and he seems to have accepted with equanimity, and always recognized with gratitude, his dependence upon a generous father.

At twenty-one, Browning published, anonymously, 'Pauline, a Fragment of a Confession'. It was kindly reviewed by the editor of *The Monthly Repository*, Mr. W. J. Fox, who had known Browning when he was a boy and became his patron and friend; but it made no impact on other critics, and Browning himself regarded it in after years with something like aversion, calling it 'altogether foolish and *not* boylike - - - ambiguous, feverish'.[1] At this time of his life he was profoundly influenced by Shelley, and later wished perhaps to forget how passionately he had invoked him in this poem: 'Sun-treader, life and light be thine for ever!' During the next twelve years, he wrote prolifically: 'Paracelsus'; 'Sordello'; 'Pippa Passes' and 'Dramatic Lyrics' (Nos. I and III of the pamphlet series, 'Bells and Pomegranates'); and five plays – 'Strafford', 'King Victor and King Charles', 'The Return of the Druses', 'A Blot in the 'Scutcheon' and 'Colombe's Birthday'. But his genius was very far from being fully recognized; it is strange, indeed, to reflect that in 1845 Elizabeth Barrett was probably the better-known and more greatly-admired poet of the two. He had had no success as a playwright; his intimacy for a time with the actor Macready had led to short-lived productions of 'Strafford' and 'A Blot in the 'Scutcheon', but none of his other

[1] Letter to E.B.B., January 15th, 1846.

plays had been produced on the stage. His social life was a very full one, and he had a wide circle of literary friends, including John Forster, chief literary critic of *The Examiner* (who had immediately recognized the power and promise of 'Paracelsus', treated with 'entire contempt'[1] by other reviewers). Carlyle became an intimate and life-long friend. 'I know Carlyle and love him,' he wrote to Elizabeth;[2] and again, 'I went to Chelsea and found dear Carlyle alone - - - He was all kindness, and talked like his own self while he made me tea - - - at night he would walk as far as Vauxhall Bridge on my way home.'[3]

'Home' was now at New Cross, Hatcham, to which the Brownings had moved in 1840. Here was the intimate and unchanging family circle; in London, literary and theatrical life, abundantly exciting for a young writer – to whom, nevertheless, the encouragement of full acceptance and recognition was persistently denied. Of any strong attachments to women during these years there is no record, and on this subject his own words, later, were specific: 'I have made myself almost ridiculous by a kind of male prudery with respect to "young ladies" - - - I have seemed to imply – "If I gave you the least encouragement something would be sure to follow" ';[4] and: 'Before I knew you, women seemed not so much better than myself, – therefore, no love for them!'[5] He had made up his mind, he says, to 'the impossibility of loving any woman'.[6] But the supreme good fortune of happy love was in fact awaiting him. Soon after his return from a voyage to Italy, late in December 1844, he read Elizabeth Barrett's 'Poems', published in the preceding August. He had heard of her frequently through his friend John Kenyon, her distant cousin, and had long admired her poetry; it now occurred to him that he would write to her and say so. But he had, he says, no slightest idea of the significance of what he was doing. 'I did write, on the whole, UNWILLINGLY .. with conscious-

[1] Letter to E.B.B., December 9th, 1845.
[2] Letter to E.B.B., February 26th, 1845.
[3] Letter to E.B.B., August 8th, 1845.
[4] Letter to E.B.B., May 22nd, 1846.
[5] Letter to E.B.B., August 10th, 1846.
[6] Letter to E.B.B., September 17th, 1845.

ness of having to *speak* on a subject which I *felt* thoroughly concerning, and could not be satisfied with an imperfect expression of. As for expecting THEN what has followed .. I shall only say I was scheming how to get done with England and go to my heart in Italy.'[1] Nevertheless, on January 10th, 1845, he picked up his pen and wrote.[2]

'I love your verses with all my heart, dear Miss Barrett' – Browning plunges into his first letter without a conventional opening. He does not go on to discuss or analyse the 'verses'; indeed, he says he finds himself unable to do so; but 'into me it has gone, and part of me has it become, this great living poetry of yours, not a flower of which but took root and grew - - - I do, as I say, love these books with all my heart – and I love you too.' This last sentence stays in our memories because of what it foreshadows; but as interesting, to a perceptive ear, is that most individual phrase: 'not a flower of which but took root and grew' – might not that almost be a line of his poetry? We shall often hear in his letters these echoes or suggestions of his poetic voice.

Elizabeth in her reply acknowledges with delight her pleasure in 'the sympathy of a poet, and such a poet!' and asks for criticisms of the faults in her writing: 'the most frequent general criticism I receive is, I think, upon the style, – "if I *would* but change my style!" But that is an objection (isn't it?) to the writer bodily? Buffon says, and every sincere writer must feel, that "Le style c'est l'homme" - - -' This first exchange of letters already shows us the intellectual sympathy between their writers, which becomes even clearer in their subsequent letters – especially in the earlier, less intimately personal ones. It would perhaps be unreasonable to expect from them any really dispassionate appraisal of each other's work; but Elizabeth, especially, is often shrewd in her judgments: ' "Mist" is an infamous word for your kind of obscurity. You never *are* misty – not even in "Sordello" – never vague. Your graver cuts deep sharp lines, always – and

[1] Letter to E.B.B., November 17th, 1845.
[2] All subsequent quotations are from letters exchanged between R.B. and E.B.B.

there is an extra-distinctness in your images and thoughts, from the midst of which, crossing each other infinitely, the general significance seems to escape.' She has, too, many perceptive and often memorable things to say about other writers – Carlyle, for instance, who 'sees things in broad blazing lights, but - - - does not analyse them like a philosopher'. Most illuminating of all, however, are the letters in which she and Browning write of the poetic vision, the creative process itself. Elizabeth writes: 'What no mere critic sees, but what you, as an artist, know, is the difference between the thing desired and the thing attained, between the idea in the writer's mind and the $\epsilon\ddot{\iota}\delta\omega\lambda o\nu$ [1] in his work - - - the great chasm between the thing I say, and the thing I would say, would be quite dispiriting to me - - - if the desire did not master the despondency.' And again: 'Like to write? of course, of course I do. I seem to live while I write – it is life, for me. Why, what is to live? Not to eat and drink and breathe, – but to feel the life in you down all the fibres of being, passionately and joyfully. And thus, one lives in composition surely – not always – but when the wheel goes round and the process is uninterrupted.'

Both Browning and Elizabeth are natural, rapid writers, delighting in the expression of their thoughts on paper; and their individual voices are clear, strong and characteristic. Browning has a splendid description of a spider, who might well figure in one of his poems – 'a great fellow that housed himself, with real gusto, in the jaws of a great scull, whence he watched me as I wrote'. Elizabeth's vivid, effortless prose has a vigour of its own, quite distinct from the abrupt energy of Browning's. Her description of a tree struck by lightning[2] is brilliant, highly-coloured, rapid; it reads as if it had been written at speed. We observe, incidentally, how precise and entertaining, in a quite unsentimental way, are her descriptions of her spaniel Flush, who has 'a very good, stout vainglory of his own', and 'looks beautiful scorn out of his golden eyes, when I order him to do this or that'. (Flush, alas, bit Browning – 'he hates all unpetticoated people'.)

Everything in these letters, however, is of secondary interest

[1] Image.
[2] See p. 25.

compared with the intense and often very complex personal feelings expressed in them; they are love-letters, and it is as such that they have become part of our literature. Even in the earliest of them there is warmth and directness, and we can see how this natural sympathy becomes gradually more ardent and whole-hearted. 'Real warm Spring, dear Miss Barrett', writes Browning on February 26th (1845) - - - 'and in Spring I shall see you, surely see you – for when did I once fail to get whatever I had set my heart upon?' In the early summer the date of his first visit to 50 Wimpole Street was fixed at last, and on Tuesday May 20th they saw each other for the first time. Browning wrote to her that evening a letter full of rather incoherent happiness, ending 'I am proud and happy in your friendship – now and ever. May God bless you!' On Friday of the same week, after receiving her reply, he wrote again, and this letter is the only one in the whole series which is missing, for he destroyed it at her request. We may easily conjecture its nature. 'You do not know,' she wrote, 'what pain you give me by speaking so wildly . . you have said some intemperate things . . fancies, – which you will not say over again, nor unsay, but *forget at once.*' Browning replies, at immense length, that she has misunderstood him; Elizabeth, also at considerable length, accepts his explanation; the 'friendship and sympathy' are uninterrupted.

This was in May 1845. Three months later, the feeling between them is running very deep, and the letter written by Browning on August 30th may perhaps be regarded as crucial. Its headlong, vehement style – tortuous and parenthetical in construction, but almost agonizingly careful and lucid in choice of words – gives the impression of a man still painfully controlling an almost overwhelming emotion. Elizabeth's long answer is completely characteristic of her: analytical, fine-drawn, subtle in feeling and expression. Its theme – her sense of unworthiness, her fear of injuring him, is to be endlessly repeated, dissected, debated and re-debated between them. Elizabeth dwells on it almost obsessively; we sometimes weary (as did Browning, perhaps, in an anguished sort of way) of so much self-scrutiny, self-analysis, meticulous examination of thoughts, motives, wishes. At this point in their relationship, it cannot prevent their deepest feelings

xxii

from finding full expression at last; on October 2nd, Browning ends his letter: 'Let me kiss your hand – dearest! My heart and life – all is yours, and forever – God make you happy as I am through you – Bless you.' They love one another, and know it. But over and over again, in the months that follow, Elizabeth returns to the idea that he is making too great a sacrifice for her; that he is the giver, she the taker. Only two months before their marriage, she can agonize him by saying that it would be better for him to leave her. Yet she can also write: 'I have none in the world who will hold me to make me live in it, except only you. I have come back for you alone .. at your voice and because you have use for me.' Here are the shortest words, nearly all monosyllables, for the deepest feelings; and in the most moving of their letters, passion and tenderness are often so expressed. But in their most intimate words of love we often find, too, the poet's delight in imagery, which for them is the natural language of the heart – as when Elizabeth writes of her life before she knew Browning – ('the long wilderness *without* the blossoming rose .. and the capacity for happiness, like a black gaping hole, before this silver flooding') – or Browning of his joy in her letters – ('the old treasure is piled undiminished and still the new comes glittering in').

The period covered by these letters is twenty months – from January 10th, 1845, to September 18th, 1846. On September 11th, Elizabeth wrote to Browning for the last time before their marriage – ('Dearest, I write one word, and have one will which is yours - - -'). A tremendous decision had been taken, after weeks of increasing strain, uncertainty, danger; only by reading the letters of these last two months can we realize exactly and intimately what degree of courage had been needed on both sides before this great moment of achievement was reached.

The ominous figure of Elizabeth's father now dominates the situation – has indeed dominated it from the outset. His relations with his daughter could well form the subject of a complete separate study; but we are here concerned with him only as he figures in these letters. Generous and affectionate as are many of her references to him, she leaves Browning (and us) in no doubt about his rigid authoritarianism, and his intolerance of any challenge to it. She knew, of course, and told Browning, that the idea of marriage on the part of any of his children was in his eyes an intolerable assertion of independence; his implacable opposition to hers must be expected as a certainty. (In one of her letters, she recalls the 'dreadful scenes' in which her sister Henrietta has been involved, 'only because she had seemed to feel a little. I hear how her knees were made to ring upon the floor, now!') Her father's presence became increasingly oppressive to her as the plans for a secret marriage began to take definite shape; and her emotions were made more complex, and therefore more torturing, by the clear-sighted affection which she still felt for him. 'In that strange, stern nature there is a capacity to love – and I love him – and I shall suffer, in causing him to suffer.' To understand something of Elizabeth's feelings during these last months before her marriage, we have also to realize – and her letters make it easy for us to do so – how much she was distressed by the necessity for conceal-ment and evasion with such personal friends as Mrs. Jameson and Mr. Kenyon; and it was inevitable too that she should dread, chiefly for Browning's sake, the general censure which both of them anticipated and were prepared to face, but which might react upon, for instance, his parents. Browning, in June, wanted to tell them everything, but Elizabeth hesitated painfully: 'You should avoid committing them further than is necessary, and so exposing them to unpleasant remarks and reproaches from *my family* - - - yet I may be wrong here, .. and you, in any case, are the master, to act as you see best.'

The heavy, almost fearful, responsibility lay, indeed, with Browning. The letters in which he and Elizabeth discuss their future financial position show that this was not a serious anxiety to him; but the risk to her health, possibly to her life, was grim enough, and the long strain of delay was perhaps almost more intolerable for him than for her. (In April 1846, he writes: 'Any obstacle now, would be more than I could bear – I feel I *must* live with you, – if but for a year, a month – to express the love which words cannot express.') The six weeks preceding their marriage were full of painful and increasing tension. It was Elizabeth who had to suffer all the incidental alarms, the half-suspicions, the dangers of discovery; her sisters knew of her engagement, but others only guessed at it. We get the impression that she was living a kind of knife-edge existence which she could hardly have endured much longer – ('I am so nervous that my own footsteps startle me' - - - 'To hear the voice of my father and meet his eye makes me shrink back – to talk to my brothers leaves my nerves all trembling.') Browning wrote, on August 31st, of 'the hatefulness of this state of things which is prolonged so uselessly'. For the last two months they had been considering ways and means – dates, routes, destinations; final decisions on these matters were now imminent. (There was an unhappy interlude, involving much incidental misery for Elizabeth: Flush was stolen, and not returned to her until ransom money had been paid for him.) What finally precipitated events, and made their marriage and departure a matter of sudden and extreme urgency, was Mr. Barrett's 'edict' on September 10th that 50 Wimpole Street was to be left 'empty for a month in order to its cleaning', and a house taken for the family at Dover, Reigate or Tunbridge Wells. 'We are to go therefore and not delay', wrote Elizabeth. Browning's reply was decisive: 'We must be *married directly* and go to Italy - - - Your words, first and last, have been that you "would not fail me".' 'I shall not fail to you – I do not, I will not,' answered Elizabeth. They were secretly married in St. Marylebone Parish Church on September 12th.

There was to be another week of strain for Elizabeth, living under her father's roof as before, her marriage unsuspected by her family – ('I did hate so, to have to take off the ring!') She is haunted by the thought of her father: 'I will put myself under his feet, to be forgiven a little, .. enough to be taken up again into his arms. I love him – he is my father – he has good and high qualities after all - - - Surely I may say to him - - - "with the exception of this act, I have submitted to the least of your wishes all my life long. Set the life against the act, and forgive me, for the sake of the daughter you once loved".' Remembering such tender and compassionate words, we find it difficult indeed to forgive her father for his implacable, life-long refusal of reconciliation and love.

Elizabeth wrote her last letter to Browning on the night of

September 18th. ('- - - Do you pray for me to-night, Robert? Pray for me, and love me, that I may have courage, feeling both.') Next day, accompanied by her maid Wilson and taking Flush with them, she and her husband left for Italy together. She was to have nearly fifteen years of happy and creative married life, to bear her husband a son, and in 1861 to die peacefully in his arms.

To read these letters is to be given a marvellously clear vision of great love, and great courage; and to understand something also of the complexity of human relationships. That these two poets wrote to each other with so much joy, so much power to express what for most men is inexpressible in language – this is our great good fortune. For Browning and Elizabeth themselves, these written words were a necessity of their love, strongly woven into its very pattern. Browning himself wrote their regretful little epitaph:

'How strange it will be to have no more letters!'

New Cross, Hatcham, Surrey
(Post-mark, January 10, 1845)

I love your verses with all my heart, dear Miss Barrett, – and this is no off-hand complimentary letter that I shall write, – whatever else, no prompt matter-of-course recognition of your genius, and there a graceful and natural end of the thing. Since the day last week when I first read your poems, I quite laugh to remember how I have been turning and turning again in my mind what I should be able to tell you of their effect upon me, for in the first flush of delight I thought I would this once get out of my habit of purely passive enjoyment, when I do really enjoy, and thoroughly justify my admiration – perhaps even, as a loyal fellow-craftsman should, try and find fault and do you some little good to be proud of hereafter! – but nothing comes of it all – so into me has it gone, and part of me has it become, this great living poetry of yours, not a flower of which but took root and grew – Oh, how different that is from lying to be dried and pressed flat, and prized highly, and put in a book with a proper account at top and bottom, and shut up and put away .. and the book called a 'Flora', besides! After all, I need not give up the thought of doing that, too, in time; because even now, talking with whoever is worthy, I can give a reason for my faith in one and another excellence, the fresh strange music, the affluent language, the exquisite pathos and true new brave thought; but in this addressing myself to you – your own self, and for the first time, my feeling rises altogether. I do, as I say, love these books with all my heart – and I love you too. Do you know I was once not very far from seeing – really seeing you?

1

Mr. Kenyon[1] said to me one morning 'Would you like to see Miss Barrett?' then he went to announce me, – then he returned .. you were too unwell, and now it is years ago, and I feel as at some untoward passage in my travels, as if I had been close, so close, to some world's-wonder in chapel or crypt, only a screen to push and I might have entered, but there was some slight, so it now seems, slight and just sufficient bar to admission, and the half-opened door shut, and I went home my thousands of miles, and the sight was never to be?

Well, these Poems were to be, and this true thankful joy and pride with which I feel myself,

Yours ever faithfully,

ROBERT BROWNING

E.B.B. TO R.B.

50 Wimpole Street: Jan. 11, 1845

I thank you, dear Mr. Browning, from the bottom of my heart. You meant to give me pleasure by your letter – and even if the object had not been answered, I ought still to thank you. But it is thoroughly answered. Such a letter from such a hand! Sympathy is dear – very dear to me: but the sympathy of a poet, and of such a poet, is the quintessence of sympathy to me! Will you take back my gratitude for it? – agreeing, too, that of all the commerce done in the world, from Tyre to Carthage, the exchange of sympathy for gratitude is the most princely thing!

For the rest you draw me on with your kindness. It is difficult to get rid of people when you once have given them too much pleasure – *that* is a fact, and we will not stop for the moral of it. What I was going to say – after a little natural hesitation – is, that if ever you emerge without inconvenient effort from your 'passive state', and will *tell* me of such faults as rise to the surface and strike you as important in my poems, (for of course, I do not think of troubling you with criticism in detail) you will confer a lasting obligation on me, and one which I shall value so much,

[1] John Kenyon, 1784–1856; poet and philanthropist; E.B.B.'s distant cousin.

that I covet it at a distance. I do not pretend to any extraordinary meekness under criticism and it is possible enough that I might not be altogether obedient to yours. But with my high respect for your power in your Art and for your experience as an artist, it would be quite impossible for me to hear a general observation of yours on what appear to you my master-faults, without being the better for it hereafter in some way. I ask for only a sentence or two of general observation – and I do not ask even for *that*, so as to tease you – but in the humble, low voice, which is so excellent a thing in women – particularly when they go a-begging! The most frequent general criticism I receive, is, I think, upon the style, – 'if I *would* but change my style'! But *that* is an objection (isn't it?) to the writer bodily? Buffon says, and every sincere writer must feel, that 'Le style c'est l'homme'; a fact, however, scarcely calculated to lessen the objection with certain critics.

Is it indeed true that I was so near to the pleasure and honour of making your acquaintance? and can it be true that you look back upon the lost opportunity with any regret? *But* – you know – if you had entered the 'crypt', you might have caught cold, or been tired to death, and *wished* yourself 'a thousand miles off'; which would have been worse than travelling them. It is not my interest, however, to put such thoughts in your head about its being 'all for the best'; and I would rather hope (as I do) that what I lost by one chance I may recover by some future one. Winters shut me up as they do dormouse's eyes; in the spring, *we shall see*: and I am so much better that I seem turning round to the outward world again. And in the meantime I have learnt to know your voice, not merely from the poetry but from the kindness in it. Mr. Kenyon often speaks of you – dear Mr. Kenyon! – who most unspeakably, or only speakably with tears in my eyes, – has been my friend and helper, and my book's friend and helper! critic and sympathiser, true friend of all hours! You know him well enough, I think, to understand that I must be grateful to him.

I am writing too much, – and notwithstanding that I am writing too much, I will write of one thing more. I will say that I am your debtor, not only for this cordial letter and for all the pleasure which came with it, but in other ways, and those the highest:

3

and I will say that while I live to follow this divine art of poetry, in proportion to my love for it and my devotion to it, I must be a devout admirer and student of your works. This is in my heart to say to you – and I say it.

And, for the rest, I am proud to remain

Your obliged and faithful

ELIZABETH B. BARRETT

R.B. TO E.B.B.

New Cross, Hatcham, Surrey
Jan. 13, 1845

Dear Miss Barrett,

- - - What 'struck me as faults', were not matters on the removal of which, one was to have – poetry, or high poetry, – but the very highest poetry, so I thought, and that, to universal recognition. For myself, or any artist, in many of the cases there would be a positive loss of time, peculiar artist's pleasure – for an instructed eye loves to see where the brush has dipped twice in a lustrous colour, has lain insistingly along a favourite outline, dwelt lovingly in a grand shadow; for these 'too muches' for the everybody's picture are so many helps to the making out the real painter's picture as he had it in his brain. And all of the Titian's Naples Magdalen must have once been golden in its degree to justify that heap of hair in her hands – the *only* gold effected now!

But about this soon – for night is drawing on and I go out, yet cannot, quiet at conscience, till I report (to *myself*, for I never said it to you, I think) that your poetry must be, cannot but be, infinitely more to me than mine to you – for you *do* what I always wanted, hoped to do, and only seem now likely to do for the first time. You speak out, *you*, – I only make men and women speak – give you truth broken into prismatic hues, and fear the pure white light, even if it is in me, but I am going to try; so it will be no small comfort to have your company just now, seeing that when you have your men and women aforesaid, you are busied with them, whereas it seems bleak, melancholy work, this talking to the wind (for I have begun) – yet I don't think I shall let *you* hear, after all, the savage things about Popes and imaginative religions that I must say - - -

4

You will never more, I hope, talk of 'the honour of my acquaintance', but I will joyfully wait for the delight of your friendship, and the spring, and my Chapel-sight after all!

Ever yours most faithfully,

R. BROWNING

50 Wimpole Street: Jan. 15, 1845

Dear Mr. Browning,

The fault was clearly with me and not with you.

When I had an Italian master, years ago, he told me that there was an unpronounceable English word which absolutely expressed me, and which he would say in his own tongue, as he could not in mine – 'testa lunga'. Of course, the signor meant *headlong*! – and now I have had enough to tame me, and might be expected to stand still in my stall. But you see I do not. Headlong I was at first, and headlong I continue – precipitously rushing forward through all manner of nettles and briars instead of keeping the path; guessing at the meaning of unknown words instead of looking into the dictionary – tearing open letters, and never untying a string, – and expecting everything to be done in a minute, and the thunder to be quick as the lightning. And so, at your half word I flew at the whole one, with all its possible consequences, and wrote what you read - - -

In art, however, I understand that it does not do to be headlong, but patient and laborious – and there is a love strong enough, even in me, to overcome nature. I apprehend what you mean in the criticism you just intimate, and shall turn it over and over in my mind until I get practical good from it. What no mere critic sees, but what you, an artist, know, is the difference between the thing desired and the thing attained, between the idea in the writer's mind and the εἰδωλον[1] cast off in his work. All the effort – the quick'ning of the breath and beating of the heart in pursuit, which is ruffling and injurious to the general effect of a composition; all of which you call 'insistency', and which many would call superfluity, and which *is* superfluous in a sense – *you* can pardon, because you understand. The great chasm between

[1] Image.

5

the thing I say, and the thing I would say, would be quite dispiriting to me, in spite even of such kindnesses as yours, if the desire did not master the despondency. 'Oh for a horse with wings!' - - -

In one thing, however, you are wrong. Why should you deny the full measure of my delight and benefit from your writings? I could tell you why you should not. You have in your vision two worlds, or to use the language of the schools of the day, you are both subjective and objective in the habits of your mind. You can deal both with abstract thought and with human passion in the most passionate sense. Thus, you have an immense grasp in Art; and no one at all accustomed to consider the usual forms of it, could help regarding with reverence and gladness the gradual expansion of your powers. Then you are 'masculine' to the height – and I, as a woman, have studied some of your gestures of language and intonation wistfully, as a thing beyond me far! and the more admirable for being beyond - - -

I did not talk of the 'honour of your acquaintance' without a true sense of honour, indeed; but I shall willingly exchange it all (and *now*, if you please, at this moment, for fear of worldly mutabilities) for the 'delight of your friendship'.

Believe me, therefore, dear Mr. Browning,

Faithfully yours, and gratefully,

ELIZABETH B. BARRETT

R.B. TO E.B.B.

New Cross, Hatcham, Monday Night
(Post-mark, January 28, 1845)

Dear Miss Barrett,

Your books lie on my table here, at arm's length from me, in this old room where I sit all day: and when my head aches or wanders or strikes work, as it now or then will, I take my chance for either green-covered volume, as if it were so much fresh trefoil to feel in one's hands this winter-time, – and round I turn, and, putting a decisive elbow on three or four half-done-with 'Bells'[1] of mine, read, read, read, and just as I have shut up the

[1] *Bells and Pomegranates*, poems by R.B., published in pamphlet form between 1841 and 1846.

6

book and walked to the window, I recollect that you wanted me to find faults there, and that, in an unwise hour I engaged to do so. Meantime the days go by (the whitethroat is come and sings now) and as I would not have you 'look down on me from your white heights' as promise breaker, evader, or forgetter, if I could help: and as, if I am very candid and contrite, you may find it in your heart to write to me again – who knows? – I shall say at once that the said faults cannot be lost, must be *somewhere*, and shall be faithfully brought you back whenever they turn up, – as people tell one of missing matters - - -

If you hate writing to me as I hate writing to nearly everybody, I pray you never write – if you do, as you say, care for anything I have done. I will simply assure you, that meaning to begin work in deep earnest, *begin* without affectation, God knows, – I do not know what will help me more than hearing from you, – and therefore, if you do not so very much hate it, I know I *shall* hear from you – and very little more about your 'tiring me'.

Ever yours faithfully,
ROBERT BROWNING

E.B.B. TO R.B.

50 Wimpole Street: Feb. 3, 1845

Why how could I hate to write to you, dear Mr. Browning? Could you believe in such a thing? If nobody likes writing to everybody (except such professional letter writers as you and I are *not*), yet everybody likes writing to somebody, and it would be strange and contradictory if I were not always delighted both to hear from *you* and to write to *you*, this talking upon paper being as good a social pleasure as another, when our means are somewhat straitened - - -

And if you will only promise to treat me en bon camarade, without reference to the conventionalities of 'ladies and gentlemen', taking no thought for your sentences (nor for mine), nor for your blots (nor for mine), nor for your blunt speaking (nor for mine), nor for your badd speling (nor for mine), and if you agree to send me a blotted thought whenever you are in the mind for it, and with as little ceremony and less legibility

B

than you would think it necessary to employ towards your printer – why, *then*, I am ready to sign and seal the contract, and to rejoice in being 'articled' as your correspondent. Only *don't* let us have any constraint, any ceremony! *Don't* be civil to me when you feel rude, – nor loquacious when you incline to silence, – nor yielding in the manners when you are perverse in the mind. See how out of the world I am! Suffer me to profit by it in almost the only profitable circumstance, and let us rest from the bowing and the courtesying, you and I, on each side. You will find me an honest man on the whole, if rather hasty and prejudging, which is a different thing from prejudice at the worst. And we have great sympathies in common, and I am inclined to look up to you in many things, and to learn as much of everything as you will teach me. On the other hand you must prepare yourself to forbear and to forgive – will you? While I throw off the ceremony, I hold the faster to the kindness - - -

Ever faithfully yours,
ELIZABETH B. BARRETT

R.B. TO E.B.B.

Wednesday morning – Spring!
(Post-mark, February 26, 1845)

Real warm Spring, dear Miss Barrett, and the birds know it; and in Spring I shall see you, surely see you – for when did I once fail to get whatever I had set my heart upon? As I ask myself sometimes, with a strange fear - - -

I know Tennyson 'face to face', – no more than that. I know Carlyle and love him – know him so well, that I would have told you he had shaken that grand head of his at 'singing', so thoroughly does he love and live by it. When I last saw him, a fortnight ago, he turned, from I don't know what other talk, quite abruptly on me with, 'Did you never try to write a *Song*? Of all things in the world, *that* I should be proudest to do.' Then came his definition of a song – then, with an appealing look to Mrs. C., 'I always say that some day in *spite of nature and my stars*, I shall burst into a song' - - - and then he began to recite an old Scotch song, stopping at the first rude couplet, "The beginning

8

words are merely to set the tune, they tell me' – and then again at the couplet about – or, to the effect that – 'give me' (but in broad Scotch) 'give me but my lass, I care not for my cogie'. '*He says*,' quoth Carlyle magisterially, 'that if you allow him the love of his lass, you may take away all else, even his cogie, his cup or can, and he cares not,' just as a professor expounds Lycophron. And just before I left England, six months ago, did not I hear him croon, if not certainly sing, 'Charlie is my darling' ('my *darling*' with an adoring emphasis), and then he stood back, as it were, from the song, to look at it better, and said 'How must that notion of ideal wondrous perfection have impressed itself in this old Jacobite's "young Cavalier" – ("They go to save their land, and the *young Cavalier*!!") – when I who care nothing about such a rag of a man, cannot but feel as he felt in speaking his words after him!' - - -

Who told you of my sculls and spider webs – Horne?[1] Last year I petted extraordinarily a fine fellow, (a *garden* spider – there was the singularity, – the thin clever-even-for a spider-sort, and they are *so* 'spirited and sly', all of them – this kind makes a long cone of web, with a square chamber of vantage at the end, and there he sits loosely and looks about), a great fellow that housed himself, with real gusto, in the jaws of a great scull, whence he watched me as I wrote, and I remember speaking to Horne about his good points. Phrenologists look gravely at that great scull, by the way, and hope, in their grim manner, that its owner made a good end. He looks quietly, now, out at the green little hill behind - - -

Ever yours faithfully,

ROBERT BROWNING

E.B.B. TO R.B.

50 Wimpole Street: Feb. 27, 1845

Yes, but, dear Mr. Browning, I want the spring according to the new 'style' (mine), and not the old one of you and the rest

---

[1] Richard Hengist Horne (1803–1884), a prolific and versatile writer, chiefly remembered for his epic poem 'Orion'; one of the E.B.B.'s correspondents.

of the poets. To me unhappily, the snowdrop is much the same as the snow – it feels as cold underfoot – and I have grown sceptical about 'the voice of the turtle', the east winds blow so loud. April is a Parthian with a dart, and May (at least the early part of it) a spy in the camp. *That* is my idea of what you call spring; mine, in the *new style*! A little later comes my spring; and indeed after such severe weather, from which I have just escaped with my life, I may thank it for coming at all. How happy you are, to be able to listen to the 'birds' without the commentary of the east wind, which, like other commentaries spoils the music. And how happy I am to listen to you, when you write such kind open-hearted letters to me! I am delighted to hear all you say to me of yourself, and 'Luria',[1] and the spider, and to do him no dishonour in the association, of the great teacher of the age, Carlyle, who is also yours and mine. He fills the office of a poet – does he not? – by analysing humanity back into its elements, to the destruction of the conventions of the hour. That is – strictly speaking – the office of the poet, is it not? – and he discharges it fully, and with a wider intelligibility perhaps as far as the contemporary period is concerned, than if he did forthwith 'burst into a song'.

But how I do wander! – I meant to say, and I will call myself back to say, that spring will really come some day I hope and believe, and the warm settled weather with it, and that then I shall be probably fitter for certain pleasures than I can appear even to myself now - - -

Ever faithfully yours,
E.B.B.

R.B. TO E.B.B.

Sunday Night, March 1 (1845)

Dear Miss Barrett,

I seem to find of a sudden – surely I knew before – anyhow, I *do* find now, that with the octaves on octaves of quite new golden strings you enlarged the compass of my life's harp with, there is added, too, such a tragic chord, that which you touched, so gently, in the beginning of your letter I got this morning, 'just

[1] R.B.'s tragedy – ('all in my brain yet') – published in 1846.

escaping' &c. But if my truest heart's wishes avail, as they have hitherto done, you shall laugh at East winds yet, as I do! See how, this sad feeling is so strange to me, that I must write it out, *must*, and you might give me great, the greatest pleasure for years and yet find me as passive as a stone used to wine libations, and as ready in expressing my sense of them, but when I am pained, I find the old theory of the uselessness of communicating the circumstances of it, singularly untenable. I have been 'spoiled' in this world – to such an extent, indeed, that I often *reason* out – make clear to myself – that I might very properly, so far as myself am concerned, take any step that would peril the whole of my future happiness – because the past is gained, secure, and on record; and, though not another of the old days should dawn on me, I shall not have lost my life, no! Out of all which you are – please – to make a sort of sense, if you can, so as to express that I have been deeply struck to find a new real unmistakable sorrow along with these as real but not so new joys you have given me - - -

Yours ever,
R.B.

E.B.B. TO R.B.

March 5, 1845

But I did not mean to strike a 'tragic chord'; indeed I did not! Sometimes one's melancholy will be uppermost and sometimes one's mirth, – the world goes round, you know – and I suppose that in that letter of mine the melancholy took the turn. As to 'escaping with my life', it was just a phrase – at least it did not signify more than that the sense of mortality, and discomfort of it, is peculiarly strong with me when east winds are blowing and waters freezing. For the rest, I am *essentially better*, and have been for several winters; and I feel as if it were intended for me to live and not die, and I am reconciled to the feeling - - -

You are not to think – whatever I may have written or implied – that I lean either to the philosophy or affectation which beholds the world through darkness instead of light, and speaks of it wailingly. Now, may God forbid that it should be so with me.

I am not desponding by nature, and after a course of bitter mental discipline and long bodily seclusion, I come out with two learnt lessons (as I sometimes say and oftener feel), – the wisdom of cheerfulness – and the duty of social intercourse. Anguish has instructed me in joy, and solitude in society; it has been a wholesome and not unnatural reaction. And altogether, I may say that the earth looks the brighter to me in proportion to my own deprivations. The laburnum trees and rose trees are plucked up by the roots – but the sunshine is in their places, and the root of the sunshine is above the storms. What we call Life is a condition of the soul, and the soul must improve in happiness and wisdom, except by its own'fault. These tears in our eyes, these faintings of the flesh, will not hinder such improvement - - -

Also, writing as from friend to friend – as you say rightly that we are – I ought to confess that of one class of griefs (which has been called too the bitterest), I know as little as you. The cruelty of the world, and the treason of it – the unworthiness of the dearest; of these griefs I have scanty knowledge. It seems to me from my personal experience that there is kindness everywhere in different proportions, and more goodness and tenderheartedness than we read of in the moralists. People have been kind to *me*, without understanding me, and pitiful to me, without approving of me: – nay, have not the very critics tamed their beardom for me, and roared delicately as sucking doves, on behalf of me? I have no harm to say of your world, though I am not of it, as you see. And I have the cream of it in your friendship, and a little more, and I do not envy much the milkers of the cows.

How kind you are! – how kindly and gently you speak to me! Some things you say are very touching, and some, surprising; and although I am aware that you unconsciously exaggerate what I can be to you, yet it is delightful to be broad awake and think of you as my friend.

May God bless you!

Faithfully yours,
ELIZABETH B. BARRETT

Tuesday Morning
(Post-mark, March 12, 1845)

- - - You think - - - that I 'unconsciously exaggerate what you are to me'. Now, you don't know what *that* is, nor can I very well tell you, because the language with which I talk to myself of these matters is spiritual Attic, and 'loves contractions', as grammarians say; but I read it myself, and well know what it means, that's why I told you I was self-conscious – I meant that I never yet mistook my own feelings, one for another – there! - - - Do you think I shall see you in two months, three months? I may travel, perhaps. So you have got to like society, and would enjoy it, you think? For me, I always hated it – have put up with it these six or seven years past, lest by foregoing it I should let some unknown good escape me, in the true time of it, and only discover my fault when too late; and now that I have done most of what is to be done, *any* lodge in a garden of cucumbers for me! I don't even care about reading now – the world, and pictures of it, rather than writings about the world! But you must read books in order to get words and forms for 'the public' if you *write*, and *that* you needs must do, if you fear God. I have no pleasure in writing myself – none, in the mere act – though all pleasure in the sense of fulfilling a duty, whence if I have done my real best, judge how heart-breaking a matter must it be to be pronounced a poor creature by critic this and acquaintance the other! But I think you like the operation of writing as I should like that of painting or making music, do you not? After all, there is a great delight in the heart of the thing; and use and forethought have made me ready at all times to set to work – but – I don't know why – my heart sinks whenever I open this desk, and rises when I shut it. Yet but for what I have written you would never have heard of me – and *through* what you have written, not properly *for* it, I love and wish you well! Now, will you remember - - - how you have promised to let me know if my wishing takes effect, and if you still continue better? And not even .. (since we are learned in magnanimity) don't even tell me that or anything else, if it teases you, but wait your own good

13

time, and know me for .. if these words were but my own, and
fresh-minted for this moment's use! ..

Yours ever faithfully,
R. BROWNING

E.B.B. TO R.B.

50 Wimpole Street: March 20,1845

- - - What you say of society draws me on to many comparative
thoughts of your life and mine. You seem to have drunken of the
cup of life full, with the sun shining on it. I have lived only
inwardly; or with *sorrow*, for a strong emotion. Before this
seclusion of my illness, I was secluded still, and there are few of
the youngest women in the world who have not seen more, heard
more, known more, of society, than I, who am scarcely to be
called young now. I grew up in the country – had no social
opportunities, had my heart in books and poetry, and my experience in reveries. My sympathies drooped towards the ground like
an untrained honeysuckle – and but for *one*, in my own house –
but of this I cannot speak. It was a lonely life, growing green
like the grass around it. Books and dreams were what I lived in –
and domestic life only seemed to buzz gently around, like the
bees about the grass. And so time passed, and passed – and afterwards, when my illness came and I seemed to stand at the edge of
the world with all done, and no prospect (as appeared at one
time) of ever passing the threshold of one room again; why then,
I turned to thinking with some bitterness (after the greatest
sorrow of my life had given me room and time to breathe) that I
had stood blind in this temple I was about to leave – that I had
seen no Human nature, that my brothers and sisters of the earth
were *names* to me, that I had beheld no great mountain or river,
nothing in fact. I was as a man dying who had not read Shakespeare and it was too late! do you understand? And do you also
know what a disadvantage this ignorance is to my art? Why, if I
live on and yet do not escape from this seclusion, do you
not perceive that I labour under signal disadvantages – that I am,
in a manner, as a *blind poet*? Certainly, there is a compensation

to a degree. I have had much of the inner life, and from the habit of self-consciousness and self-analysis, I make great guesses at Human nature in the main. But how willingly I would as a poet exchange some of this lumbering, ponderous, helpless knowledge of books, for some experience of life and man, for some ..

But all grumbling is a vile thing. We should all thank God for our measures of life, and think them enough for each of us - - - I have lived all my chief *joys*, and indeed nearly all emotions that go warmly by that name and relate to myself personally, in poetry and poetry alone. Like to write? Of course, of course I do. I seem to live while I write – it is life, for me. Why, what is to live? Not to eat and drink and breathe, – but to feel the life in you down all the fibres of being, passionately and joyfully. And thus, one lives in composition surely – not always – but when the wheel goes round and the procession is uninterrupted. Is it not so with you? oh – it must be so. For the rest, there will be necessarily a reaction; and, in my own particular case, whenever I see a poem of mine in print, or even smoothly transcribed, the reaction is most painful. The pleasure, the sense of power, without which I could not write a line, is gone in a moment; and nothing remains but disappointment and humiliation. I never wrote a poem which you could not persuade me to tear to pieces if you took me at the right moment! I have a *seasonable* humility, I do assure you - - -

May God Bless you!

Ever and truly yours,

E.B.B.

R.B. TO E.B.B.

Tuesday Morning
(Post-mark, May 13, 1845)

- - - 'If you ask me, I must ask myself'[1] – that is, when I am to see you – I will *never* ask you! You do *not* know what I shall estimate that permission at, – nor do I, quite – but you do – do

[1] In her previous letter, E.B.B. had written: 'Shall I have courage to see you soon, I wonder! If you ask me, I must ask myself.'

15

not you? know so much of me as to make my 'asking' worse than a form – I do not 'ask' you to write to me – not *directly* ask, at least.

I will tell you – I ask you *not* to see me so long as you are unwell, or mistrustful of –

No, no, that is being too grand! Do see me when you can, and let me not be only writing myself,

Yours
R.B.

E.B.B. TO R.B.

Thursday
(Post-mark, May 16, 1845)

But how 'mistrustfulness'? - - - What have I said or done, *I*, who am not apt to be mistrustful of anybody and should be a miraculous monster if I began with *you*! What can I have said, I say to myself again and again - - -

Well! – but this is to prove that I am not mistrustful, and to say, that if you care to come to see me you can come; and that it is my gain (as I feel it to be) and not yours, whenever you do come. You will not talk of having come afterwards I know, because although I am 'fast bound' to see one or two persons this summer (besides yourself, whom I receive of choice and willingly) I *cannot* admit visitors in a general way – and putting the question of health quite aside, it would be unbecoming to lie here on the sofa and make a company-show of an infirmity, and hold a beggar's hat for sympathy. I should blame it in another woman –and the sense of it has had its weight with me sometimes - - -

Also, . . as to the how and when - - - you must choose whether you would like best to come with Mr. Kenyon or to come alone – and if you would come alone, you must just tell me on what day, and I will see you on any day unless there should be an unforeseen obstacle, . . any day after two, or before six. And my sister will bring you up-stairs to me; and we will talk; or *you* will talk; and you will try to be indulgent, and like me as well as you can. If, on the other hand, you would rather come with Mr. Kenyon, you must wait, I imagine, till June, – because he goes away on Monday and is not likely immediately to return – no, on Saturday, tomorrow.

In the meantime, why I should be 'thanked', is an absolute mystery to me – but I leave it!

You are generous and impetuous; *that*, I can see and feel; and so far from being of an inclination to mistrust you or distrust you, I do profess to have as much faith in your full, pure loyalty, as if I had known you personally as many years as I have appreciated your genius. Believe this of me – for it is spoken truly - - -

Always your friend,

E.B.B.

R.B. TO E.B.B.

Tuesday Evening[1]
(Post-mark, May 21, 1845)

I trust to you for a true account of how you are – if tired, if not tired, if I did wrong in any thing, – or, if you please, *right* in any thing – (only, not one more word about my 'kindness', which, to get done with, I will grant is exceptive) – but, let us so arrange matters if possible, – and why should it not be – that my great happiness, such as it will be if I see you, as this morning, from time to time, may be obtained at the cost of as little inconvenience to you as we can contrive. For an instance – just what strikes me – they all say here I speak very loud – (a trick caught from having often to talk with a deaf relative of mine). And did I stay too long?

I will tell *you* unhesitatingly of such 'corrigenda' – nay I will again say, do not humiliate me – *do not* again, – by calling me 'kind' in that way.

I am proud and happy in your friendship – now and ever. May God bless you!

R.B.

[1] R.B. had that day paid his first visit to E.B.B., lasting one and a half hours.

Wednesday Morning
(Post-mark, May 22, 1845)

Indeed there was nothing wrong – how could there be? And there was everything right – as how should there not be? And as for the 'loud speaking', I did not hear any – and, instead of being worse, I ought to be better for what was certainly (to speak it, or be silent of it,) happiness and honour to me yesterday.

Which reminds me to observe that you are so restricting our vocabulary, as to be ominous of silence in a full sense, presently. First, one word is not to be spoken – and then, another is not. And why? Why deny me the use of such words as have natural feelings belonging to them – and how can the use of such be 'humiliating' to *you*? If my heart were open to you, you could see nothing offensive to you in any thought there or trace of thought that has been there – but it is hard for you to understand, with all your psychology (and to be reminded of it I have just been looking at the preface of some poems by some Mr. Gurney where he speaks of 'the reflective wisdom of a Wordsworth and the profound psychological utterances of a Browning') it is hard for you to understand what my mental position is after the peculiar experience I have suffered, and what $\tau i \ \dot{\epsilon} \mu o i \ \kappa a i \ \sigma o i$[1] a sort of feeling is irrepressible from me to you, when, from the height of your brilliant happy sphere, you ask, as you did ask, for personal intercourse with me. What words but 'kindness' .. but 'gratitude' – but I will not in any case be *un*kind and *un*grateful, and do what is displeasing to you. And let us both leave the subject with the words – because we perceive in it from different points of view; we stand on the black and white sides of the shield; and there is no coming to a conclusion.

But you will come really on Tuesday – and again, when you like and can together – and it will not be more 'inconvenient' to me to be pleased, I suppose, than it is to people in general – will it, do you think? Ah – how you misjudge! Why it must obviously and naturally be delightful to me to receive you here when you

[1] 'What have I to do with thee?'

18

like to come, and it cannot be necessary for me to say so in set words – believe it of

Your friend,
E.B.B.

Friday Evening
(Post-mark, May 24, 1845)

I intended to write to you last night and this morning, and could not, – you do not know what pain you give me in speaking so wildly. And if I disobey you, my dear friend, in speaking, (I for my part) of your wild speaking, I do it, not to displease you, but to be in my own eyes, and before God, a little more worthy, or less unworthy, of a generosity from which I recoil by instinct and at the first glance, yet conclusively; and because my silence would be the most disloyal of all means of expression, in reference to it. Listen to me then in this. You have said some intemperate things .. fancies, – which you will not say over again, nor unsay, but *forget at once*, and *for ever, having said at all*; and which (so) will die out between *you and me alone*, like a misprint between you and the printer. And this you will do *for my sake* who am your friend (and you have none truer) – and this I ask, because it is a condition necessary to our future liberty of intercourse. You remember – surely you do – that I am in the most exceptional of positions; and that, just *because of it*, I am able to receive you as I did on Tuesday; and that, for me to listen to 'unconscious exaggerations', is as unbecoming to the humilities of my position, as unpropitious (which is of more consequence) to the prosperities of yours. Now, if there should be one word of answer attempted to this; or of reference; *I must not* .. I *will not see you again* – and you will justify me later in your heart. So for my sake you will not say it – I think you will not – and spare me the sadness of having to break through an intercourse just as it is promising pleasure to me; to me who have so many sadnesses and so few pleasures. You will! – and I need not be uneasy – and I shall

---

[1] The letter from R.B. to which this one refers was sent back to him by E.B.B. and destroyed at her request; see pp. 23 and 120–1.

19

owe you that tranquillity, as one gift of many. For, that I have much to receive from you in all the free gifts of thinking, teaching, master-spirits, .. *that*, I know! – it is my own praise that I appreciate you, as none can more. Your influence and help in poetry will be full of good and gladness to me – for with many to love me in this house, there is no one to judge me .. *now*. Your friendship and sympathy will be dear and precious to me all my life, if you indeed leave them with me so long or so little. Your mistakes in me .. which *I* cannot mistake (– and which have humbled me by too much honouring –) I put away gently, and with grateful tears in my eyes; because *all that hail* will beat down and spoil crowns, as well as 'blossoms'.

If I put off next Tuesday to the week after – I mean your visit, – shall you care much? For the relations I named to you, are to be in London next week; and I am to see one of my aunts whom I love, and have not met since my great affliction – and it will all seem to come over again, and I shall be out of spirits and nerves. On Tuesday week you can bring a tomahawk and do the criticism, and I shall try to have my courage ready for it – Oh, you will do me so much good – and Mr. Kenyon calls me 'docile' sometimes I assure you; when he wants to flatter me out of being obstinate – and in good earnest, I believe I shall do everything you tell me - - -

You are not displeased with me? *no, that* would be hail and lightning together – I do not write as I might, of some words of yours – but you know that I am not a stone, even if silent like one. And if in the *un*silence, I have said one word to vex you, pity me for having had to say it – and for the rest, may God bless you far beyond the reach of vexation from my words or my deeds!

Your friend in grateful regard,

E.B.B.

R.B. TO E.B.B.

Saturday Morning
(Post-mark, May 24, 1845)

Don't you remember I told you, once on a time, that you 'knew nothing of me'? whereat you demurred – but I meant what I said, and knew it was so. To be grand in a simile, for every poor speck of a Vesuvius or a Stromboli in my microcosm there are huge layers of ice and pits of black cold water – and I make the most of my two or three fire-eyes, because I know by experience, alas, how these tend to extinction – and the ice grows and grows – still this last is true part of me, most characteristic part, *best* part perhaps, and I disown nothing – only, – when you talked of 'knowing me'! Still, I am utterly unused, of these late years particularly, to dream of communicating anything about *that* to another person (all my writings are purely dramatic as I am always anxious to say) that when I make never so little an attempt, no wonder if I *bungle* notably – 'language', too, is an organ that never studded this heavy heavy head of mine. Will you not think me very brutal if I tell you I could almost smile at your misapprehension of what I meant to write? – Yet I *will* tell you, because it will undo the bad effect of my thoughtlessness, and at the same time exemplify the point I have all along been honestly earnest to set you right upon .. my real inferiority to you; just that and no more. I wrote to you, in an unwise moment, on the spur of being again 'thanked', and, unwisely writing just as if thinking to myself, said what must have looked absurd enough as seen apart from the horrible counterbalancing never-to-be-written *rest of me* – by the side of which, could it be written and put before you, my note would sink to its proper and relative place, and become a mere 'thank you' for your good opinion – which I assure you is far too generous – for I really believe you to be my superior in many respects, and feel uncomfortable till *you* see that, too – since I hope for your sympathy and assistance, and frankness is everything in such a case - - - I am, from my heart, sorry that by a foolish fit of inconsideration I should have given pain for a minute to you, towards whom, on every account, I would rather soften and 'sleeken every word as to a bird' .. (and, not such a bird as my black self that go screeching about the world for 'dead horse' – corvus (picus) – mirandola!). I, too, who have been at such pains to acquire the reputation I enjoy in the world, – (ask Mr. Kenyon,) and who dine, and wine, and dance and enhance the company's pleasure till they make me ill and I keep house, as of late: Mr. Kenyon, (for I only quote where you may verify if you please) *he* says my common sense strikes him,

21

and its contrast with my muddy metaphysical poetry! And so it shall strike you – for though I am glad that, since you *did* misunderstand me, you said so, and have given me an opportunity of doing by another way what I wished to do in *that*, – yet, if you had *not* alluded to my writing, as I meant you should not, you would have certainly understood *something* of its drift when you found me next Tuesday precisely the same quiet (no, for I feel I speak too loudly, in spite of your kind disclaimer, but –) the same mild man-about-town you were gracious to, the other morning – for, indeed, my own way of worldly life is marked out long ago, as precisely as yours can be, and I am set going with a hand, winkerwise, on each side of my head, and a directing finger before my eyes, to say nothing of an instinctive dread I have that a certain whip-lash is vibrating somewhere in the neighbourhood in playful readiness! So 'I hope here be proofs', Dogberry's satisfaction that, first, I am but a very poor creature compared to you and entitled by my wants to look up to you, – all I meant to say from the first of the first – and that, next, I shall be too much punished if, for this piece of mere inconsideration, you deprive me, more or less, or sooner or later, of the pleasure of seeing you, – a little over boisterous gratitude for which, perhaps, caused all the mischief! - - - Pray write me a line to say, 'Oh .. if *that's* all!' and remember me for good (which is very compatible with a moment's stupidity) and let me not for one fault, (and that the only one that shall be), lose *any pleasure* .. for your friendship I am sure I have not lost – God bless you, my dear friend!

R. BROWNING

And by the way, will it not be better, as co-operating with you more effectually in your kind promise to forget the 'printer's error' in my blotted proof, to send me back that same 'proof', if you have not inflicted proper and summary justice on it? - - -

E.B.B. TO R.B.

Sunday
(May 25, 1845)

I owe you the most humble of apologies dear Mr. Browning, for having spent so much solemnity on so simple a matter, and I hasten to pay it; confessing at the same time (as why should I not?) that I am quite as much ashamed of myself as I ought to be, which is not a little - - - I may say however, in a poor justice to myself, that I wrote what I wrote so unfortunately, *through reverence for you*, and not at all from vanity on my own account .. although I do feel palpably while I write these words here and now, that I might as well leave them unwritten; for that no man of the world who ever lived in the world (not even *you*) could be expected to believe them, though said, sung, and sworn.

So I here enclose to you your letter back again, as you wisely desire; although you never could doubt, I hope for a moment, of its safety with me in the completest of senses: and then, from the heights of my superior .. stultity, and other qualities of the like order, .. I venture to advise you .. however (to speak of the letter critically, and as the dramatic composition it is) it is to be admitted to be very beautiful, and well worthy of the rest of its kin in the portfolio, .. 'Lays of the Poets', or otherwise, .. I venture to advise you to burn it at once - - - After which friendly turn, you will do me the one last kindness of forgetting all this exquisite nonsense, and of refraining from mentioning it, by breath or pen, *to me or another*. Now I trust you so far: – you will put it with the date of the battle of Waterloo – and I, with every date in chronology; seeing that I can remember none of them. And we will shuffle the cards and take patience, and begin the game again, if you please - - - And you can come this week if you do like it – because our relations don't come till the end of it, it appears – not that I made a pretence 'out of kindness' – pray don't judge me so outrageously – but if you like to come .. not on Tuesday .. but on Wednesday at three o'clock, I shall be very glad to see you; and I, for one, shall have forgotten everything by that time; being quick at forgetting my own faults usually. If Wednesday does not suit you, I am not sure that I *can* see you this week – but it depends on circumstances. Only don't think yourself *obliged* to come on Wednesday. You know I *began* by entreating you to be open and sincere with me – and no more – I *require* no 'sleekening of every word'. I love the truth and can bear it – whether in word or deed – and those who

23

have known me longest would tell you so fullest. Well! – May
God bless you. We shall know each other some day perhaps – and
I am

Always and faithfully your friend,

E.B.B.

(Post-mark, June 14, 1845)

- - - I have always been jealous of my own musical faculty (I
can write music). – Now that I see the uselessness of such jealousy,
and am for loosing and letting it go, it may be cramped possibly.
Your music is more various and exquisite than any modern
writer's to my ear. One should study the mechanical part of the
art, as nearly all that there is to be studied – for the more one sits
and thinks over the creative process, the more it confirms itself
as 'inspiration', nothing more nor less. Or, at worst, you write
down old inspirations, what you remember of them .. but with
that it begins. 'Reflection' is exactly what it names itself – a *re-*
presentation, in scattered rays from every angle of incidence, of
what first of all became present in a great light, a whole one. So
tell me how these lights are born, if you can! But I can tell
anybody how to make melodious verse – let him do it therefore –
it should be exacted of all writers.

You do not understand what a new feeling it is for me to have
someone who is to like my verses or I shall not ever like them
after! So far differently was I circumstanced of old, that I used
rather to go about for a subject of offence to people; writing ugly
things in order to warn the ungenial and timorous off my grounds
at once. I shall never do so again at least! - - -

I thank God that you are better: do pray make fresh endeavours
to profit by this partial respite of the weather! All about you must
urge that: but even from my distance some effect might come of
such wishes. But you *are* better – look so and speak so! God bless
you.

R.B.

(Post-mark, July 12, 1845)

You understand that it was not a resolution passed in favour of
formality, when I said what I did yesterday about not going out
at the time you were coming – surely you do; whatever you might
signify to a different effect. If it were necessary for me to go out
every day, or most days even, it would be otherwise; but as it is,
I may certainly keep the day you come, free from the fear of
carriages, let the sun shine its best or worst, without doing
despite to you or injury to me – and that's all I meant to insist
upon indeed and indeed. You see, Jupiter Tonans was good
enough to come today on purpose to deliver me – one evil for
another! for I confess with shame and contrition, that I never
wait to enquire whether it thunders to the left or the right, to be
frightened most ingloriously. Isn't it a disgrace to anyone with a
pretension to poetry? Dr. Chambers,[1] a part of whose office it is,
Papa says, 'to reconcile foolish women to their follies', used to
take the side of my vanity, and discourse at length on the passive
obedience of some nervous systems to electrical influences; but
perhaps my faintheartedness is besides traceable to a half-reason-
able terror of a great storm in Herefordshire, where great storms
most do congregate, (such storms!) round the Malvern Hills,
those mountains of England. We lived four miles from their
roots, through all my childhood and early youth, in a Turkish
house my father built himself,[2] crowded with minarets and domes,
and crowned with metal spires and crescents, to the provocation
(as people used to observe) of every lightning of heaven. Once a
storm of storms happened, and we all thought the house was
struck – and a tree was so really, within two hundred yards of the
windows while I looked out – the bark, rent from the top to
the bottom .. torn into long ribbons by the dreadful fiery hands,
and dashed out into the air, over the heads of other trees, or left
twisted in their branches – torn into shreds in a moment, as a
flower might be, by a child! Did you ever see a tree after it has
been struck by lightning? The whole trunk of that tree was bare

[1] E.B.B.'s doctor.
[2] Hope End.

and peeled – and up that new whiteness of it, ran the finger-mark of the lightning in a bright beautiful rose-colour (none of your roses brighter or more beautiful!) the fever-sign of the certain death – though the branches themselves were for the most part untouched, and spread from the peeled trunk in their full summer foliage; and birds singing in them three hours after-wards! - - -

I am yours,

E.B.B.

R.B. TO E.B.B.

Sunday Morning
(Post-mark, July 14, 1845)

- - - What a grand sight your tree was – *is*, for I see it. My father has a print of a tree so struck – torn to ribbons, as you describe – but the rose-mark is striking and new to me. We had a good storm on our last voyage, but I went to bed at the end, as I thought – and only found there had been lightning next day by the bare poles under which we were riding: but the finest moun-tain fit of the kind I ever saw has an unfortunately ludicrous association. It was at Possagno, among the Euganean Hills, and I was at a poor house in the town – an old woman was before a little picture of the Virgin, and at every fresh clap she lighted, with the oddest sputtering muttering mouthful of prayer imagin-able, an inch of guttery candle, which, the instant the last echo had rolled away, she as constantly blew out again for saving's sake – having, of course, to *light the smoke* of it, about an instant after that: the expenditure in wax at which the elements might be propitiated, you see, was a matter for curious calculation. I suppose I ought to have bought the whole taper for some four or five centesimi (100 of which make 8d English) and so kept the countryside safe for about a century of bad weather. Leigh Hunt tells you a story he had from Byron, of kindred philosophy in a Jew who was surprised by a thunderstorm while he was dining on bacon – he tried to eat between-whiles, but the flashes were as pertinacious as he, so at last he pushed his plate away, just remarking with a compassionate shrug, 'all this fuss about a piece of pork!' By the way, what a characteristic of an Italian *late* evening is Summer-lightning – it hangs in broad slow sheets, dropping from cloud to cloud, so long in dropping and dying off. The 'bora',[1] which you only get at Trieste, brings wonderful lightning – you are in glorious June-weather, fancy, of an evening, under green shock-headed acacias, so thick and green, with the cicalas stunning you above, and all about you men, women, rich and poor, sitting standing and coming and going – and through all the laughter and screaming and singing, the loud clink of the spoons against the glasses, the way of calling for fresh 'sorbetti'[2] – for all the world is at open-coffee-house at such an hour – when suddenly there is a stop in the sunshine, a blackness drops down, then a great white column of dust drives straight on like a wedge, and you see the acacia heads snap off, now one, then another – and all the people scream 'la bora, la bora!' and you are caught up in their whirl and landed in some interior, the man with the guitar on one side of you, and the boy with a cageful of little brown owls for sale, on the other – meanwhile, the thunder claps, claps, with such a persistence, and the rain, for a finale, falls in a mass, as if you had knocked out the whole bottom of a huge tank at once – then there is a second stop – out comes the sun – somebody clinks at his glass, all the world bursts out laughing, and prepares to pour out again, – but *you*, the stranger, *do* make the best of your way out, with no preparation at all; whereupon you infallibly put your foot (and half your leg) into a river, really that, of rainwater – that's a *Bora* (and that comment of yours, a justifiable pun!). Such things you get in Italy, but better, better, the best of all things you do not (*I* do not) get those - - - And now goodbye – I am to see you on Wednesday I trust – and to hear you say you are better, still better, much better? God grant that, and all else good for you, dear friend, and so for R.B.

ever yours

---

[1] The north-east wind.
[2] Dishes made with ice-cream or sherbet.

Monday
(Post-mark, July 21, 1845)

- - - The *Hood* poems[1] have delighted me - - - the St. Praxed's
- - - is of course the finest and most powerful .. and indeed full of
the power of life .. and of death. It has impressed me very much.
Then the 'Angel and Child', with all its beauty and significance! –
and the 'Garden Fancies' .. some of the stanzas about the name
of the flower, with such exquisite music in them, and grace of
every kind – and with that beautiful and musical use of the word
'meandering', which I never remember having seen used in
relation to *sound* before. It does to mate with your '*simmering
quiet*' in Sordello, which brings the summer air into the room as
sure as you read it. Then I like your burial of the pedant[2] so
much! – you have quite the damp smell of funguses and the sense
of creeping things through and through it. And the 'Laboratory'
is hideous as you meant to make it: – only I object a little to
your tendency .. which is almost a habit, and is very observable
in this poem I think, .. of making lines difficult for the reader to
read .. see the opening lines of this poem. Not that music is
required everywhere, nor in *them* certainly, but that the uncertainty of rhythm throws the reader's mind off the *rail* .. and
interrupts his progress with you and your influence with him.
Where we have not direct pleasure from rhythm, and where no
peculiar impression is to be produced by the changes in it, we
should be encouraged by the poet to *forget it altogether*; should we
not? I am quite wrong perhaps – but you see how I do not
conceal my wrongnesses where they mix themselves up with my
sincere impressions - - -

May God bless you my dear friend, my ever dear friend! –

E.B.B.

[1] Six poems by R.B. published in *Hood's Magazine* in 1844 and 1845:
'The Laboratory', 'Claret and Tokay', 'Garden Fancies', 'The Boy and the
Angel', 'The Flight of the Duchess', and 'The Tomb of St. Praxed's' (afterwards re-named 'The Bishop Orders His Tomb at Saint Praxed's Church').
[2] 'Sibrandus Schafnaburgensis' – one of the 'Garden Fancies'.

- - - *Sunday.* – I wrote so much yesterday and then went out, not knowing very well how to speak or how to be silent (is it better today?) of some expressions of yours .. and of your interest in me – which are deeply affecting to my feelings – whatever else remains to be said of them. And do you know that you make great mistakes, .. of fennel for hemlock, of four o'clocks for five o'clocks, and of other things of more consequence, one for another; and may not be quite right besides as to my getting well '*if I please!*' .. which reminds me a little of what Papa says sometimes when he comes into this room unexpectedly and convicts me of having dry toast for dinner, and declares angrily that obstinacy and dry toast have brought me to my present condition, and that if I *pleased* to have porter and beefsteaks instead, I should be as well as ever I was, in a month! .. But where is the need of talking of it? What I wished to say was this – that if I get better or worse .. as long as I live and to the last moment of life, I shall remember with an emotion which cannot change its character, all the generous interest and feeling you have spent on me – *wasted* on me I was going to write – but I would not provoke any answering – and in one obvious sense, it need not be so. I never shall forget these things, my dearest friend; nor remember them more coldly. God's goodness! – I believe in it, as in His sunshine here – which makes my head ache a little, while it comes in at the window, and makes most other people gayer – it does *me* good too in a different way. And so, may God bless you! and me in this .. just this, .. that I may never have the sense, .. intolerable in the remotest apprehension of it .. of being, in any way, directly or indirectly, the means of ruffling your smooth path by so much as one of my flint-stones! – In the meantime you do not tire me indeed even when you go later for sooner .. and I do not tire myself even when I write longer and duller letters to you (if the last is possible) than the one I am ending now .. as the most grateful (leave me that word) of your friends.

E.B.B.

(Post-mark, July 28, 1845)

How must I feel, and what can, or could I say even if you let me say all? I am most grateful, most happy – most happy, come what will!

Will you let me try and answer your note tomorrow – before Wednesday when I am to see you? I will not hide from you that my head aches now; and I have let the hours go by one after one – I am better all the same, and will write as I say – 'Am I better' you ask!

Yours I am, ever yours my dear friend R.B.

R.B. TO E.B.B.

Thursday
(Post-mark, July 31, 1845)

In all I say to you, write to you, I know very well that I trust to your understanding me almost beyond the warrant of any human capacity – but as I began, so I shall end. I shall believe you remember what I am forced to remember – you who do me the superabundant justice on every possible occasion, – you will never do me injustice when I sit by you and talk about Italy and the rest.

– Today I cannot write – though I am very well otherwise – but I shall soon get into my old self-command and write with as much 'ineffectual fire' as before: but meantime, *you* will write to me, I hope – telling me how you are? I have but one greater delight in the world than in hearing from you.

God bless you, my best, dearest friend – think what I would speak –

Ever yours,
R.B.

R.B.B. TO R.B.

(Post-mark, August 11, 1845)

- - - You would smile, as I have often done in the midst of my vexation, if you knew the persecution I have been subjected to by the people who call themselves (*lucus a non lucendo*) 'the faculty', and set themselves against the exercise of other people's faculties, as a sure way to death and destruction. The modesty and simplicity with which one's physicians tell one not to think or feel, just as they would tell one not to walk out in the dew, would be quite amusing, if it were not too tryingly stupid sometimes. I had a doctor once who thought he had done everything because he had carried the inkstand out of the room – 'Now,' he said, 'You will have such a pulse tomorrow.' He gravely thought poetry a sort of disease – a sort of fungus of the brain – and held as a serious opinion, that nobody could be properly well who exercised it as an art – which was true (he maintained) even of men – he had studied the physiology of poets, 'quotha' – but that for women, it was a mortal malady and incompatible with any common show of health under any circumstances. And then came the damnatory clause in his experience .. that he had never known 'a system' approaching mine in 'excitability' .. except Miss Garrow's .. a young lady who wrote verses for Lady Blessington's annuals .. and who was the only other female rhymer he had had the misfortune of attending. And she was to die in two years, though she was dancing quadrilles then (and has lived to do the same by the polka), and *I*, of course, much sooner, if I did not ponder these things, and amend my ways, and take to reading 'a course of history'!! Indeed I do not exaggerate. And just so, for a long while I was persecuted and pestered .. vexed thoroughly sometimes .. my own family, instructed to sing the burden out all day long – until the time when the subject was suddenly changed by my heart being broken by that great stone that fell out of Heaven. Afterwards I was let do anything I could best .. which was very little until last year – and the working, last year, did much for me in giving me stronger roots down into life, .. much. But think of that absurd reasoning that went before! – the *niaiserie* of it! For, granting all the premises all round, it is not the *utterance* of a thought that *can* hurt anybody; while only the utterance is dependent on the will; and so, what can the taking away of an inkstand do? Those physicians are such metaphysicians! It's curious to listen to them. And it's wise to leave off listening: though I have met with excessive kindness among them, and do not refer to Dr. Chambers in any of this, of course - - -

May God bless you my dearest friend,

E.B.B.

E.B.B. TO R.B.

Wednesday
(Post-mark, August 25, 1845)

- - - You must not, you must not, make an unjust opinion out of what I said today. I have been uncomfortable since, lest you should – and perhaps it would have been better if I had not said it apart from all context in that way; only that you could not long be a friend of mine without knowing and seeing what so lies on the surface. But then, .. as far as I am concerned, .. no one cares less for a 'will' than I do (and this though I never had one, .. in clear opposition to your theory which holds generally nevertheless) for a will in the common things of life. Every now and then there must of course be a crossing and vexation – but in one's mere pleasures and fantasies, one would rather be crossed and vexed a little than vex a person one loves .. and it is possible to get used to the harness and run easily in it at last; and there is a side-world to hide one's thoughts in - - - and the word 'literature' has, with me, covered a good deal of liberty as you must see .. real liberty which is never enquired into – and it has happened throughout my life by an accident (as far as anything is accident) that my own sense of right and happiness on any important point of overt action, has never run contrariwise to the way of obedience required of me .. while in things not exactly *overt*, I and all of us are apt to act sometimes up to the limit of our means of acting, with shut doors and windows, and no waiting for cognisance or permission. Ah – and the last is the worst of it all perhaps! to be forced into concealments from the heart naturally nearest to us; and forced away from the natural source of counsel and strength! – and then, the disingenuousness – the cowardice – the 'vices of slaves'! – and everyone you see .. all my brothers, .. constrained *bodily* into submission .. apparent submission at least .. by that worst and most dishonouring of necessities, the necessity of *living*, everyone of them all, except myself, you see? But what you do *not* see, what you *cannot* see, is the deep tender affection behind and below all those patriarchal ideas of governing grown up children 'in the way they *must* go!' and there never was (under the strata) a truer affection in a father's heart .. no, nor a worthier heart in itself .. a heart loyaller and purer, and more compelling to gratitude and reverence, than his, as I see it! The evil is in the system – and he simply takes it to be his duty to rule, and to make happy according to his own views of the propriety of happiness – he takes it to be his duty to rule like the Kings of Christendom, by divine right. But he loves us through and through it – and *I*, for one, love *him*! and when, five years ago, I lost what I loved best in the world[1] beyond comparison and rivalship .. far better than himself as he knew .. for everyone who knew *me* could not choose but know what was my first and chiefest affection .. when I lost *that*, .. I felt that he stood the nearest to me on the closed grave .. or by the unclosing sea .. I do not know which nor could ask. And I will tell you that not only he has been kind and patient and forbearing to me through the tedious trial of this illness (far more trying to standers by than you have an idea of perhaps) but that he was generous and forbearing in that hour of bitter trial, and never reproached me as he might have done and as my own soul has not spared – never once said to me then or since that if it had not been for *me*, the crown of his house would not have fallen. He *never did* .. and he might have said it, and more – and I could have answered nothing. Nothing, except that I had paid my own price – and that the price I paid was greater than his *loss* .. his!! For see how it was; and how, 'not with my hand but heart', I was the cause or occasion of that misery – and though not with the intention of my heart but with its weakness, yet the *occasion*, any way!

They sent me down you know to Torquay – Dr. Chambers saying that I could not live a winter in London. The worst – what people call the worst – was apprehended for me at that time. So I was sent down with my sister to my aunt there – and he, my brother whom I loved so, was sent too, to take us there

[1] Her eldest brother, Edward, drowned in 1840.

and return. And when the time came for him to leave me, *I*, to whom he was the dearest of friends and brothers in one .. the only one of my family who .. well, but I cannot write of these things; and it is enough to tell you that he was above us all, better than us all, and kindest and noblest and dearest to *me*, beyond comparison, any comparison, as I said – and when the time came for him to leave me *I*, weakened by illness, could not master my spirits or drive back my tears – and my aunt kissed them away instead of reproving me as she should have done; and said that *she* would take care that I should not be grieved .. *she*! .. and so she sate down and wrote a letter to Papa to tell him that he would 'break my heart' if he persisted in calling away my brother – As if hearts were broken *so*! I have thought bitterly since that my heart did not break for a good deal more than *that*! And Papa's answer was – burnt into me, as with fire, it is – that 'under such circumstances he did not refuse to suspend his purpose, but that he considered it to be *very wrong in me to exact such a thing*'. So there was no separation *then*: and month after month passed – and sometimes I was better and sometimes worse – and the medical men continued to say that they would not answer for my life .. they! if I were agitated – and so there was no more talk of a separation. And once *he* held my hand, .. how I remember! and said that he 'loved me better than them all and that he *would not* leave me .. till I was well', he said! how I remember *that*! And ten days from that day the boat had left the shore which never returned; never – and he *had* left me! gone! For three days we waited – and I hoped while I could – oh – that awful agony of three days! And the sun shone as it shines today, and there was no more wind than now; and the sea under the windows was like this paper for smoothness – and my sisters drew the curtains back that I might see for myself how smooth the sea was, and how it could hurt nobody – and other boats came back one by one.

Remember how you wrote in your 'Gismond'

> What says the body when they spring
> Some monstrous torture-engine's whole
> Strength on it? No more says the soul,

and you never wrote anything which *lived* with me more than *that*. It is such a dreadful truth. But you knew it for truth, I hope, by your genius, and not by such proof as mine – I, who could not speak or shed a tear, but lay for weeks and months half conscious, half unconscious, with a wandering mind, and too near to God under the crushing of His hand, to pray at all. I expiated all my weak tears before, by not being able to shed then one tear – and yet they were forbearing – and no voice said 'You have done this'.

Do not notice what I have written to you, my dearest friend. I have never said so much to a living being – I never *could* speak or write of it. I asked no question from the moment when my last hope went: and since then, it has been impossible for me to speak what was in me. I have borne to do it today and to you, but perhaps if you were to write – so do not let this be noticed between us again – *do not*! And besides there is no need! I do not reproach myself with such acrid thoughts as I had once – I *know* that I would have died ten times over for *him*, and that therefore though it was wrong of me to be weak, and I have suffered for it and shall learn by it I hope; *remorse* is not precisely the word for me – not at least in its full sense. Still you will comprehend from what I have told you how the spring of life must have seemed to break within me *then*; and how natural it has been for me to loathe the living on – and to lose faith (even without the loathing), to lose faith in myself .. which I have done on some points utterly. It is not from the cause of illness – no. And you will comprehend too that I have strong reasons for being grateful to the forbearance .. It would have been *cruel*, you think, to reproach me. Perhaps so! yet the kindness and patience of the desisting from reproach, are positive things all the same.

- - - And so goodbye until Tuesday. Perhaps I shall .. not .. hear from you tonight. Don't let the tragedy or aught else do you harm – will you? and try not to be 'weary in your soul' any more – and forgive me this gloomy letter I half shrink from sending you, yet will send.

May God bless you,
E.B.B.

Wednesday Morning
(Post-mark, August 27, 1845)

On the subject of your letter – quite irrespective of the injunction in it – I would not have dared speak; now, at least. But I may permit myself, perhaps, to say I am *most* grateful, *most grateful*, dearest friend, for this admission to participate, in any degree, in these feelings. There is a better thing than being happy in your happiness; I feel, now that you teach me, it is so. I will write no more now; though that sentence of 'what you are *expecting*, – that I shall be tired of you &c.', – though I *could* blot that out of your mind for ever by a very few words *now*, – for you *would believe* me at this moment, close on the other subject: – but I will take no such advantage – I will wait.

I have many things (indifferent things, after those) to say; will you write, if but a few lines, to change the associations for that purpose? Then I will write too. –

May God bless you, – in what is past and to come! I pray that from my heart, being yours,

R.B.

Wednesday Morning—
(Post-mark, August 27, 1845)

But your 'Saul' is unobjectionable as far as I can see, my dear friend. He was tormented by an evil spirit – but how, we are not told .. and the consolation is not obliged to be definite, .. is it? A singer was sent for as a singer – and all that you are called upon to be true to, are the general characteristics of David the chosen, standing between his sheep and his dawning hereafter, between innocence and holiness, and with what you speak of as the 'gracious gold locks' besides the chrism of the prophet, on his own head – and surely you have been happy in the tone and spirit of these lyrics .. broken as you have left them. Where is the wrong in all this? For the right and beauty, they are more obvious – and I cannot tell you how the poem holds me and will not let me go until it blesses me .. and, so, where are the 'sixty lines' thrown away? I do beseech you .. you who forget nothing, .. to remember them directly, and to go on with the rest .. *as* directly (be it understood) as is not injurious to your health. The whole conception of the poem, I like .. and the execution is exquisite up to this point – and the sight of Saul in the tent, just struck out of the dark by that sunbeam, 'a thing to see', .. not to say that afterwards when he is visibly 'caught in his pangs' like the king serpent, .. the sight is grander still. How could you doubt about this poem ..

At the moment of writing which, I receive your note. Do *you* receive my assurances from the deepest of my heart that I never did otherwise than *'believe' you* .. never did nor shall do .. and that you completely misinterpreted my words if you drew another meaning from them. Believe *me* in this – will you? I could not believe *you* any more for anything you could say, now or hereafter – and so do not avenge yourself on my unwary sentences by remembering them against me for evil. I did not mean to vex you .. still less to suspect you – indeed I did not! and moreover it was quite your fault that I did not blot it out after it was written, whatever the meaning was. So you forgive me (altogether) for your own sins: you must:–

For my part, though I have been sorry since to have written you such a gloomy letter, the sorrow unmakes itself in hearing you speak so kindly. Your sympathy is precious to me, I may say. May God bless you. Write and tell me among the 'indifferent things' something not indifferent, how you are yourself, I mean .. for I fear you are not well and thought you were not looking so yesterday.

Dearest friend, I remain yours,

E.B.B.

E.B.B. TO R.B.

Friday Evening
(Post-mark, August 30, 1845)

I do not hear; and come to you to ask the alms of just one line, having taken it into my head that something is the matter. It is not so much exactingness on my part, as that you spoke of meaning to write as soon as you received a note of mine .. which went to you five minutes afterwards .. which is three days ago, or will be when you read this. Are you not well – or what? Though I have tried and *wished* to remember having written in the last note something very or even a little offensive to you, I failed in it and go back to the worse fear. For you could not be vexed with me for talking of what was 'your fault' .. 'your own fault', viz. in having to read sentences which, but for your commands would have been blotted out. You could not very well take *that* for serious blame! from *me* too, who have so much reason and provocation for blaming the archangel Gabriel. – No – you could not misinterpret so, – and if you could not, and if you are not displeased with me, you must be unwell, I think. I took for granted yesterday that you had gone out as before – but tonight it is different – and so I come to ask you to be kind enough to write one word for me by some post tomorrow. Now remember .. I am not asking for a letter – but for a *word* .. or line strictly speaking.

Ever yours, dear friend,

E.B.B.

R.B. TO E.B.B.

(Post-mark, August 30, 1845)

Can you understand me *so*, dearest friend, after all? Do you see me – when I am away, or with you – 'taking offence' at words, 'being vexed' at words, or deeds of yours, even if I could not immediately trace them to their source of entire, pure kindness; as I have hitherto done in every smallest instance?

I believe in *you* absolutely, utterly – I believe that when you bade me, that time, be silent – that such was your bidding, and I was silent – dare I say I think you did not know at that time the power I have over myself, that I could sit and speak and listen as I have done since? Let me say now – *this only once* – that I loved you from my soul, and gave you my life, so much of it as you would take, – and all that is *done*, not to be altered now: it was, in the nature of the proceeding, wholly independent of any return

38

on your part. I will not think on extremes you might have resorted to; as it is, the assurance of your friendship, the intimacy to which you admit me, *now*, make the truest, deepest joy of my life – a joy I can never think fugitive while we are in life, because I *know*, as to me, I *could* not willingly displease you, – while, as to you, your goodness and understanding will always see to the bottom of involuntary or ignorant faults – always help me to correct them. I have done now. If I thought you were like other women I have known, I should say so much! – but – (my first and last word – I *believe* in you!) – what you could and would give me, of your affection, you would give nobly and simply and as a giver – you would not need that I tell you (*tell* you!) – what would be supreme happiness to me in the event – however distant –

I repeat .. I call on your justice to remember, on your intelligence to believe .. that this is merely a more precise stating the *first* subject; to put an end to any possible misunderstanding – to prevent your henceforth believing that because I *do not write*, from thinking too deeply of you, I am offended, vexed &c. &c. I will never recur to this, nor shall you see the least difference in my manner next Monday: it is indeed, always before me .. how I know nothing of you and yours. But I think I ought to have spoken when I did – and to speak clearly .. or more clearly what I do, as it is my pride and duty to fall back, now, on the feeling with which I have been in the meantime – Yours – God bless you –

R.B.

E.B.B. TO R.B.

Sunday
(August 31, 1845)

- - - My dearest friend – you have followed the most *generous* of impulses in your whole bearing to me – and I have recognised and called by its name, in my heart, each one of them. Yet I cannot help adding that, of us two, yours has not been quite the hardest part .. I mean, to a generous nature like your own, to which every sort of nobleness comes easily. Mine has been more difficult – and I have sunk under it again and again: and the sinking and the effort to recover the duty of a lost position, may have given me an appearance of vacillation and lightness, unworthy at least of *you*, and perhaps of both of us. Notwithstanding which appearance, it was right and just (only just) of you, to believe in me – in my truth – because I have never failed to you in it, nor been capable of *such* failure: the thing I have said, I have meant . . always: and in things I have not said, the silence has had a reason somewhere different perhaps from where you looked for it. And this brings me to complaining that you, who profess to believe in me, do yet obviously believe that it was only merely silence, which I required of you on one occasion – and that if I had 'known your power over yourself', I should not have minded . . no! In other words you believe of me that I was thinking just of my own (what shall I call it for a motive base and small enough?) my own scrupulousness . . freedom from embarrassment! of myself in the least of me; in the tying of my shoestrings, say! – so much and no more! Now this is so wrong, as to make me impatient sometimes in feeling it to be your impression: I asked for silence – but *also* and chiefly for the putting away of . . you know very well what I asked for. And this was sincerely done, I attest to you. You wrote once to me . . oh, long before May and the day we met: that you 'had been so happy, you should be now justified to yourself in taking any step most hazardous to the happiness of your life' – but if you were justified, could *I* be therefore justified in abetting such a step, – the step of wasting, in a sense, your best feelings . . of emptying your water gourds into the sand? What I thought then I think now – just what any third person, knowing you, would think, I think and feel. I thought too, at first, that the feeling on your part was a mere generous impulse, likely to expend itself in a week perhaps. It affects me and has affected me, very deeply, more than I dare attempt to say, that you should persist *so* – and if sometimes I have felt, by a sort of instinct, that after all you would not go on to persist, and that (being a man, you know) you might mistake, a little unconsciously, the strength of your own feeling; you ought not to be surprised; when I felt it was more advantageous and happier for you that it should be so. *In any case*, I shall never regret my own share in the events of this summer, and your friendship will be dear to me to the last. You know that I told you so – not long since. And as to what you say otherwise, you are right in thinking that I would not hold by unworthy motives in avoiding to speak what you had any claim to hear. But what could I speak that would not be unjust to you? Your life! if you gave it to me and I put my whole heart into it: what should I put but anxiety, and more sadness than you were born to? What could I give you, which it would not be ungenerous to give? Therefore we must leave this subject – and I must trust you to leave it without one word more; (too many have been said already – but I could not let your letter pass quite silently .. as if I had nothing to do but to receive all as matter of course *so*!) while you may well trust *me* to remember to my life's end, as the grateful remember; and to feel, as those do who have felt sorrow (for where these pits are dug, the water will stand), the full price of your regard. May God bless you, my dearest friend. I shall send this letter after I have seen you, and hope you may not have expected to hear sooner.

Ever yours,

E.B.B.

R.B. TO E.B.B.

Saturday Morning
(Post-mark, September 13, 1845)

Now, dearest, I will try and write the little I shall be able, in reply to your letter of last week – and first of all I have to entreat you, now more than ever, to help me and understand from the few words the feelings behind them – (I should *speak* rather more easily, I think – but I dare not run the risk: and I know, after all, you will be just and kind where you can.) I have read your letter again and again. I will tell you – no, not *you*, but any imaginary other person, who should hear what I am going to avow; I would tell that person most sincerely there is not a particle of fatuity, shall I call it, in that avowal; cannot be, seeing that from the beginning and at this moment I never dreamed of winning your *love*. I can hardly write this word, so incongruous and impossible does it seem; such a change of our places does it

41

imply – nor, next to that, though long after, *would* I, if I *could*, supplant one of any of the affections that I know to have taken root in you – *that* great and solemn one, for instance. I feel that if I could get myself *remade*, as if turned to gold, I WOULD not even then desire to become more than the mere setting to *that* diamond you must always wear. The regard and esteem you now give me, in this letter, and which I press to my heart and bow my head upon, is all I can take and all too embarrassing, using *all* my gratitude. And yet, with that contented pride in being infinitely your debtor as it is, bound to you for ever as it is; when I read your letter with all the determination to be just to us both; I dare not so far withstand the light I am master of, as to refuse seeing that whatever is recorded as an objection to your disposing of that life of mine I would give you, has reference to some supposed good in that life which your accepting it would destroy (of which fancy I shall speak presently) – I say, wonder as I may at this, I cannot but find it there, surely there. I could no more 'bind *you* by words', than you have bound me, as you say – but if I misunderstand you, one assurance to that effect will be but too intelligible to me – but, as it *is*, I have difficulty in imagining that while one of so many reasons, which I am not obliged to repeat to myself, but which any one easily conceives; while *any one* of those reasons would impose silence on me *for ever* (for, as I observed, I love you as you now are, and *would* not remove one affection that is already part of you,) – *would* you, being able to speak *so*, only say *that you* desire not to put 'more sadness than I was born to', into my life? – that you 'could give me only what it were ungenerous to give'?

Have I your meaning here? In so many words, is it on my account that you bid me 'leave this subject'? I think if it were so, I would for once call my advantages round me. I am not what your generous self-forgetting appreciation would sometimes make me out – but it is not since yesterday, nor ten nor twenty years before, that I began to look into my own life, and study its end, and requirements, what would turn to its good or its loss – and I *know*, if one may know anything, that to make that life yours and increase it by union with yours, would render me *supremely happy*, as I said, and say, and feel. My whole suit to you is, in that sense, *selfish* – not that I am ignorant that *your* nature would most surely attain happiness in being conscious that it made another happy – but *that best, best end of all*, would like the rest, come from yourself, be a reflection of your own gift.

Dearest, I will end here – words, persuasion, arguments, if they were at my service I would not use them – I believe in you, altogether have faith in you – in you. I will not think of insulting by trying to reassure you on one point which certain phrases in your letter might at first glance seem to imply – you do not understand me to be living and labouring and writing (and *not* writing) in order to be successful in the world's sense? I even convinced the people *here* what was my true 'honourable position in society', &c. &c. therefore I shall not have to inform *you* that I desire to be very rich, very great; but not in reading Law gratis with dear foolish old Basil Montagu, as he ever and anon bothers me to do; – much less – enough of this nonsense.

'Tell me what I have a claim to hear': I can hear it, and be as grateful as I was before and am now – your friendship is my pride and happiness. If you told me your love was bestowed elsewhere, and that it was in my power to serve you *there*, to serve you there would still be my pride and happiness. I look on and on over the prospect of my love, it is all *on*wards – and all possible forms of unkindness .. I quite laugh to think how they are *behind* .. cannot be encountered in the route we are travelling! I submit to you and will obey you implicitly – obey what I am able to conceive of your least desire, much more of your expressed wish. But it was necessary to make this avowal, among other reasons, for one which the world would recognize too. My whole scheme of life (with its wants, material wants at least, closely cut down) was long ago calculated – and it supposed *you*, the finding such an one as you, utterly impossible – because in calculating one goes upon *chances*, not on providence – how could I expect you? So for my own future way in the world I have always refused to care – any one who can live a couple of years and more on bread and potatoes as I did once on a time and who prefers a blouse and a blue shirt (such as I now write in) to all manner of dress and gentlemanly appointment, and who can, if necessary, groom a horse not so badly, or at all events would rather do it all day long than succeed Mr. Fitzroy Kelly in the Solicitor-Generalship, – such an one need not very much concern himself beyond considering the lilies how they grow. But now I see you near this life, all changes – and at a word, I will do all that ought to be done, that every one used to say could be done, and let 'all my powers find sweet employ' as Dr. Watts sings, in getting whatever is to be got – not very much surely. I would print these things, get them away, and do this now, and go to you at Pisa with the news – at Pisa where one may live for some £100 a year – while, lo, I seem to remember, I *do* remember, that Charles Kean[1] offered to give me 500 of those pounds for any play that might suit him – to say nothing of Mr. Colburn[2] saying confidentially that he wanted more than his dinner 'a novel on the subject of *Napoleon*'! So may one make money, if one does not live in a house in a row, and feel impelled to take the Princess's Theatre for a laudable development and exhibition of one's faculty.

Take the sense of all this, I beseech you, dearest – all you shall say will be best – I am yours –

Yes, Yours ever. God bless you for all you have been, and are, and will certainly be to me, come what He shall please!

R.B.

E.B.B. TO R.B.

(Post-mark, September 16, 1845)

I scarcely know how to write what is to be written nor indeed why it is to be written and to what end. I have tried in vain – and you are waiting to hear from me. I am unhappy enough even where I am happy – but ungrateful nowhere – and I thank you from my heart – profoundly from the depths of my heart .. which is nearly all I can do.

One letter I began to write and asked in it how it could become me to speak at all if '*from the beginning and at this moment you never dreamed of*' .. and there, I stopped and tore the paper; because I felt that you were too loyal and generous, for me to

---

[1] The actor (1811?–1868); son of Edmund Kean.

[2] Henry Colburn (d. 1855); publisher and journalist.

bear to take a moment's advantage of the same, and bend down the very flowering branch of your generosity (as it might be) to thicken a little the fence of a woman's caution and reserve. You will not say that you have not acted as if you 'dreamed' – and I will answer therefore to the general sense of your letter and former letters, and admit at once that I *did* state to you the difficulties most difficult to myself .. though not all .. and that if I had been worthier of you I should have been proportionably less in haste to 'bid you leave that subject'. I do not understand how you can seem at the same moment to have faith in my integrity and to have doubt whether all this time I may not have felt a preference for another .. which you are ready 'to serve', you say. Which is generous in you – but in *me*, where were the integrity? Could you really hold me to be blameless, and do you think that true-hearted women act usually so? Can it be necessary for me to tell you that I could not have acted so, and did not? And shall I shrink from telling you besides .. you, who have been generous to me and have a right to hear it .. and have spoken to me in the name of an affection and memory most precious and holy to me, in this same letter .. that neither now nor formerly has any man been to my feelings what you are .. and that if I were different in some respects and free in others by the providence of God, I would accept the great trust of your happiness, gladly, proudly, and gratefully; and give away my own life and soul to that end. I *would* do it .. *not, I do* .. observe! it is a truth without a consequence; only meaning that I am not all stone – only proving that I am not likely to consent to help you in wrong against yourself. You see in me what is not: – *that*, I know: and you overlook in me what is unsuitable to you .. *that* I know, and have sometimes told you. Still, because a strong feeling from some sources is self-vindicating and ennobling to the object of it, I will not say that, if it were proved to me that you felt this for me, I would persist in putting the sense of my own unworthiness between you and me – not being heroic, you know, nor pretending to be so. But something worse than even a sense of unworthiness, *God* has put between us! and judge yourself if to beat your thoughts against the immovable marble of it, can be anything but pain and vexation of spirit, waste and wear of spirit to you .. judge! The present is here to be seen .. speaking for itself! and the best future you can imagine for me, what a precarious thing it must be .. a thing for making burdens out of .. only not for your carrying, as I have vowed to my own soul. As dear Mr. Kenyon said to me today in his smiling kindness .. 'In ten years you may be strong perhaps' – or 'almost strong'! that being the encouragement of my best friends! What would he say, do you think, if he could know or guess ..! what *could* he say but that you were .. a poet! – and I .. still worse! *Never* let him know or guess!

And so if you are wise and would be happy (and you have excellent practical sense after all and should exercise it) you must leave me – these thoughts of me, I mean .. for if we might not be true friends for ever, I should have less courage to say the other truth. But we may be friends always .. and cannot be so separated, that your happiness, in the knowledge of it, will not increase mine. And if you will be persuaded by me, as you say, you will be persuaded *thus* .. and consent to take a resolution and force your mind at once into another channel. Perhaps I might bring you reasons of the class which you tell me 'would silence you for ever'. I might certainly tell you that my own father, if he knew that you had written to me *so*, and that I had answered you – *so*, even, would not forgive me at the end of ten years – and this, from none of the causes mentioned by me here and in no disrespect to your name and your position .. though he does not over-value poetry even in his daughter, and is apt to take the world's measures of the means of life .. but for the singular reason that he never *does* tolerate in his family (sons or daughters) the development of one class of feelings. Such an objection I could not bring to you of my own will – it rang hollow in my ears – perhaps I thought even too little of it: – and I brought to you what I thought much of, and cannot cease to think much of equally. Worldly thoughts, these are not at all, nor have been: there need be no soiling of the heart with any such: – and I will say, in reply to some words of yours, that you cannot despise the gold and gauds of the world more than I do, and should do even if I found a use for them. And if I *wished* to be very poor, in the world's sense of poverty, I *could not*, with three or four hundred a year of which no living will can dispossess me. And is it not the chief good of money, the being free from the need of thinking of it? It seems so to me.

The obstacles then are of another character, and the stronger for being so. Believe that I am grateful to you – *how* grateful, cannot be shown in words nor even in tears .. grateful enough to be truthful in all ways. You know I might have hidden myself from you – but I would not: and by the truth told of myself, you may believe in the earnestness with which I tell the other truths – of you .. and of this subject. The subject will not bear consideration – it breaks in our hands. But that God is stronger than we cannot be a bitter thought to you but a holy thought .. while He lets me, as much as I can be anyone's, be only yours.

E.B.B.

R.B. TO E.B.B.
(Post-mark, September 17, 1845)

I do not know whether you imagine the precise effect of your letter on me – very likely you do, and write it just for that – for I conceive *all* from your goodness. But before I tell you what is that effect, let me say in as few words as possible what shall stop any fear – though only for a moment and on the outset – that you have been misunderstood, that the goodness *outside*, and round and over all, hides all or anything. I understand you to signify to me that you see, at this present, insurmountable obstacles to that – can I speak it – entire gift, which I shall own, was, while I dared ask it, above my hopes – and wishes, even, so it seems to me .. and yet could not but be asked, so plainly was it dictated to me, by something quite out of those hopes and wishes. Will it help me to say that once in this Aladdin-cavern I knew I ought to stop for no heaps of jewel-fruit on the trees from the very beginning, but go on to the lamp, *the* prize, the last and best of all? Well, I understand you to pronounce that at present you believe this gift impossible – and I acquiesce entirely – I submit wholly to you; repose on you in all the faith of which I am capable. Those obstacles are solely for *you* to see and to declare .. had *I* seen them, be sure I should never have mocked you or

47

myself by affecting to pass them over .. what *were* obstacles, I mean: but you *do* see them, I must think, – and perhaps they strike me the more from my true, honest unfeigned inability to imagine what they are, – not that I shall endeavour. After what you *also* apprise me of, I know and am joyfully confident that if ever they cease to be what you now consider them, you who see now *for me*, whom I implicitly trust in to see for me; you will *then*, too, see and remember me, and how I trust, and shall then be still trusting. And until you so see, and so inform me, I shall never utter a word – for that would involve the vilest of implications. I thank God – I *do* thank him, that in this whole matter I have been, to the utmost of my power, not unworthy of his introducing you to me, in this respect that, being no longer in the first freshness of life, and having for many years now made up my mind to the impossibility of loving any woman .. having wondered at this in the beginning, and fought not a little against it, having acquiesced in it at last, and accounted for it all to myself, and become, if anything, rather proud of it than sorry .. I say, when real love, making itself at once recognised as such, *did* reveal itself to me at last, I *did* open my heart to it with a cry – nor care for its overturning all my theory – nor mistrust its effect upon a mind set in ultimate order, so I fancied, for the few years more – nor apprehend in the least that the new element would harm what was already organised without its help. Nor have I, either, been guilty of the more pardonable folly, of treating the new feeling after the pedantic fashions and instances of the world. I have not spoken when *it* did not speak, because 'one' might speak, or has spoken, or *should* speak, and 'plead' and all that miserable work which, after all, I may well continue proud that I am not called to attempt. *Here* for instance, *now* .. 'one' should despair; but 'try' again first, and work blindly at removing those obstacles (– if I saw them, I should be silent, and only speak when a month hence, ten years hence, I could bid you look where they *were*) – and 'one' would do all this, not for the *play-acting's* sake, or to 'look the character' .. (*that* would be something quite different from folly ..) but from a not unreasonable anxiety lest by too sudden a silence, too complete an acceptance of your will; the earnestness and endurance and unabatedness .. the *truth*, in fact, of what had already been professed, should get to be questioned – But I believe that you believe me – And now that all is clear between us I will say, what you will hear, without fearing for me or yourself, that I am utterly contented .. ('grateful' I have done with .. it must go –) I accept what you give me, what those words deliver to me, as – not all I asked for .. as I said .. but as more than I ever hoped for, – *all*, in the best sense, that I deserve. That phrase in my letter which you objected to, and the other – may stand, too – I never attempted to declare, describe my feeling for you – one word of course stood for it all .. but having to put down some one *point*, so to speak, of it – you could not wonder if I took any extreme one *first* .. never minding all the untold portion that *led* up to it, made it possible and natural – it is true, 'I could not dream of *that*' – that I was eager to get the horrible notion away from never so flitting a visit to you, that you were thus and thus to me *on condition* of my proving just the same to you – just as if we had waited to acknowledge that the moon lighted us till we ascertained within these two or three hundred years that the earth happens to light the moon as well! But I felt that, and so said it: – now you have declared what I should never have presumed to hope – and I repeat to you that I, with all to be thankful for to God, am most of all thankful for this the last of his providences .. which is no doubt, the natural and inevitable feeling, could one always see clearly. Your regard for me is *all* success – let the rest come, or not come. In my heart's thankfulness I would .. I am sure I would promise anything that would gratify you .. but it would *not* do that, to agree, in words, to change my affections, put them elsewhere &c. &c. That would be pure foolish talking, and quite foreign to the practical results which you will attain in a better way from a higher motive. I will cheerfully promise you, however, to be 'bound by no words', blind to no miracle; in sober earnest, it is not because I renounced once for all oxen and the owning and having to do with them, that I will obstinately turn away from any unicorn when such an apparition blesses me .. but meantime I shall walk at peace on our hills here nor go looking in all corners for the bright curved horn! And as for you .. if I did not dare 'to dream of that' – now

49

it is mine, my pride and joy prevent in no manner my taking the whole consolation of it at once, *now* – I will be confident that, if I obey you, I shall get no wrong for it – if, endeavouring to spare you fruitless pain, I do not eternally revert to the subject; do indeed 'quit' it just now, when no good can come of dwelling on it to you; you will never say to yourself – so I said – 'the "generous impulse" *has* worn itself out' .. time is doing his usual work – this was to be expected' &c. &c. You will be the first to say to me 'such an obstacle has ceased to exist .. or is now become one palpable to *you*, one *you* may try and overcome' – and I shall be there, and ready – ten years hence as now – if alive.

One final word on the other matters – the 'worldly matters' – I shall own I alluded to them rather ostentatiously, because – because *that would be* the *one* poor sacrifice I could make you – one I would cheerfully make, but a sacrifice, and the only one: this careless 'sweet habitude of living' – this absolute independence of mine, which, if I had it not, my heart would starve and die for, I feel, and which I have fought so many good battles to preserve – for that has happened, too – this light rational life I lead, and know so well that I lead; this I could give up for nothing less than – what you know – but I *would* give it up, not for you merely, but for those whose disappointment might re-act on you – and I should break no promise to myself – the money getting would not be for the sake of *it*; 'the labour not for that which is nought' – indeed the necessity of doing this, if at all, *now*, was one of the reasons which make me go on to that *last request of all* – at once; one must not be too old, they say, to begin their ways. But, in spite of all the babble, I feel sure that whenever I make up my mind to that, I can be rich enough and to spare – because along with what you have thought *genius* in me, is certainly talent, what the world recognises as such; and I have tried it in various ways, just to be sure that I *was* a little magnanimous in never intending to use it. Thus, in more than one of the reviews and newspapers that laughed my 'Paracelsus' to scorn ten years ago – in the same column, often, of these reviews, would follow a most laudatory notice of an Elementary French book, on a new plan, which I *'did'* for my old French master, and he published – '*that* was really an useful work'! – So that when the only obstacle is only that there is so much *per annum* to be producible, you will tell me. After all it would be unfair in me not to confess that this was always intended to be *my* own single stipulation – 'an objection' which I could see, certainly, – but meant to treat myself to the little luxury of removing.

So, now, dearest – let me once think of that, and of you as my own, my dearest – this once – dearest, I have done with words for the present. I will wait. God bless you and reward you – I kiss your hands *now*. This is my comfort, that if you accept my feeling as all but *un*expressed now, more and more will become spoken – or understood, that is – we both live on – you will know better *what* it was, how much and manifold, what one little word had to give out.

God bless you –
Your R.B.

E.B.B. TO R.B.

Wednesday Evening
(Post-mark, September 18, 1845)

But one word before we leave the subject - - - if I were in a position to accept sacrifices from you, I would not accept *such* a sacrifice .. amounting to a sacrifice of duty and dignity as well as of ease and satisfaction .. to an exchange of higher work for lower work .. and of the special work you are called to, for that which is work for anybody. I am not so ignorant of the right uses and destinies of what you have and are - - -

And for all the rest I thank you – believe that I thank you .. and that the feeling is not so weak as the word. That *you* should care at all for *me* has been a matter of unaffected wonder to me from the first hour until now – and I cannot help the pain I feel sometimes, in thinking that it would have been better for you if you never had known me. May God turn back the evil of me! - - - And here I have done. I had done *living*, I thought, when you came and sought me out! and why? and to what end? *That*, I cannot help thinking now. Perhaps just that I may pray for you –

which were a sufficient end. If you come on Saturday I trust
you to leave this subject untouched, – as it must be indeed henceforth.

I am yours,

E.B.B.

E.B.B. TO R.B.

Wednesday
(Post-mark, September 18, 1845)

- - - Papa has been walking to and fro in this room, looking
thoughtfully and talking leisurely – and every moment I have
expected I confess, some word (that did not come) about Pisa.[1]
Mr. Kenyon thinks it cannot end so – and I do sometimes – and
in the meantime I do confess to a little 'savageness' also – at
heart! All I asked him to say the other day, was that he was not
displeased with me – *and he wouldn't;* and for me to walk across
his displeasure spread on the threshold of the door, and moreover
take a sister and brother with me, and do such a thing for the
sake of going to Italy and securing a personal advantage, were
altogether impossible, obviously impossible! So poor Papa is
quite in disgrace with me just now – if he would but care for
that! - - -

Ever yours,

E.B.B.

E.B.B. TO R.B.

(Post-mark, September 25, 1845)

I have spoken again, and the result is that we are in precisely
the same position; only with bitterer feelings on one side. If I
go or stay they *must* be bitter: words have been said that I cannot
easily forget, nor remember without pain; and yet I really do
almost smile in the midst of it all, to think how I was treated this
morning as an undutiful daughter because I tried to put on my
gloves .. for there was no worse provocation. At least he

[1] E.B.B. had been strongly advised by her doctor to spend the winter in
Italy, and was hoping to go to Pisa.

complained of the undutifulness and rebellion (!!!) of everyone in the house – and when I asked if he meant that reproach for *me*, the answer was that he meant it for all of us, one with another. And I could not get an answer. He would not even grant me the consolation of thinking that I sacrificed what I supposed to be good, to *him*. I told him that my prospects of health seemed to me to depend on taking this step, but that through my affection for him, I was ready to sacrifice those to his pleasure if he exacted it – only it was necessary to my self-satisfaction in future years, to understand definitely that the sacrifice *was* exacted by him and *was* made to him, .. and not thrown away blindly and by a misapprehension. And he would not answer *that*. I might do my own way, he said – *he* would not speak – *he* would not say that he was not displeased with me, nor the contrary: - I had better do what I liked: – for his part, he washed his hands of me altogether - - -

Well! – and what do you think? Might it be desirable for me to give up the whole? Tell me. I feel aggrieved of course and wounded – and whether I go or stay that feeling must last – I cannot help it. But my spirits sink altogether at the thought of leaving England *so* – and then I doubt about Arabel[1] and Stormie[2] .. and it seems to me that I *ought not* to mix them up in a business of this kind where the advantage is merely personal to myself. On the other side, George[3] holds that if I give up and stay even, there will be displeasure just the same, .. and that, when once gone, the irritation will exhaust and smooth itself away – which however does not touch my chief objection. Would it be better .. more *right* .. to give it up? Think for me. Even if I hold on to the last, at the last I shall be thrown off – *that* is my conviction. But .. shall I give up *at once?* Do think for me - - -

May God bless you.

Ever yours,
E.B.B.

[1] The younger of E.B.B.'s two sisters.
[2] Charles John, her eldest surviving brother.
[3] Her fourth brother.

(Post-mark, September 25, 1845)

You have said to me more than once that you wished I might never know certain feelings *you* had been forced to endure. I suppose all of us have the proper place where a blow should fall to be felt most – and I truly wish *you* may never feel what I have to bear in looking on, quite powerless, and silent, while you are subjected to this treatment, which I refuse to characterise – so blind is it *for* blindness. I think I ought to understand what a father may exact, and a child should comply with; and I respect the most ambiguous of love's caprices if they give never so slight a clue to their all-justifying source. Did I, when you signified to me the probable objections – you remember what – to myself, my own happiness, – did I once allude to, much less argue against, or refuse to acknowledge those objections? For I wholly sympathise, however it go against me, with the highest, wariest, pride and love for you, and the proper jealousy and vigilance they entail – but now, and here, the jewel is not being over guarded, but ruined, cast away. And whoever is privileged to interfere should do so in the possessor's own interest – all common sense interferes – all rationality against absolute no-reason at all. And you ask whether you ought to obey this no-reason? I will tell you: all passive obedience and implicit submission of will and intellect is by far too easy, if well considered, to be the course prescribed by God to Man in this life of probation – for they *evade* probation altogether, though foolish people think otherwise. Chop off your legs, you will never go astray; stifle your reason altogether and you will find it is difficult to reason ill. 'It is hard to make these sacrifices!' – not so hard as to lose the reward or incur the penalty of an Eternity to come; 'hard to effect them, then, and go through with them' – *not* hard, when the leg is to be *cut off* – that it is rather harder to keep it quiet on a stool, I know very well. The partial indulgence, the proper exercise of one's faculties, there is the difficulty and problem for solution, set by that Providence which might have made the laws of Religion as indubitable as those of vitality, and revealed the articles of belief as certainly as that condition, for instance, by which we breathe so many times in a minute to support life. But there is no reward proposed for the feat of breathing, and a great one for that of believing – consequently there must go a great deal more of voluntary effort to this latter than is implied in the getting absolutely rid of it at once, by adopting the direction of an infallible church, or private judgment of another – for all our life is some form of religion, and all our action some belief, and there is but one law, however modified, for the greater and the less. In your case I do think you are called upon to do your duty to yourself; that is, to God in the end. Your own reason should examine the whole matter in dispute by every light which can be put in requisition; and every interest that appears to be affected by your conduct should have its utmost claims considered – your father's in the first place; and that interest, not in the miserable limits of a few days' pique or whim in which it would seem to express itself; but in its whole extent .. the *hereafter* which all momentary passion prevents him seeing .. indeed, the *present* on either side which everyone else must see. And this examination made, with whatever earnestness you will, I do think and am sure that on its conclusion you should act, in confidence that a duty has been performed .. *difficult*, or how were it a duty? Will it *not* be infinitely harder to act so than to blindly adopt his pleasure, and die under it? Who can *not* do that?

I fling these hasty rough words over the paper, fast as they will fall – knowing to whom I cast them, and that any sense they may contain or point to, will be caught and understood, and presented in a better light. The hard thing .. this is all I want to say .. is to act on one's own best conviction – not to abjure it and accept another will, and say '*there* is my plain duty' – easy it is, whether plain or no!

'How all changes!' When I first knew you – you know what followed. I supposed you to labour under an incurable complaint and, of course, to be completely dependent on your father for its commonest alleviations; the moment after that inconsiderate letter, I reproached myself bitterly with the selfishness apparently involved in any proposition I might then have made – for though I have never been at all frightened of the world, nor mistrustful of my power to deal with it, and get my purpose out of it if once I thought it worth while, yet I could not but feel the consideration, of *what* failure would *now* be, paralyse all effort even in fancy. When you told me lately that 'you could never be poor' – all my solicitude was at an end – I had but myself to care about, and I told you, what I believed and believe, that I can at any time amply provide for that, and that I could cheerfully and confidently undertake the removing *that* obstacle. Now again the circumstances shift – and you are in what I should wonder at as the veriest slavery – and I who *could* free you from it, I am here scarcely daring to write .. though I know you must feel for me and forgive what forces itself from me .. what retires so mutely into my heart at your least word .. what *shall not* be again written or spoken, if you so will .. that I should be made happy beyond all hope of expression by. Now while I *dream*, let me once dream! I would marry you now and thus – I would come when you let me, and go when you bade me – I would be no more than one of your brothers – '*no more*' – that is, instead of getting tomorrow for Saturday, I should get Saturday as well – two hours for one – when your head ached I should be *here*. I deliberately choose the realisation of that dream (– of sitting simply by you for an hour every day) rather than any other, excluding you, I am able to form for this world, or any world I know – And it will continue but a dream.

God bless my dearest E.B.B.

R.B.

E.B.B. TO R.B.

Friday Evening
(Post-mark, September 27, 1845)

I had your letter late last night, everyone almost, being out of the house by an accident, so that it was left in the letter-box, and if I had wished to answer it before I saw you, it had scarcely been possible.

But it will be the same thing – for you know as well as if you saw my answer, what it must be, what it cannot choose but be, on pain of sinking me so infinitely below not merely your level but my own, that the depth cannot bear a glance down. Yet, though I am not made of such clay as to admit of my taking a base advantage of certain noble extravagances, (and that I am not I thank God for your sake) I will say, I must say, that your words in this letter have done me good and made me happy, .. that I thank and bless you for them, .. and that to receive such a proof of attachment from *you*, not only overpowers every present evil, but seems to me a full and abundant amends for the merely personal sufferings of my whole life. When I had read that letter last night I *did* think so. I looked round and round for the small bitternesses which for several days had been bitter to me, and I could not find one of them. The tear-marks went away in the moisture of new, happy tears. Why, how else could I have felt? how else do you think I could? How would any woman have felt .. who could feel at all .. hearing such words said (though 'in a dream' indeed) by such a speaker?

And now listen to me in turn. You have touched me more profoundly than I thought even *you* could have touched me – my heart was full when you came here today. Henceforward I am yours for everything but to do you harm – and I am yours too much, in my heart, ever to consent to do you harm in that way. If I could consent to do it, not only should I be less loyal .. but in one sense, less yours. I say this to you without drawback and reserve, because it is all I am able to say, and perhaps all I *shall* be able to say. However this may be, a promise goes to you in it that none, except God and your will, shall interpose between you and me, .. I mean, that if He should free me within a moderate time from the trailing chain of this weakness, I will then be to you whatever at that hour you shall choose .. whether friend or more than friend .. a friend to the last in any case. So it rests with God and with you – only in the meanwhile you are most absolutely free .. 'unentangled' (as they call it) by the breadth of a thread – and if I did not know that you considered yourself so, I would not see you any more, let the effort cost me what it might. You may force me to *feel*: .. but you cannot force me to *think* contrary to my first thought .. that it were better for you to forget me at once in one relation. And if better for *you*, can it be bad for *me*? which flings me down on the stone-pavement of the logicians - - -

Dear Mr. Kenyon has been here again, and talking so (in his kindness too) about the probabilities as to Pisa being against me .. about all depending 'on one throw' and the 'dice being loaded' &c. .. that I looked at him aghast as if he looked at the future through the folded curtain and was licensed to speak oracles : – and ever since I have been out of spirits .. oh, out of spirits – and must write myself back again, or try - - -

Well – George will probably speak before *he* leaves town, which will be on Monday! and now that the hour approaches, I do feel as if the house stood upon gunpowder, and as if I held Guy Fawkes's lantern in my right hand. And no: I shall not go. The obstacles will not be those of Mr. Kenyon's finding – and what their precise character will be I do not see distinctly. Only that they will be sufficient, and thrown by one hand just where the wheel should turn, .. *that*, I see – and you will, in a few days - - -

To show the significance of the omission of those evening or rather night visits of Papa's – for they came sometimes at eleven, and sometimes at twelve – I will tell you that he used to sit and talk in them, and then *always* kneel and pray with me and for me – which I used of course to feel as a proof of very kind and affectionate sympathy on his part, and which has proportionably pained me in the withdrawing. They were no ordinary visits, you observe, .. and he could not well throw me further from him than by ceasing to pay them – the thing is quite expressively significant. Not that I pretend to complain, nor to have reason to complain. One should not be grateful for kindness, only while it lasts: *that* would be a short-breathed gratitude. I just tell you the fact proving that it cannot be accidental - - -

May God bless you – I am quite heavy-hearted today, but never less yours,

E.B.B.

- - - Do not be angry with me – do not think it my fault – but *I do not go to Italy* .. it has ended as I feared. What passed between George and Papa there is no need of telling: only the latter said that I 'might go if I pleased, but that going it would be under his heaviest displeasure'. George, in great indignation, pressed the question fully: but all was vain .. and I am left in this position .. to go, if I please, with his displeasure over me, (which after what you have said and after what Mr. Kenyon has said, and after what my own conscience and deepest moral convictions say aloud, I would unhesitatingly do at this hour!) and necessarily run the risk of exposing my sister and brother to that same displeasure .. from which risk I shrink and fall back and feel that to incur it, is impossible. Dear Mr. Kenyon has been here and we have been talking – and he sees what I see .. that I am justified in going myself, but not in bringing others into difficulty. The very kindness and goodness with which they desire me (both my sisters) 'not to think of them', naturally makes me think more of them. And so, tell me that I am not wrong in taking up my chain again and acquiescing in this hard necessity. The bitterest 'fact' of all is, that I had believed Papa to have loved me more than he obviously does: but I never regret knowledge .. I mean I never would *un*know anything .. even were it the taste of the apples by the Dead sea – and this must be accepted like the rest. In the meantime your letter comes – and if I could seem to be very unhappy after reading it .. why it would be 'all pretence' on my part, believe me. Can you care for me so much .. *you*? Then *that* is light enough to account for all the shadows, and to make them almost unregarded – the shadows of the life behind - - -

And now that you are not well,[1] will you take care? and not come on Wednesday unless you are better? and never again bring me *wet flowers*, which probably did all the harm on Thursday? I was afraid for you then, though I said nothing. May God bless you.

Ever yours I am – your own.

[1] R.B. had 'a cold, influenza or some unpleasant thing'.

Tuesday Morning
(Post-mark, October 14, 1845)

Be sure, my own, dearest love, that this is for the best; will be seen for the best in the end. It is hard to bear now – but *you* have to bear it; any other person could not, and you will, I know, knowing you – *will* be well this one winter if you can, and then – since I am *not* selfish in this love to you, my own conscience tells me, – I desire, more earnestly than I ever knew what desiring was, to be yours and with you and, as far as may be in this life and world, YOU – and no hindrance to that, but one, gives me a moment's care or tear; but that one is just your little hand, as I could fancy it raised in any least interest of yours – and before that, I am, and would ever be, still silent. But now – what is to make you raise that hand? I will not speak *now;* not seem to take advantage of your present feelings, – we will be rational, and all-considering and weighing consequences, and foreseeing them – but first I will prove . . if *that* has to be done, why – but I begin speaking, and I should not, I know.

Bless you, love!
R.B.

E.B.B. TO R.B.

(Post-mark, October 22, 1845)

- - - I did not say half I thought about the poems[1] yesterday – and their various power and beauty will be striking and surprising to your most accustomed readers. 'St. Praxed' – 'Pictor Ignotus' – 'The Ride' – 'The Duchess'! – Of the new poems I like supremely the first and last . . that 'Lost Leader' which strikes so broadly and deep . . which nobody can ever forget – and which is worth all the journalising and pamphleteering in the world! – and then, the last 'Thought'[2] which is quite to be grudged to that place of fragments . . those grand sea-sights in the long lines. Should

[1] R.B.'s 'Dramatic Romances and Lyrics' (No. VII of *Bells and Pomegranates*).
[2] 'Home Thoughts from the Sea'.

not these fragments be severed otherwise than by numbers? The last stanza but one of the 'Lost Mistress' seemed obscure to me. Is it so really? The end you have put to 'England in Italy' gives unity to the whole .. just what the poem wanted. Also you have given some nobler lines to the middle than met me there before. 'The Duchess' appears to me more than ever a new-minted golden coin – the rhythm of it answering to your own description, 'Speech half asleep, or song half awake?' You have right of trove to these novel effects of rhythm. Now if people do not cry out about these poems, what are we to think of the world?

May God bless you always – send me the next proof *in any case.*

Your
E.B.B.

Friday
(Post-mark, October 25, 1845)

- - - First I will say that you are not to fancy any the least danger of my falling under displeasure through your visits – there is no sort of risk of it *for the present* – and if I ran the risk of making you uncomfortable about *that*, I did foolishly, and what I meant to do was different. I wish you also to understand that *even if you came here every day*, my brothers and sisters would simply care to know if I liked it, and then be glad if I was glad: – the caution referred to one person alone. In relation to *whom*, however, there will be no 'getting over' – you might as well think to sweep off a third of the stars of Heaven with the motion of your eyelashes – this, for matter of fact and certainty – and this, as I said before, the keeping of a general rule and from no disrespect towards individuals: a great peculiarity *in the individual* of course. But .. though I have been a submissive daughter, and this from no effort, but for love's sake .. because I loved him tenderly (and love him), .. and hoped that he loved me back again even if the proofs came untenderly sometimes – yet I have reserved for myself *always* that right over my own affections which is the most strictly personal of all things, and which involves principles and consequences of infinite importance and scope – even though I *never* thought (except perhaps when the door of life was just about to open .. before it opened) never thought it probable or possible that I should have occasion for the exercise; from without and from within at once. I have too much need to look up. For friends, I can look any way .. round, and *down* even – the merest thread of a sympathy will draw me sometimes – or even the least look of kind eyes over a dyspathy – 'Cela se peut facilement'. But for another relation – it was all different – and rightly so – and so very different – 'Cela ne se peut nullement' – as in Malherbe - - -

May God bless you – and me as I am

Yours,

E.B.B.

E.B.B. TO R.B.

Thursday Evening

(Post-mark, November 7, 1845)

- - - I do hold that nobody with an ordinary understanding has the slightest pretence for attaching a charge of obscurity to this new number[1] – there are lights enough for the critics to scan one another's dull blank of visage by. One verse indeed in that expressive lyric of the 'Lost Mistress', does still seem questionable to me, though you have changed a word since I saw it; and still I fancy that I rather leap at the meaning than reach it – but it is my own fault probably .. I am not sure. With that one exception I *am quite* sure that people who shall complain of darkness are blind .. I mean, that the construction is clear and unembarrassed everywhere. Subtleties of thought which are not directly apprehensible by minds of a common range, are here as elsewhere in your writings – but if to utter things 'hard to understand' from *that* cause be an offence, why we may begin with 'our beloved brother Paul', you know, and go down through all the geniuses of the world, and bid them put away their inspirations. You must descend to the level of critic A or B, that he may look into your

[1] No. VII of *Bells and Pomegranates* (see also E.B.B.'s letter of October 22nd).

face .. Ah well! – 'Let them rave'. You will live when all *those* are under the willows. In the meantime there is something better, as you said, even than your poetry – as the giver is better than the gift, and the maker than the creature, and *you* than *yours*. Yes – *you* than *yours* .. (I did not mean it so when I wrote it first .. but I accept the 'bona verba', and use the phrase for the end of my letter) .. as *you* are better than *yours*; even when so much yours as your own

E.B.B.

R.B. TO E.B.B.

Sunday Evening
(Post-mark, November 10, 1845)

When I come back from seeing you, and think over it all, there never is a least word of yours I could not occupy myself with, and wish to return to you with some .. not to say, all .. the thoughts and fancies it is sure to call out of me. There is nothing in you that does not draw out all of me. You possess me, dearest .. and there is no help for the expressing it all, no voice nor hand, but these of mine which shrink and turn away from the attempt. So you must go on, patiently, knowing me more and more, and your entire power on me, and I will console myself, to the full extent, with your knowledge – penetration, intuition – *somehow* I must believe you can get to what is here, in me, without the pretence of my telling or writing it. But, because I give up the great achievements, there is no reason I should not secure any occasion of making clear one of the less important points that arise in our intercourse .. if I fancy I can do it with the least success. For instance, it is on my mind to explain what I meant yesterday by trusting that the entire happiness I feel in the letters, and the help in the criticising might not be hurt by the surmise, even, that those labours to which you were born, might be suspended, in any degree, through such generosity to *me*. Dearest, I believed in your glorious genius and knew it for a true star from the moment I saw it; long before I had the blessing of knowing it was MY star, with my fortune and futurity in it. And, when I draw back from myself, and look better and more clearly, then I *do* feel, with you, that the writing a few letters more or less, reading many or few rhymes of any other person, would not interfere in any material degree with that power of yours – that you might easily make one so happy and yet go on writing 'Geraldines' and 'Berthas'[1] – but – how can I, dearest, leave my heart's treasures long, even to look at your genius? .. and when I come back and find all safe, find the comfort of you, the traces of you .. *will* it do – tell me – to trust all that as a light effort, an easy matter?

Yet, if you can lift me with one hand, while the other suffices to crown you – there is queenliness in *that*, too! - - -

Ever your own

R.B.

Two letters in one – Wednesday
(Post-mark, November 15, 1845)

I shall see you tomorrow and yet am writing what you will have to read perhaps. When you spoke of 'stars' and 'geniuses' in that letter, I did not seem to hear; I was listening to those words of the letter which were of a better silver in the sound than even your praise could be: and now that at last I come to hear them in their extravagance (oh such pure extravagance about 'glorious geniuses' –) I can't help telling you they were heard last, and deserved it.

Shall I tell you besides? – The first moment in which I seemed to admit to myself in a flash of lightning the *possibility* of your affection for me being more than dreamwork .. the first moment was *that* when you intimated (as you have done since repeatedly) that you cared for me not for a reason, but because you cared for me.[2] Now such a 'parceque' which reasonable people would take to be irrational, was just the only one fitted to the uses of my understanding on the particular question we were upon .. just the 'woman's reason' suitable to the woman ..: for I could

[1] 'Lady Geraldine's Courtship' and 'Bertha in the Lane' were two of E.B.B.'s 1844 *Poems*.

[2] Cf. *Sonnets from the Portuguese*, No. XIV, p. 210.

64

understand that it might be as you said, and, if so, that it was altogether unanswerable .. do you see? If a fact includes its own cause .. why there it stands for ever – one of 'earth's immortalities' – *as long as it includes it*.

And when unreasonableness stands for a reason, it is a promising state of things, we may both admit, and proves what it would be as well not too curiously to enquire into. But then .. to look at it in a brighter aspect, .. I do remember how, years ago, when talking the foolishnesses which women will talk when they are by themselves, and not forced to be sensible, .. one of my friends thought it 'safest to begin with a little aversion',[1] and another, wisest to begin with a great deal of esteem, and how the best attachments were produced so and so, .. I took it into my head to say that the best was where there was no cause at all for it, and the more wholly unreasonable, the better still; that the motive should lie in the feeling itself and not in the object of it – and that the affection which could (if it could) throw itself out on an idiot with a goitre would be more admirable than Abelard's. Whereupon everybody laughed, and someone thought it affected of me and no true opinion, and others said plainly that it was immoral, and somebody else hoped, in a sarcasm, that I meant to act out my theory for the advantage of the world. To which I replied quite gravely that I had not virtue enough – and so, people laughed as it is fair to laugh when other people are esteemed to talk nonsense. And all this came back to me in the south wind of your 'parceque', and I tell it as it came .. now - - -

When you write will you say exactly how you are? and will you write? And I want to explain to you that although I don't make a profession of equable spirits, (as a matter of temperament, my spirits were always given to rock a little, up and down) yet that I did not mean to be so ungrateful and wicked as to complain of low spirits now and to you.[2] It would not be true either: and I said 'low' to express a merely bodily state. My opium comes in to keep the pulse from fluttering and fainting .. to give the right composure and point of balance to the nervous system. I don't take it for 'my spirits' in the usual sense; you must not

---

[1] The sentiment was originally Mrs. Malaprop's: 'The Rivals', I-2.

[2] Cf. *Sonnets from the Portuguese*, No. XXV.

think such a thing. The medical man who came to see me made me take it the other day when he was in the room, before the right hour and when I was talking quite cheerfully, just for the need he observed in the pulse. 'It was a necessity of my position', he said. Also I do not suffer from it in any way, as people usually do who take opium. I am not even subject to an opium-headache. As to the low spirits I will not say that mine *have not* been low enough and with cause enough; but *even then*, .. why if you were to ask the nearest witnesses, .. say, even my own sisters, .. everybody would tell you, I think, that the 'cheerfulness' even *then*, was the remarkable thing in me – certainly it has been remarked about me again and again. Nobody has known that it was an effort (a habit of effort) to throw the light on the outside, – I do abhor so that ignoble groaning aloud of the 'groans of Testy and Sensitude' – yet I may say that for three years I never was conscious of one movement of pleasure in anything. Think if I could mean to complain of 'low spirits' now, and to you. Why it would be like complaining of not being able to see at noon – which would simply prove that I was very blind. And you, who are not blind, cannot make out what is written – so you *need not try*. May God bless you long after you have done blessing me!

Your own E.B.B.

R.B. TO E.B.B.

Friday Night
(Post-mark, November 22, 1845)

- - - When I spread out my riches before me and think *what* the hour and more means that you endow me with, I *do* – not to say *could* – I *do* form resolutions, and say to myself – 'If next time I am bidden stay away a FORTNIGHT, I will not reply by a word beyond the grateful assent.' I *do*, God knows, lay up in my heart these pricelss treasures, – shall I tell you? I never in my life kept a journal, a register of sights, or fancies, or feelings - - - But I have, from the first, recorded the date and the duration of every visit to you; the numbers of minutes you have given me .. and I put them together till they make .. nearly two days now; four-and-twenty-hour-long-days, that I have been *by you* – and I enter the room determining to get up and go sooner .. and I go away into the light street repenting that I went so soon by I don't know how many minutes – for, love, what is it all, this love for you, but an earnest desiring to include you in myself, if that might be; to feel you in my very heart and hold you there for ever, through all chance and earthly changes!

There, I had better leave off; the words! - - -

I am *very* well – quite well; yes, dearest! The pain is quite gone; and the inconvenience, hard on its trace. You will write to me again, will you not? And be as brief as your heart lets you, to me who hoard up your words and get remote and imperfect ideas of what .. shall it be written ? .. anger at you could mean, when I see a line blotted out; a *second-thoughted* finger-tip rapidly put forth upon one of my gold pieces! - - -

E.B.B. TO R.B.

Monday
(Post-mark, November 24, 1845)

- - - I never gave away what you ask me to give *you*,[1] to a human being, except my nearest relatives and once or twice or thrice to female friends, .. never, though reproached for it; and it is just three weeks since I said last to an asker that I was 'too great a prude for such a thing'! it was best to anticipate the accusation! – And, prude or not, I could not – I never could – *something* would not let me. And now .. what am I to do .. 'for my own sake and not yours?' Should you have it, or not? Why I suppose .. *yes*. I suppose that 'for my own sense of justice and in order to show that I was wrong' (which is wrong – you wrote a wrong word there .. 'right', you meant!) 'to show that I was *right* and am no longer so', .. I suppose you must have it. 'Oh, *You*', .. who have your way in everything! Which does not mean .. Oh, vous qui avez toujours raison – far from it.

Also .. which does not mean that I shall give you what you ask for, *tomorrow*, – because I shall not – and one of my conditions is (with others to follow) that *not a word be said tomorrow,*

---

[1] A lock of her hair. She sent him one, in the setting of a ring, a week later. (Cf. *Sonnets from the Portuguese*, Nos. XVIII and XIX.)

you understand. Some day I will send it perhaps .. as you *knew* I should .. ah, as you knew I should .. notwithstanding that 'getting up' .. that 'imitation' .. of humility: as you knew *too* well I should! - - -

Your

E.B.B.

R.B. TO E.B.B.

Tuesday

(Post-mark, December 2, 1845)

I was happy, so happy before! But I am happier and richer now. My love – no words could serve here, but there is life before us, and to the end of it the vibration now struck will extend – I will live and die with your beautiful ring, your beloved hair – comforting me, blessing me.

Let me write tomorrow – when I think on all you have been and are to me, on the wonder of it and the deliciousness, it makes the paper words that come seem vainer than ever – Tomorrow I will write.

May God bless you, my own, my precious –

I am all your own

R.B.

E.B.B. TO R.B.

Friday

(Post-mark, December 13, 1845)

Do not blame me in your thoughts for what I said yesterday or wrote a day before, or think perhaps on the dark side of some other days when I cannot help it .. always when I cannot help it – you could not blame me if you saw the full motives as I feel them. If it is distrust, it is not of *you*, dearest of all! – but of myself rather: – it is not doubt *of* you, but *for* you. From the beginning I have been subject to the too reasonable fear which rises as my spirits fall, that your happiness might suffer in the end through your having known me: – it is for *you*, I fear, whenever I fear: – and if you were less to me, .. *should* I fear do you think? – if you were to me only what I am to myself for instance, . . if your happiness were only as precious as my own in my own eyes, . . should I fear, do you think, *then*? Think, and do not blame me - - -

As to unfavourable influences, . . I can speak of them quietly, having foreseen them from the first, . . and it is true, I have been thinking since yesterday, that I might be prevented from receiving you here, and *should*, if all were known: but with that act, the adverse power would end. It is not my fault if I have to choose between two affections; only my pain; and I have not to choose between two duties, I feel, . . since I am yours, while I am of any worth to you at all. For the plan of the sealed letter, it would correct no evil, – ah, you do not see, you do not understand. The danger does not come from the side to which a reason may go. Only one person holds the thunder – and I shall be thundered at; I shall not be reasoned with – it is impossible. I could tell you some dreary chronicles made for laughing and crying over; and you know that if I once thought I might be loved enough to be spared above others, I cannot think so now. In the meanwhile we need not for the present be afraid. Let there be ever so many suspectors, there will be no informers. I suspect the suspectors, but the informers are out of the world, I am very sure: – and then, the one person, by a curious anomaly, *never* draws an inference of this order, until the bare blade of it is thrust palpably into his hand, point outwards. So it has been in other cases than ours – and so it is, at this moment in the house, with others than ourselves - - -

For 'conditions' – now I will tell you what I said once in a jest . .

'If a prince of Eldorado should come, with a pedigree of lineal descent from some signory in the moon in one hand, and a ticket of good-behaviour from the nearest Independent chapel, in the other' –?

'Why even *then*,' said my sister Arabel, 'it would not *do*.' And she was right, and we all agreed that she was right. It is an obliquity of the will – and one laughs at it till the turn comes for crying - - -

Your

E.B.B.

E.B.B. TO R.B.

Tuesday Evening
(Post-mark, December 17, 1845)

Henrietta[1] had a note from Mr. Kenyon to the effect that he was 'coming to see *Ba*'[2] today if in any way he found it possible. Now he has not come – and the inference is that he will come tomorrow – in which case you will be convicted of not wishing to be with him perhaps. So .. would it not be advisable for you to call at his door for a moment – and *before* you come here? Think of it. You know it would not do to vex him – would it?

Your

E.B.B.

R.B. TO E.B.B.

Friday Morning
(Post-mark, December 19, 1845)

- - - You never before heard me love and bless and send my heart after – 'Ba' – did you? Ba .. and that is you! I TRIED .. (more than *wanted*) to call you *that*, on Wednesday! I have a flower here – rather, a tree, a mimosa, which must be turned and turned, the side to the light changing in a little time to the *leafy* side, where all the fans lean and spread .. so I turn your name to me, that side I have not last seen: you cannot tell how I feel glad that you will not part with the name – Barrett – seeing you have two of the same – and must always, moreover, remain my EBB! - - -

Bless you, my own sweetest. You will write to me, I know in my heart! Ever may God bless you!

R.B.

E.B.B. TO R.B.

Thursday Evening
(Post-mark, December 20, 1845)

Dearest, you know how to say what makes me happiest, you who never think, you say, of making me happy! For my part I do

[1] The elder of E.B.B.'s two sisters.

[2] The family nick-name by which she was invariably called. (Cf. *Sonnets from the Portuguese*, No. **XXXIII**.)

70

not think of it either; I simply understand you *are* my happiness, and that therefore you could not make another happiness for me, such as would be worth having – not even *you*! Why, how could you? *That* was in my mind to speak yesterday, but I could not speak it – to write it, is easier.

Talking of happiness – shall I tell you? Promise not to be angry and I will tell you. I have thought sometimes that, if I considered myself wholly, I should choose to die this winter – now – before I had disappointed you in anything. But because you are better and dearer and more to be considered than I, I do *not* choose it. I *cannot* choose to give you any pain, even on the chance of its being a less pain, a less evil, than what may follow perhaps (who can say?), if I should prove the burden of your life.

For if you make me happy with some words, you frighten me with others – as with the extravagance yesterday – and seriously – *too* seriously, when the moment for smiling at them is past – I am frightened, I tremble! When you come to know me as well as I know myself, what can save me, do you think, from disappointing and displeasing you? I ask the question, and find no answer.

It is a poor answer, to say that I can do one thing well .. that I have one capacity largely - - - The capacity of loving is the largest of my powers I think – I thought so before knowing you – and one form of feeling. And although any woman might love you – *every* woman, – with understanding enough to discern you by – (oh, do not fancy that I am unduly magnifying mine office) yet I persist in persuading myself that! Because I have the capacity, as I said – and besides I owe more to you than others could, it seems to me: let me boast of it. To many, you might be better than all things while one of all things: to me you are instead of all – to many, a crowning happiness – to me, the happiness itself. From out of the deep dark pits men see the stars more gloriously – and *de profundis amavi* - - -

As your letter does not come it is a good opportunity for asking what sort of ill humour, or (to be more correct) bad temper, you most particularly admire – sulkiness? – the divine gift of sitting aloof in a cloud like any god for three weeks together perhaps – pettishness? .. which will get you up a storm about a crooked pin or a straight one either? obstinacy? – which

D

is an agreeable form of temper I can assure you, and describes itself – or the good open passion which lies on the floor and kicks, like one of my cousins? – Certainly I prefer the last, and should, I think, prefer it (as an evil), even if it were not the born weakness of my own nature – though I humbly confess (to *you*, who seem to think differently of these things) that never since I was a child have I upset all the chairs and tables and thrown the books about the room in a fury – I am afraid I do not even 'kick', like my cousin, now. Those demonstrations were all done by the 'light of other days' – not a very full light, I used to be accustomed to think: – but *you*, – *you* think otherwise, *you* take a fury to be the opposite of 'indifference', as if there could be no such thing as self-control! Now for my part, I do believe that the worst-tempered persons in the world are less so through sensibility than selfishness – they spare nobody's heart, on the ground of being themselves pricked by a straw. Now see if it isn't so. What, after all, is a good temper but generosity in trifles – and what, without it, is the happiness of life? We have only to look round us. I *saw* a woman, once, burst into tears, because her husband cut the bread and butter too thick. I saw *that* with my own eyes. Was it *sensibility*, I wonder! They were at least real tears and ran down her cheeks. 'You *always* do it!' she said.

Why how you must sympathize with the heroes and heroines of the French romances (*do* you sympathize with them very much?) when at the slightest provocation they break up the tables and chairs, (a degree beyond the deeds of my childhood! – *I* only used to upset them) break up the tables and chairs and chiffoniers, and dash the china to atoms. The men *do* the furniture, and the women the porcelain: and pray observe that they always set about this as a matter of course! When they have broken everything in the room, they sink down quite (and very naturally) *abattus*. I remember a particular case of a hero of Frederic Soulié's, who, in the course of an 'emotion', takes up a chair *unconsciously*, and breaks it into very small pieces, and then proceeds with his soliloquy. Well! – the clearest idea this excites in *me*, is of the low condition in Paris, of moral government and of upholstery. Because – just consider for yourself – how *you* would succeed in breaking to pieces even a three-legged stool if it were properly put together – as stools are in England – just yourself, without a hammer and a screw! You might work at it *comme quatre*, and find it hard to finish, I imagine - - -

Your own –

R.B. TO E.B.B.   *Saturday*
(Post-mark, December 20, 1845)

I do not, nor will not think, dearest, of ever 'making you happy' – I can imagine no way of working that end, which does not go straight to my own truest, only true happiness – yet in every such effort there is implied some distinction, some supererogatory grace, or why speak of it at all? *You* it is, are my happiness, and all that ever can be: YOU – dearest!

But never, if you would not, what you will not do I know, never revert to *that* frightful wish.[1] 'Disappoint me?' 'I speak what I know and testify what I have seen' – you shall 'mystery' again and again – I do not dispute that, but do not *you* dispute, neither, that mysteries are. But it is simply because I do most justice to the mystical part of what I feel for you, because I consent to lay most stress on that fact of facts that I love you, beyond admiration, and respect, and esteem, and affection even, and do not adduce any reason which stops short of accounting for *that*, whatever else it would account for, because I do this, in pure logical justice – *you* are able to turn and wonder (if you *do* .. *now*) what causes it all! My love, only wait, only believe in me, and it cannot be but I shall, little by little, become known to you – after long years, perhaps, but still one day: I *would* say *this* now – but I will write more tomorrow. God bless my sweetest – ever, love, I am your

R.B.

E.B.B. TO R.B.   *Sunday Night*
(Post-mark, December 24, 1845)

- - - People used to say to me, 'You expect too much – you are too romantic.' And my answer always was that 'I could not

[1] Cf. *Sonnets from the Portuguese*, No. XXIII, for her comment.

expect too much when I expected nothing at all' .. which was the truth – for I never thought (and how often I have *said that!*) I never thought that anyone whom *I* could love, would stoop to love *me* .. the two things seemed clearly incompatible to my understanding.

And now when it comes in a miracle, you wonder at me for looking twice, thrice, four times, to see if it comes through ivory or *horn*. You wonder that it should seem to me at first all illusion – illusion for you, – illusion for me as a consequence. But how natural.

It is true of me – very true – that I have not a high appreciation of what passes in the world - - - under the name of love; and that a distrust of the thing had grown to be a habit of mind with me when I knew you first. It has appeared to me, through all the seclusion of my life and the narrow experience it admitted of, that in nothing men – and women too – were so apt to mistake their own feelings, as in this one thing. Putting *falseness* quite on one side, quite out of sight and consideration, an honest mistaking of feeling appears wonderfully common, and no mistake has such frightful results – none can. Self-love and generosity, a mistake may come from either – from pity, from admiration, from any blind impulse – oh, when I look at the histories of my own female friends – to go no step further! And if it is true of the *women*, what must the other side be? To see the marriages which are made every day! worse than solitudes and more desolate! In the case of the two happiest I ever knew, one of the husbands said in confidence to a brother of mine – not much in confidence or I should not have heard it, but in a sort of smoking frankness, – that he had 'ruined his prospects by marrying'; and the other said to himself at the very moment of professing an extraordinary happiness, .. 'But I should have done as well if I had not married *her.*'

Then for the falseness – the first time I ever, in my own experience, heard that word which rhymes to glove and comes as easily off and on (on some hands!) – it was from a man of whose attentions to another woman I was at that *time her confidante*. I was bound so to silence for her sake, that I could not even speak the scorn that was in me – and in fact my uppermost feeling was a sort of horror .. a terror – for I was very young then, and the world did, at the moment, look ghastly!

The falseness and the calculations! – why how can you, who are *just*, *blame women* .. when you must know what the 'system' of man is towards them, – and of men not ungenerous otherwise? Why are women to be blamed if they act as if they had to do with swindlers? – is it not the mere instinct of preservation which makes them do it? These make women what they are. And your 'honourable men', the most loyal of them, (for instance) is it not a rule with them (unless when taken unaware through a want of self-government) to force a woman (trying all means) to force a woman to stand committed in her affections .. (they with their feet lifted all the time to trample on her for want of delicacy) before *they* risk the pin-prick to their own personal pitiful vanities? Oh – to see how these things are set about by *men*! to see how a man carefully holding up on each side the skirts of an embroidered vanity to keep it quite safe from the wet, will contrive to tell you in so many words that he .. might love you if the sun shone! And women are to be blamed! Why there are, to be sure, cold and heartless, light and changeable, ungenerous and calculating women in the world! – that is sure. But for the most part, they are only what they are made .. and far better than the nature of the making .. of that I am confident. The loyal make the loyal, the disloyal the disloyal. And I give no more discredit to those women you speak of, than I myself can take any credit in this thing – I. Because who could be disloyal with *you* .. with whatever corrupt inclination? *you*, who are the noblest of all? If you judge me so, .. it is my privilege rather than my merit .. as I feel of myself - - -

I shall hear from you, I hope .. I *ask* you to let me hear soon. I write all sorts of things to you, rightly and wrongly perhaps; when wrongly, forgive it. I think of you always. May God bless you. 'Love me for ever', as

Your

BA

Tuesday
(Post-mark, December 30, 1845)

When you are gone I find your flowers; and you never spoke of nor showed them to me – so instead of yesterday I thank you today – thank you. Count among the miracles that your flowers live with me – I accept *that* for an omen, dear – dearest! Flowers in general, all other flowers, die of despair when they come into the same atmosphere . . used to do it so constantly and observably that it made me melancholy and I left off for the most part having them here. Now you see how they put up with the close room, and condescend to me and the dust – it is true and no fancy! To be sure they know that I care for them and that I stand up by the table myself to change their water and cut their stalk freshly at intervals – *that* may make a difference perhaps. Only the great reason must be that they are yours, and that you teach them to bear with me patiently.

Do not pretend even to misunderstand what I meant to say yesterday of dear Mr. Kenyon. His blame would fall as my blame of myself has fallen: he would say – will say – 'it is ungenerous of her to let such a risk be run! I thought she would have been more generous.' There, is Mr. Kenyon's opinion as I foresee it! Not that it would be spoken, you know! he is too kind. And then, he said to me last summer, somewhere à propos to the flies or butterflies, that he had 'long ceased to wonder at any extreme of foolishness produced by – *love*'. He will of course think you very very foolish, but not ungenerously foolish like other people.

Never mind. I do not mind indeed. I mean, that, having said to myself worse than the worst perhaps of what can be said against me by any who regard me at all, and feeling it put to silence by the fact that you *do* feel so and so for me; feeling that fact to be an answer to all, – I cannot mind much, in comparison, the railing at second remove. There will be a nine days' railing of it and no more: and if on the ninth day you should not exactly wish never to have known me, the better reason will be demonstrated to stand with us. On this one point the wise man cannot judge for the fool his neighbour. If you *do* love me, the inference is that you would be happier with than without me – and whether you do, you know better than another: so I think of *you* and not of *them* – always of you! When I talked of being afraid of dear Mr. Kenyon, I just meant that he makes me nervous with his all-scrutinising spectacles, put on for great occasions, and his questions which seem to belong to the spectacles, they go together so: – and then I have no presence of mind, as you may see without the spectacles. My only way of hiding (when people set themselves to look for me) would be the old child's way of getting behind the window curtains or under the sofa: – and even *that* might not be effectual if I had recourse to it now. Do you think it would? Two or three times I fancied that Mr. Kenyon suspected something – but if he ever *did*, his only reproof was a reduplicated praise of *you* – he praises you always and in relation to every sort of subject - - -

May God bless you – and mind to say how you are *exactly*, and don't neglect the walking, *pray* do not.

Your own

R.B. TO E.B.B.

Sunday Night
(Post-mark, January 5, 1846)

- - - I suspect, par parenthèse, you have found out by this time my odd liking for 'vermin' – you once wrote '*your* snails' – and certainly snails are old clients of mine – but efts! - - - Never try and catch a speckled gray lizard when we are in Italy, love, and you see his tail hang out of the chink of a wall, his winter-house – because the strange tail will snap off, drop from him and stay in your fingers – and though you afterwards learn that there is more desperation in it and glorious determination to be free, than positive pain (so people say who have no tails to be twisted off) – and though, moreover, the tail grows again after a sort – *yet* .. don't do it, for it will give you a thrill! What a fine fellow our English water-eft is; 'Triton paludis Linnaei' – e come guizza[1] (that you can't say in another language; cannot preserve the little in-and-out motion along with the straightforwardness!) –

[1] How it flickers,

I always loved all those wild creatures God '*sets up for themselves*' so independently of us, so successfully, with their strange happy minute inch of a candle, as it were, to light them; while we run about and against each other with our great cressets and fire-pots. I once saw a solitary bee nipping a leaf round till it exactly fitted the front of a hole; his nest, no doubt; or tomb, perhaps - - - Well, it seemed awful to watch that bee – he seemed so *instantly* from the teaching of God! - - -

E.B.B. TO R.B.

Sunday
(Post-mark, January 6, 1846)

- - - You never guessed perhaps, what I look back to at this moment in the psychology of our intercourse, the curious double feeling I had about you – you personally, and you as the writer of these letters, and the crisis of the feeling, when I was positively vexed and jealous of myself for not succeeding better in making a unity of the two. I could not! And moreover I could not help but that the writer of the letters seemed nearer to me, long .. long .. and in spite of the postmark, than did the personal visitor who confounded me, and left me constantly under such an impression of its being all dream-work on his side, that I have stamped my feet on this floor with impatience to think of having to wait so many hours before the 'candid' closing letter could come with its confessional of an illusion. 'People say', I used to think, 'that women *always* know, and certainly I do not know, and therefore .. therefore.' – The logic crushed on like Juggernaut's car. But in the letters it was different – the dear letters took me on the side of my own ideal life where I was able to stand a little upright and look round. I could read such letters for ever and answer them after a fashion .. that, I felt from the beginning. But *you* – ! - - -

Do you know, I think I like frogs too – particularly the very little leaping frogs, which are so high-hearted as to emulate the birds. I remember being scolded by my nurses for taking them up in my hands and letting them leap from one hand to the other.

But for the toad! – why, at the end of the row of narrow beds which we called our gardens when we were children, grew an old thorn, and in the hollow of the root of the thorn, lived a toad, a great ancient toad, whom I, for one, never dared approach too nearly. That he 'wore a jewel in his head' I doubted nothing at all. You must see it glitter if you stooped and looked steadily into the hole. And on days when he came out and sate swelling his black sides, I never looked steadily; I would run a hundred yards round through the shrubs, deeper than knee-deep in the long wet grass and nettles, rather than go past him where he sate; being steadily of opinion, in the profundity of my natural history-learning, that if he took it into his toad's head to spit at me I should drop down dead in a moment, poisoned as by one of the Medici.

Oh – and I had a field-mouse for a pet once, and should have joined my sisters in a rat's nest if I had not been ill at the time (as it was, the little rats were tenderly smothered by over-love!): and blue-bottle flies I used to feed, and hated your spiders for them; yet no, not much. My aversion proper .. call it horror rather .. was for the silent, cold, clinging, gliding *bat;* and even now, I think, I could not sleep in the room with that strange bird-mouse-creature, as it glides round the ceiling silently, silently as its shadow does on the floor. If you listen or look, there is not a wave of the wing – the wing never waves! A bird without a feather! a beast that flies! and so cold! as cold as a fish! It is the most supernatural-seeming of natural things. And then to see how when the windows are open at night those bats come sailing .. without a sound – and go .. you cannot guess where! – fade with the night-blackness! - - -

Your own –

E.B.B. TO R.B.

Saturday
(Post-mark, January 10, 1846)

- - - Do you know, when you have told me to think of you, I have been feeling ashamed of thinking of you so much, of thinking of only you – which *is* too much, perhaps. Shall I tell you? it seems to me, to myself, that no man was ever before to any woman what you are to me – the fulness must be in proportion, you know, to the vacancy .. and only *I* know what was behind – the long wilderness *without* the blossoming rose .. and the capacity for happiness, like a black gaping hole, before this silver flooding. Is it wonderful that I should stand as in a dream, and disbelieve – not *you* – but my own fate? Was ever any one taken suddenly from a lampless dungeon and placed upon the pinnacle of a mountain, without the head turning round and the heart turning faint, as mine do? And you love me *more*, you say? – Shall I thank you or God? Both, – indeed – and there is no possible return from me to either of you! I thank you as the unworthy may .. and as we all thank God. How shall I ever prove what my heart is to you? how will you ever see it as I feel it? I ask myself in vain.

Have so much faith in me, my only beloved, as to use me simply for your own advantage and happiness, and to your own ends without a thought of any others – *that* is all I could ask you without any disquiet as to the granting of it – May God bless you! –

Your

B A

R.B. TO E.B.B.

Sunday
(Post-mark, January 12, 1846)

I have no words for you, my dearest, – I shall never have.

You are mine, I am yours. Now, here is one sign of what I said .. that I must love you more than at first .. a little sign, and to be looked narrowly for or it escapes me, but then the increase it shows *can* only be little, so very little now – and as the fine French Chemical Analysts bring themselves to appreciate matter in its refined stages by *millionths*, so –! At first I only thought of being *happy* in you, – in your happiness: now I most think of you in the dark hours that must come – I shall grow old with you, and die with you – as far as I can look into the night I see the light with me. And surely with that provision of comfort one should turn with fresh joy and renewed sense of security to the sunny middle of the day. I am in the full sunshine now; and *after*, all seems cared for, – is it too homely an illustration if I say the day's visit is not crossed by uncertainties as to the return through the wild country at nightfall? – Now Keats speaks of 'Beauty, that must *die* – and Joy whose hand is ever at his lips, bidding farewell!'[1] And *who* spoke of – looking up into the eyes and asking 'And *how long* will you love us?' – There is a Beauty that will not die, a Joy that bids no farewell, dear dearest eyes that will love for ever! - - -

See, love, – a year is gone by – we were in one relation when you wrote at the end of a letter 'Do not say I do not tire you' (by writing) – '*I am sure I do*'. A year has gone by – *Did you tire me then? Now*, you tell me what is told; for my sake, sweet, let the few years go by; we are married, and my arms are round you, and my face touches yours, and I am asking you, '*Were you not* to me, in that dim beginning of 1846, a joy behind all joys, a life added to and transforming mine, the good I choose from all the possible gifts of God on this earth, for which I seemed to have lived; which accepting, I thankfully step aside and let the rest get what they can; what, it is very likely, they esteem more – for why should my eye be evil because God's is good; why should I grudge that, giving them, I do believe, infinitely less, he gives them a content in the inferior good and belief in its worth? I should have wished *that* further concession, that illusion as I believe it, for their sakes – but I cannot undervalue my own treasure and so scant the only tribute of mere gratitude which is in my power to pay.' Hear this said *now before* the few years, and believe in it *now, for then*, dearest! - - -

R.B. TO E.B.B.

Thursday
(Post-mark, January 15, 1846)

- - - My Ba, you are to consider now for me. Your health, your strength, it is all wonderful; that is not my dream, you know – but what all see. Now, steadily care for us both – take

[1] Keats wrote 'Adieu'.

time, take counsel if you choose; but at the end tell me what you will do for your part – thinking of me as utterly devoted, soul and body, to you, living wholly in your life, seeing good and ill only as you see, – being yours as your hand is, – or as your Flush,[1] rather. Then I will, on my side, prepare. When I say 'take counsel' – I reserve my last right, the man's right of first speech. *I* stipulate, too, and require to say my own speech in my own words or by letter – remember! But this living without you is too tormenting now. So begin thinking, – as for Spring, as for a New Year, as for a new life - - -

Now, bless you, my precious Ba – I am your own –

– Your own R

E.B.B. TO R.B.

Thursday Morning
(Post-mark, January 17, 1846)

- - - 'Pauline,'[2] I must have *some day* – why not without the emendations? But if you insist on them, I will agree to wait a little – if you promise *at last* to let me see the book, which I will not show. Some day, then! you shall not be vexed nor hurried for the day – some day. Am I not generous? And *I* was 'precocious', too, and used to make rhymes over my bread and milk when I was nearly a baby .. only really it was mere echo-verse, that of mine, and had nothing of mark or of indication, such as I do not doubt that yours had. I used to write of virtue with a large 'V', and 'Oh Muse' with a harp, and things of that sort. At nine years old I wrote what I called 'an epic' – and at ten, various tragedies, French and English, which we used to act in the nursery. There was a French 'hexameter' tragedy on the subject of Regulus – but I cannot even smile to think of it now, there are so many grave memories – which time has made grave – hung around it. How I remember sitting in 'my house under the sideboard', in the dining-room, concocting one of the soliloquies beginning

[1] E.B.B.'s spaniel.
[2] R.B.'s first published work (1833).

82

Que suis je? autrefois un général Romain:
Maintenant esclave de Carthage je souffre en vain.

Poor Regulus! – Can't you conceive how fine it must have been altogether? And these were my 'maturer works', you are to understand, .. and the 'moon was bright at ten o'clock at night' years before. As to the gods and goddesses, I believed in them all quite seriously, and reconciled them to Christianity, which I believed in too after a fashion, as some greater philosophers have done – and went out one day with my pinafore full of little sticks (and a match from the housemaid's cupboard) to sacrifice to the blue-eyed Minerva who was my favourite goddess on the whole because she cared for Athens. As soon as I began to doubt about my goddesses, I fell into a vague sort of general scepticism, .. and though I went on saying 'the Lord's prayer' at nights and mornings, and the 'Bless all my kind friends' afterwards, by the childish custom .. yet I ended this liturgy with a supplication which I found in 'King's Memoirs' and which took my fancy and met my general views exactly .. 'O God, if there be a God, save my soul if I have a soul.' Perhaps the theology of many thoughtful children is scarcely more orthodox than this: but indeed it is wonderful to myself sometimes how I came to escape, on the whole, as well as I have done, considering the commonplaces of education in which I was set, with strength and opportunity for breaking the bonds all round into liberty and license. Papa used to say .. 'Don't read Gibbon's history – it's not a proper book. Don't read "Tom Jones" – and none of the books on *this* side, mind!' So I was very obedient and never touched the books on *that* side, and only read instead Tom Paine's 'Age of Reason', and Voltaire's 'Philosophical Dictionary', and Hume's 'Essays', and Werther, and Rousseau, and Mary Wollstonecraft .. books, which I was never suspected of looking towards, and which were not 'on *that* side' certainly, but which did as well.

How I am writing! – And what are the questions you did not answer? I shall remember them by the answers I suppose – but your letters always have a fulness to me and I never seem to wish for what is not in them.

But this is the end *indeed*.

Thursday Night.
(In the same envelope with the preceding letter)

Ever dearest – how you can write touching things to me; and how my whole being vibrates, as a string, to these! How have I deserved from God and you all that I thank you for? Too unworthy I am of all! - - -

I will think as you desire: but I have thought a great deal, and there are certainties which I know; and I hope we *both* are aware that nothing can be more hopeless than our position in some relations and aspects, though you do not guess perhaps that the very approach to the subject is shut up by dangers, and that from the moment of a suspicion entering *one* mind, we should be able to meet never again in this room, nor to have intercourse by letter through the ordinary channel. I mean, that letters of yours, addressed to me here, would infallibly be stopped and destroyed – if not opened. Therefore it is advisable to hurry on nothing – on these grounds it is advisable. What should I do if I did not see you nor hear from you, without being able to feel that it was for your happiness? What should I do for a month even? And, then, I might be thrown out of the window or its equivalent – I look back shuddering to the dreadful scenes in which poor Henrietta was involved who never offended as I have offended .. years ago which seem as present as today. She had forbidden the subject to be referred to until that consent was obtained – and at a word she gave up all – at a word. In fact she had no true attachment, as I observed to Arabel at the time – a child never submitted more meekly to a revoked holiday. Yet how she was made to suffer. Oh, the dreadful scenes! and only because she had seemed to feel a little. I told you, I think, that there was an obliquity – an eccentricity, or something beyond – on one class of subjects. I hear how her knees were made to ring upon the floor, now! she was carried out of the room in strong hysterics, and I, who rose up to follow her, though I was quite well at that time and suffered only by sympathy, fell flat down upon my face in a fainting-fit. Arabel thought I was dead.

I have tried to forget it all – but now I must remember – and throughout our intercourse *I have remembered*. It is necessary to remember so much as to avoid such evils as are inevitable, and for this reason I would conceal nothing from you. Do *you* remember, besides, that there can be no faltering on my 'part', and that, if I should remain well, which is not proved yet, I will do for you what you please and as you please to have it done. But there is time for considering!

Only .. as you speak of 'counsel', I will take courage to tell you that my *sisters know*. Arabel is in most of my confidences, and being often in the room with me, taxed me with the truth long ago – she saw that I was affected from some cause – and I told her. We are as safe with both of them as possible .. and they thoroughly understand that *if there should be any change it would not be your fault* .. I made them understand that thoroughly. From themselves I have received nothing but the most smiling words of kindness and satisfaction (I thought I might tell you so much), they have too much tenderness for me to fail in it now. My brothers, it is quite necessary not to draw into a dangerous responsibility. I have felt that from the beginning, and shall continue to feel it – though I hear and can observe that they are full of suspicions and conjectures, which are never un-kindly expressed. I told you once that we held hands the faster in this house for the weight over our heads. But the absolute *knowledge* would be dangerous for my brothers: with my sisters it is different, and I could not continue to conceal from *them* what they had under their eyes; and then, Henrietta is in a like position. It was not wrong of me to let them know it? – no?

Yet of what consequence is all this to the other side of the question? What, if *you* should give pain and disappointment where you owe such pure gratitude. But we need not talk of these things now. Only you have more to consider than *I*, I imagine, while the future comes on - - -

Sunday
(Post-mark, January 19, 1846)

- - - And you call the *Athenaeum* 'kind and satisfactory'? Well – I was angry instead. To make us wait so long for an 'article' like *that*, was not over-kind certainly, nor was it 'satisfactory' to class your peculiar qualities with other contemporary ones, as if they were not peculiar. It seemed to me cold and cautious, from the causes perhaps which you mention, but the extracts will work their own way with everybody who knows what poetry is, and for others, let the critic do his worst with them. For what is said of 'mist' I have no patience because I who know when you are obscure and never think of denying it in some of your former works do hold that this last number[1] is as clear and self-sufficing to a common understanding, as far as the expression and medium goes, as any book in the world, and that Mr. Chorley[2] was bound in verity to say so. If I except that one stanza, you know, it is to make the general observation stronger. And then 'mist' is an infamous word for your kind of obscurity. You never *are* misty, not even in 'Sordello' – never vague. Your graver cuts deep sharp lines, always – and there is an extra-distinctness in your images and thoughts, from the midst of which, crossing each other infinitely, the general significance seems to escape. So that to talk of a 'mist', when you are obscurest, is an impotent thing to do. Indeed it makes me angry - - -

Now, shall I tell you what I did yesterday? It was so warm, so warm, the thermometer at 68 in this room, that I took it into my head to call it April instead of January, and put on a cloak and walked down-stairs into the drawing-room – walked, mind. Before, I was carried by one of my brothers, – even to the last autumn-day when I went out – I never walked a step for fear of the cold in the passages. But yesterday it was so wonderfully warm, and I so strong besides – it was a feat worthy of the day – and I surprised them all as much as if I had walked out of the

[1] Cf. *Bells and Pomegranates* (see pp. 60 and 62).

[2] Henry Fothergill Chorley, 1808–1872. Author and reviewer; literary and musical critic on the staff of the *Athenaeum*.

Robert Browning, from a painting by M. Gordigiani, 1858

Elizabeth Barrett Browning, from a painting by M. Gordigiani, 1858

Wednesday.

Ever dearest – I will say, as you desire,
nothing on that subject – but this
strictly for myself: you engaged me to
consult my own good in the keeping
or breaking our engagement; not
your good as it might seem
to me; much less seem to
another: my only good in
this world, – that against which
all the world goes for nothing
– is to spend my life with you,
and be yours. You know this

Facsimile reproduction of a letter from Miss Barrett to Robert Browning,
15 July 1846

window instead. That kind dear Stormie, who with all his shyness and awkwardness has the most loving of hearts in him, said that he was '*so* glad to see me!'

Well! – setting aside the glory of it, it would have been as wise perhaps if I had abstained; our damp detestable climate reaches us otherwise than by cold, and I am not quite as well as usual this morning after an uncomfortable feverish night – not very unwell, mind, nor unwell at all in the least degree of consequence – and I tell you, only to show how susceptible I really am still, though 'scarcely an invalid', say the complimenters - - -

Your own

BA

R.B. TO E.B.B. *Sunday Evening*
(Post-mark, January 26, 1846)

- - - That remark of your sister's delights me – you remember? – that the anger[1] would not be so formidable. I have exactly the fear of encountering *that*, which the sense of having to deal with a ghost would induce: there's no striking at it with one's partizan. Well, God is above all! It is not my fault if it so happens that by returning my love you make me exquisitely blessed; I believe – more than hope, I am *sure* I should do all I ever *now* can do, if you were never to know it – that is, my love for you was in the first instance its own reward – if one must use such phrases – and if it were possible for that .. not *anger*, which is of no good, but that *opposition* – that adverse will – to show that your good would be attained by the - - -

But it would need to be *shown* to me. You have said thus to me – in the very last letter, indeed. But with me, or any *man*, the instincts of happiness develop themselves too unmistakably where there is anything like a freedom of will. The man whose heart is set on being rich or influential after the worldly fashion, may be found far enough from the attainment of either riches or influence – but he will be in the presumed way to them – pumping at the pump, if he is really anxious for water, even though the pump be dry – but not sitting still by the dusty roadside.

[1] Mr. Barrett's.

I believe – first of all, you – but when that is done, and I am allowed to call your heart *mine*, – I cannot think you would be happy if parted from me – and *that* belief, coming to add to my own feeling in *that* case. So, this will *be* – I trust in God - - -

Monday
(Post-mark, January 27, 1846)

- - - Another mistake you made concerning Henrietta and her opinion – and there's no use nor comfort in leaving you in it. Henrietta says that the 'anger would not be so formidable after all!' Poor dearest Henrietta, who trembles at the least bending of the brows .. who has less courage than I, and the same views of the future! What she referred to, was simply the infrequency of the visits. 'Why was I afraid', she said – 'where was the danger? who would be the *informer*?' – Well! I will not say any more. It is just natural that you, in your circumstances and associations, should be unable to see what I have seen from the beginning – only you will not hereafter reproach me, in the most secret of your thoughts, for not having told you plainly. If I could have told you with greater plainness I should blame myself (and I do not) because it is not an opinion I have, but a perception. I see, I know. The result .. the end of all .. perhaps now and then I see *that* too .. in the 'lucid moments' which are not the happiest for anybody. Remember, in all cases, that I shall not repent of any part of our past intercourse; and that, therefore, when the time for decision comes, you will be free to look at the question as you saw it then for the first moment, without being hampered by considerations about 'all those yesterdays'.

For *him* .. he would rather see me dead at his foot than yield the point: and he will say so, and mean it, and persist in the meaning.

Do you ever wonder at me .. that I should write such things, and have written others so different? *I have thought that in myself very often*. Insincerity and injustice may seem the two ends, while I occupy the straight betwixt two – and I should not like you to doubt how this may be! Sometimes I have begun to show you the truth, and torn the paper; I *could* not. Yet now again I am borne on to tell you, .. to save you from some thoughts which you cannot help perhaps.

There has been no insincerity – nor is there injustice. I believe, I am certain, I have loved him better than the rest of his children. I have heard the fountain within the rock, and my heart has struggled in towards him through the stones of the rock .. thrust off .. dropping off .. turning in again and clinging! Knowing what is excellent in him well, loving him as my only parent left, and for himself dearly, notwithstanding that hardness and the miserable 'system' which made him appear harder still, I have loved him and been proud of him for his high qualities, for his courage and fortitude when he bore up so bravely years ago under the worldly reverses which he yet felt acutely – more than you and I could feel them – but the fortitude was admirable. Then came the trials of love – then, I was repulsed too often, .. made to suffer in the suffering of those by my side .. depressed by petty daily sadnesses and terrors, from which it is possible however for an elastic affection to rise again as past. Yet my friends used to say 'You look broken-spirited' – and it was true. In the midst, came my illness, – and when I was ill he grew gentler and let me draw nearer than ever I had done: and after that great stroke .. you *know* .. though *that* fell in the middle of a storm of emotion and sympathy on my part, which drove clearly against him, God seemed to strike our hearts together by the shock; and I was grateful to him for not saying aloud what I said to myself in my agony, '*If it had not been for you*' ..! And comparing my self-reproach to what I imagined his self-reproach must certainly be (for if *I* had loved selfishly, *he* had not been kind), I felt as if I could love and forgive him for two .. (I knowing that serene generous departed spirit, and seeming left to represent it) .. and I did love him better than all those left to *me* to love in the world here. I proved a little my affection for him, by coming to London at the risk of my life rather than diminish the comfort of his home by keeping a part of my family away from him. And afterwards for long and long he spoke to me kindly and gently, and of me affectionately and with too much praise; and God knows that I had as much joy as I imagined myself capable of again, in the sound of his footsteps on the stairs, and of his voice when he prayed in this room; my best hope, as I have told him since, being, to die beneath his eyes. Love is so much to me naturally – it is, to all women! and it was so much to *me* to feel sure at last that *he* loved me – to forget all blame – to pull the weeds up from that last illusion of life: – and this, till the Pisa business, which threw me off, far as ever, again – farther than ever – when George said 'he could not flatter me' and I dared not flatter myself. But do *you* believe that I never wrote what I did not feel: I never did. And I ask one kindness more .. do not notice what I have written here. Let it pass. We can alter nothing by ever so many words. After all, he is the victim. He isolates himself – and now and then he feels it .. the cold dead silence all round, which is the effect of an incredible system. If he were not stronger than most men, he could not bear it as he does. With such high qualities too! – so upright and honourable – you would esteem him, you would like him, I think. And so .. dearest .. let *that* be the last word - - -

R.B. TO E.B.B.

Wednesday
(Post-mark, January 28, 1846)

Ever dearest – I will say, as you desire, nothing on that subject – but this strictly for myself: you engaged me to consult my own good in the keeping or breaking our engagement; not *your* good as it might even seem to me; much less seem to another. My only good in this world – that against which all the world goes for nothing – is to spend my life with you, and be yours. You know that when I *claim* anything, it is really yourself in me – you *give* me a right and bid me use it, and I, in fact, am most obeying you when I appear most exacting on my own account – so, in that feeling, I dare claim, once for all, and in all possible cases (except that dreadful one of your becoming worse again .. in which case I wait till life ends with both of us), I claim your promise's fulfilment – say, at the summer's end: it cannot be for your good that this state of things should continue. We can go to Italy for a year or two and be happy as day and night are long. For me, I adore you. This is all unnecessary, I feel as I write: but you will think of the main fact as *ordained*, granted by God, will you not, dearest? – so, not to be put in doubt *ever again* – then, we can go quietly thinking of after matters. Till tomorrow, and ever after, God bless my heart's own, own Ba. All my soul follows you, love – encircles you – and I live in being yours.

E.B.B. TO R.B.

Friday Morning
(Post-mark, January 31, 1846)

Let it be this way, ever dearest. If in the time of fine weather, I am not ill, .. *then* .. *not now* .. you shall decide, and your decision shall be duty and desire to me, both – I will make no difficulties. Remember, in the meanwhile, that I *have* decided to let it be as you shall choose .. *shall* choose. That I love you enough to give you up 'for your good', is proof (to myself at least) that I love you enough for any other end: – but you thought *too much of me in the last letter.* Do not mistake me. I believe and trust in all your words – only you are generous unawares, as other men are selfish.

- - - For Italy .. you are right. We should be nearer the sun, as you say, and further from the world, as I think – out of hearing of the great storm of gossiping, when 'scirocco is loose'. Even if you liked to live altogether abroad, coming to England at intervals, it would be no sacrifice for me – and whether in Italy or England, we should have sufficient or more than sufficient means of living, without modifying by a line that 'good free life' of yours which you reasonably praise – which, if it had been necessary to modify, *we must have parted,* .. because I could not have borne to see you do it; though, that you once offered it for my sake, I never shall forget - - -

Your own

BA

Shall I have a letter?

91

Friday Evening
(Post-mark, February 2, 1846)

- - - Dearest, did I write you a cold letter the last time? Almost
it seems so to me! the reason being that my feelings were near to
overflow, and that I had to hold the cup straight to prevent the
possible dropping on your purple underneath. *Your* letter, the
letter I answered, was in my heart .. *is* in my heart – and all
the yeses in the world would not be too many for such a letter, as
I felt and feel. Also, perhaps, I gave you, at last, a merely formal
distinction – and it comes to the same thing practically without
any doubt! but I shrank, with a sort of instinct, from appearing (to
myself, mind) to take a security from your words now (said too
on an obvious impulse) for what should, would, *must*, depend on
your deliberate wishes hereafter. You understand – you will not
accuse me of over-cautiousness and the like. On the contrary,
you are all things to me, .. instead of all and better than all! You
have fallen like a great luminous blot on the whole leaf of the
world .. of life and time .. and I can see nothing beyond you,
nor wish to see it. As to all that was evil and sadness to me, I
do not feel it any longer – it may be raining still, but I am in the
shelter and can scarcely tell. If you *could* be *too dear* to me you
would be now – but you could not – I do not believe in those
supposed excesses of pure affections – God cannot be too
great - - -
May God bless you, ever dearest: –

Your own BA

Saturday
(In the same envelope with the preceding letter)

- - - For Mr. Kenyon, I only know that I have grown the most
ungrateful of human beings lately, and find myself almost glad
when he does not come, certainly uncomfortable when he does –
yes, *really* I would rather not see him at all, and when you are not
here. The sense of which, and the sorrow for which, turn me to a

hypocrite, and make me ask why he does not come &c. .. questions which never came to my lips before .. till I am more and more ashamed and sorry. Will it end, I wonder, by my ceasing to care for any one in the world, except, except ..? or is it not rather that I feel trodden down by either his too great penetration or too great unconsciousness, both being overwhelming things from him to me. From a similar cause I hate writing letters to any of my old friends – I feel as if it were the merest swindling to attempt to give the least account of myself to anybody, and when their letters come and I know that nothing very fatal has happened to them, scarcely I can read to an end afterwards through the besetting care of having to answer it all. Then I am ignoble enough to revenge myself on people for their stupidities .. which never in my life I did before nor felt the temptation to do .. and when they have a distaste for your poetry through want of understanding, I have a distaste for *them* .. cannot help it – and you need not say it is wrong, because I know the whole iniquity of it, persisting nevertheless. As for dear Mr. Kenyon – with whom we began, and who thinks of you as appreciatingly and admiringly as one man can think of another, – do not imagine that, if he *should* see anything, he can 'approve' of either your wisdom or my generosity .. *he*, with his large organs of caution, and his habit of looking right and left, and round the corner a little way. Because, you know, .. if I should be ill *before* .. why there, is a conclusion! – but if *afterward* .. what? You who talk wildly of my generosity, whereas I only and most impotently tried to be generous, must see how both suppositions have their possibility. Nevertheless you are the master to run the latter risk. You have overcome .. to your loss perhaps – unless the judgment is revised. As to taking the half of my prison .. I could not even smile at *that* if it seemed probable .. I should recoil from your affection even under a shape so fatal to you .. dearest! No! There is a better probability before us I hope and believe – in spite of the *possibility* which it is impossible to deny. And now we leave this subject for the present - - -

Here I have been reading Carlyle upon Cromwell and he is very fine, very much himself, it seems to me, everywhere. Did Mr. Kenyon make you understand that I had said there was

93

nothing in him but *manner* .. I thought he said so – and I am confident that he never heard such an opinion from me, for good or for evil, ever at all. I may have observed upon those vulgar attacks on account of the so-called *mannerism*, the obvious fact, that an individuality, carried into the medium, the expression, is a feature in all men of genius, as Buffon teaches .. 'Le style, c'est *l'homme*'. But if the *whole man* were style, if all Carlyleism were manner – why there would be no man, no Carlyle worth talking of. I wonder that Mr. Kenyon should misrepresent me so. Euphuisms there may be to the end of the world – affected parlances – just as a fop at heart may go without shoestrings to mimic the distractions of some great wandering soul – although *that* is a bad comparison, seeing that what is called Carlyle's mannerism, is not his dress, but his physiognomy – or more than *that* even.

But I do not forgive him for talking here against the 'ideals of poets' .. opposing their ideal by a mis-called *reality*, which is another sort, a baser sort, of ideal after all. He sees things in broad blazing lights – but he does not analyse them like a philosopher – do you think so? Then his praise for dumb heroic action as opposed to speech and singing, what is *that* – when all earnest thought, passion, belief, and their utterances, are as much actions surely as the cutting off of fifty heads by one right hand. As if Shakespeare's actions were not greater than Cromwell's! –

But I shall write no more. Once more, may God bless you.

Wholly and only
Your BA

R.B. TO E.B.B.

Saturday Morning
(Post-mark, February 23, 1846)

- - - Now to these letters! I do solemnly, unaffectedly wonder how you can put so much pure felicity into an envelope so as that I shall get it as from the fount head. This today, those yesterday – there is, I see, and know, thus much goodness in line after line, goodness to be scientifically appreciated, *proved there* – but over and above, is it in the writing, the dots and traces, the seal, the

paper – here does the subtle charm lie beyond all rational accounting for? The other day I stumbled on a quotation from J. Baptista
Porta – wherein he avers that any musical instrument made out of
wood possessed of medicinal properties retains, being put to
use, such virtues undiminished, – and that, for instance, a sick
man to whom you should pipe on a pipe of elder-tree would so
receive all the advantage derivable from a decoction of its berries.
From whence, by a parity of reasoning, I may discover, I think,
that the very ink and paper were – ah, what were they? Curious
thinking won't do for me and the wise head which is mine, so I
will lie and rest in my ignorance of content and understand that
without any magic at all you simply wish to make one person –
which of your free goodness proves to be your R.B. – to make
me supremely happy, and that you have your wish – you *do*
bless me! More and more, for the old treasure is piled undiminished and still the new comes glittering in. Dear, dear heart of
my heart, life of my life, *will this last*, let *me* begin to ask? Can it
be meant I shall live this to the end? Then, dearest, care also for
the life beyond, and put in my mind how to testify here that I
have felt, if I could not deserve that gift beyond all gifts! I hope
to work hard, to prove I do feel, as I say – it would be terrible to
accomplish nothing now - - -

Bless you, my sweetest. I love you with my whole heart;
ever shall love you.

E.B.B. TO R.B.

(Post-mark, February 24, 1846)

- - - With all you say of liking to have my letters (which I
like to hear quite enough indeed) you cannot pretend to think
that *yours* are not more to *me*, most to *me*! Ask my guardian-angel
and hear what he says! Yours will look another way for shame of
measuring joys with him! Because as I have said before, and as he
says now, you are all to me, all the light, all the life; I am living
for you now. And before I knew you, what was I and where?
What was the world to me, do you think? and the meaning of
life? - - -

Yet indeed I did not fancy that I was to love *you* when you came to see me – no indeed .. any more than I did your caring on your side. My ambition when we began our correspondence, was simply that you should forget I was a woman (being weary and *blasée* of the empty written gallantries, of which I have had my share and all the more perhaps from my peculiar position which made them so without consequence), that you should forget *that* and let us be friends, and consent to teach me what you knew better than I, in art and human nature, and give me your sympathy in the meanwhile. I am a great hero-worshipper and had admired your poetry for years, and to feel that you liked to write to me and be written to was a pleasure and a pride, as I used to tell you I am sure, and then your letters were not like other letters, as I must not tell you again. Also you *influenced* me, in a way in which no one else did. For instance, by two or three half words you made me see you, and other people had delivered orations on the same subject quite without effect. I surprised everybody in this house by consenting to see you. Then, when you came, you never went away. I mean I had a sense of your presence constantly. Yes .. and to prove how free that feeling was from the remotest presentiment of what has occurred, I said to Papa in my unconsciousness the next morning .. 'it is most extraordinary how the idea of Mr. Browning does beset me – I suppose it is not being used to see strangers, in some degree – but it haunts me .. it is a persecution.' On which he smiled and said that 'it was not grateful to my friend to use such a word'. When the letter came ..

Do you know that all that time I was frightened of you? frightened in this way. I felt as if you had a power over me and meant to use it, and that I could not breathe or speak very differently from what you chose to make me. As to my thoughts, I had it in my head somehow that you read *them* as you read the newspaper – examined them, and fastened them down writhing under your long entomological pins – ah, do you remember the entomology of it all?

But the power was used upon *me* – and I never doubted that you had mistaken your own mind, the strongest of us having some exceptional weakness. Turning the wonder round in all lights, I came to what you admitted yesterday .. yes, I saw *that* very early .. that you had come here with the intention of trying to love whomever you should find, .. and also that what I had said about exaggerating the amount of what I could be to you, had just operated in making you more determined to justify your own presentiment in the face of mine. Well – and if that last clause was true a little, too .. why should I be sorry now .. and why should you have fancied for a moment, that the first could make me sorry. At first and when I did not believe that you really loved me, when I thought you deceived yourself, *then*, it was different. But now .. now .. when I see and believe your attachment for me, do you think that any cause in the world (except what diminished it) could render it less a source of joy to me? I mean as far as I myself am considered. Now if you ever fancy that I am *vain* of your love for me, you will be unjust, remember. If it were less dear, and less above me, I might be vain perhaps. But I may say *before* God and you, that of all the events of my life, inclusive of its afflictions, nothing has humbled me so much as your love. Right or wrong it may be, but true it *is*, and I tell you. Your love has been to me like God's own love, which makes the receivers of it kneelers - - -

R.B. TO E.B.B.

Wednesday Morning
(Post-mark, February 25, 1846)

- - - I looked yesterday over the 'Tragedy',[1] and think it will do after all. I will bring one part at least next time, and 'Luria' take away, if you let me, so all will be off my mind, and April and May be the welcomer? Don't think I am going to take any extraordinary pains. There are some things in the 'Tragedy' I should like to preserve and print now, leaving the future to spring as it likes, in any direction, and these half-dead, half-alive works fetter it, if left behind.

Yet one thing will fetter it worse, only one thing – if *you*,

[1] 'A Soul's Tragedy', published (together with 'Luria') in 1846, as No. VIII of *Bells and Pomegranates*.

in any respect, stay behind? You that in all else help me and will help me, beyond words – beyond dreams – if, because I find you, your own works *stop* – 'then comes the Selah and the voice is hushed.'[1] Oh, no, no, dearest, *so* would the help cease to be help – the joy to be joy, Ba herself to be *quite* Ba, and my own Siren singing song for song. Dear love, will that be kind, and right, and like the rest? Write and promise that all shall be resumed, the romance-poem chiefly,[2] and I will try and feel more yours than ever now. Am I not with you in the world, proud of you – and *vain*, too, very likely, which is all the sweeter if it is a sin as you teach me. Indeed dearest, I have set my heart on your fulfilling your mission – my heart is on it! Bless you, my Ba –

Your R.B.

E.B.B. TO R.B.

(Post-mark, February 26, 1846)

- - - As for myself, I believe that you set about exhorting me to be busy, just that I might not reproach *you* for the over-business. Confess that *that* was the only meaning of the exhortation. But no, you are quite serious, you say. You even threaten me in a sort of underground murmur, which sounds like a nascent earthquake; and if I do not write so much a day directly, your stipendiary magistrateship will take away my license to be loved .. I am not to be Ba to you any longer .. you say! And is *this* right? now I ask you - - -

As for the writing, I will write .. I have written .. I am writing. You do not fancy that I have given up writing? – No. Only I have certainly been more loitering and distracted than usual in what I have done, which is not my fault – nor yours directly – and I feel an indisposition to setting about the romance, the hand of the soul shakes. I am too happy and not calm enough, I suppose, to have the right inclination. Well – it will come. But all in blots and fragments there are verses enough, to fill a volume done in the last year.[3]

---

[1] A quotation from E.B.B.'s poem 'An Essay on Mind' (1826).

[2] 'Aurora Leigh' (1857).

[3] These 'verses', almost certainly included *Sonnets from the Portuguese*.

And if there were not .. if there were none .. I hold that I should be Ba, and also *your* Ba .. which is 'insolence' .. will you say?

Sunday
(Post-mark, March 2, 1846)

You never could think that I meant any insinuation against you by a word of what was said yesterday, or that I sought or am likely to seek a 'security'! do you know it was not right of you to use such an expression – indeed no. You were angry with me for just one minute, or you would not have used it – and why? Now what did I say that was wrong or unkind even by construction? If I did say anything, it was three times wrong, and unjust as well as unkind, and wronged my own heart and consciousness of all that you are to me, more than it could *you*.

- - - And for myself, it was my compromise with my own scruples, that you should not be 'chained' to me, not in the merest metaphor, that you should not seem to be bound, in honour or otherwise, so that if you stayed with me it should be your free choice to stay, not the *consequence* of a choice so many months before. That was my compromise with my scruples, and not my doubt of your affection – and least of all, was it an intention of trifling with you sooner or later that made me wish to suspend all *decisions* as long as possible. I have decided (for me) to let it be as you shall please – now I told you that before. Either we will live on as we are, until an obstacle arises – for indeed I do not look for a 'security' where you suppose, and the very appearance of it *there*, is what most rebuts me[1] – or I will be yours in the obvious way, to go out of England the next half-hour if possible. As to the steps to be taken (or not taken) before the last step, we must think of those. The worst is that the only question is about a *form*. Virtually the evil is the same all round,

[1] The two references in this letter to 'security' are obscure, and evidently relate to something said by R.B. at their last meeting. Probably the allusion is to her father.

99

whatever we do. Dearest, it was plain to see yesterday evening when he came into this room for a moment at seven o'clock, before going to his own to dress for dinner .. plain to see, that he was not altogether pleased at finding you here in the morning. There was no pretext for objecting gravely – but it was plain that he was not pleased. Do not let this make you uncomfortable, he will forget all about it, and I was not *scolded*, do you understand. It was more manner, but my sisters thought as I did of the significance: – and it was enough to prove to me (if I had not known) what a desperate game we should be playing if we depended on a yielding nerve *there* - - -

Talking of music, I had a proposition the other day from certain of Mr. Russell's (the singer's) friends, about his setting to music my 'Cry of the Children'.[1] His programme exhibits all the horrors of the world, I see! Lifeboats .. madhouses .. gamblers' wives .. all done to the right sort of moaning. His audiences must go home delightfully miserable, I should fancy. He has set the 'Song of the Shirt'[2] .. and my 'Cry of the Children' will be acceptable, it is supposed, as a climax of agony. Do you know this Mr. Russell, and what sort of music he suits to his melancholy? But to turn my 'Cry' to a 'Song', a burden, it is said, is required – he can't sing it without a burden! and behold what has been sent 'for my approval' .. I shall copy it verbatim for you ..

And the threads twirl, twirl, twirl,
Before each boy and girl;
And the wheels, big and little, still whirl, whirl, whirl.

.. accompaniment agitato, imitating the roar of the machinery!

This is not endurable .. ought not to be .. should it now? Do tell me.

May God bless you, very dearest! Let me hear how you are – and think how I am

Your own ..

---

[1] First published in *Blackwood's Magazine* in 1843, and afterwards in E.B.B.'s 1844 *Poems*. It was a protest against the conditions of child labour at this time.

[2] By Thomas Hood (1799–1845).

Tuesday
(Post-mark, March 3, 1846)

- - - You tell me what was observed in the 'moment's' visit; by you, and (after, I suppose) by your sisters. First, I *will* always see with your eyes *there* – next, what I see I will *never* speak, if it pain you; but just this much truth I ought to say, I think. I always give myself to you for the worst I am, – full of faults, as you will find, if you have not found them. But I *will* not affect to be so bad, so wicked, as I count wickedness, as to call that conduct other than intolerable – *there*, in my conviction of *that*, is your real 'security' and mine for the future as the present. That a father choosing to give out of his whole day some five minutes to a daughter, supposed to be prevented from participating in what he, probably, in common with the whole world of sensible men, as distinguished from poets and dreamers, consider *every* pleasure of life, by a complete foregoing of society – that he, after the Pisa business and the enforced continuance, and as he must believe, permanence of this state in which any other human being would go mad – I do dare say, for the justification of God, who gave the mind to be *used* in this world, – where it saves us, we are taught, or destroys us, – and not to be sunk quietly, overlooked, and forgotten; that, under these circumstances, finding .. what, you say, unless he thinks he *does* find, he would close the door of his house instantly; a mere sympathizing man, of the same literary tastes, who comes good-naturedly, on a proper and unexceptionable introduction, to chat with and amuse a little that invalid daughter, once a month, so far as is known, for an hour perhaps – that such a father should show himself 'not *pleased* plainly', at such a circumstance .. my Ba, it is SHOCK-ING! See, I go *wholly* on the supposition that the real relation is not imagined to exist between us. I so completely could understand a repugnance to trust you to me were the truth known, that, I will confess, I have several times been afraid the very reverse of this occurrence would befall; that your father would have at some time or other thought himself obliged, by the usual feeling of people in such cases, to see me for a few minutes

and express some commonplace thanks after the customary mode
- - - and if *this* had been done, I shall not deny that my heart
would have accused me – unreasonably I *know* but still, suppres-
sion, and reserve, and apprehension – the whole of *that is*
horrible always! But this way of looking on the endeavour of
anybody, however humble, to just preserve your life, remedy in
some degree the first, if it *was* the first, unjustifiable measure, –
this being 'displeased' – is exactly what I did *not* calculate upon.
Observe, that in this *only* instance I am able to do as I shall be
done by; to take up the arms furnished by the world, the usages
of society – this is monstrous on the *world's* showing! I say this
now that I may never need recur to it – that you may understand why I keep *such* entire silence henceforth - - -

Bless you, now, my darling – I love you, ever shall love you,
ever be your own.

E.B.B. TO R.B.

Tuesday Evening
(Post-mark, March 4, 1846)

- - - You do not see aright what I meant to tell you - - - If he
was displeased, (and it was expressed by a shadow a mere nega-
tion of pleasure) it was not with you as a visitor and my friend.
You must not fancy such a thing. It was a sort of instinctive
indisposition towards seeing you here – unexplained to himself, I
have no doubt – of course unexplained, or he would have desired
me to receive you never again, *that* would have been done at
once and unscrupulously. But without defining his own feeling,
he rather disliked seeing you here – it just touched one of his
vibratory wires, brushed by and touched it – oh, we understand
in this house. He is not a nice observer, but, at intervals very
wide, he is subject to lightnings – call them fancies, sometimes
right, sometimes wrong. Certainly it was not in the character of
a 'sympathising friend' that you made him a very little cross on
Monday. And yet you never were nor will be in danger of being
thanked, he would not think of it. For the reserve, the apprehension – dreadful those things are, and desecrating to one's own

nature – but we did not make this position, we only endure it. The root of the evil is the miserable misconception of the limits and character of parental rights – it is a mistake of the intellect rather than of the heart. Then, after using one's children as one's chattels for a time, the children drop lower and lower toward the level of the chattels, and the duties of human sympathy to them become difficult in proportion. And (it seems strange to say it, yet it is true) *love*, he does not conceive of at all. He has feeling, he can be moved deeply, he is capable of affection in a peculiar way, but *that*, he does not understand, any more than he understands Chaldee, respecting it less of course.

And you fancy that I could propose Italy again? after saying too that I never would? Oh no, no – yet there is time to think of this, a superfluity of time, .. 'time, times and half a time' and to make one's head swim with leaning over a precipice is not wise. The roar of the world comes up too, as you hear and as I heard from the beginning. There will be no lack of 'lying', be sure – 'pure lying' too – and nothing you can do, dearest dearest, shall hinder my being torn to pieces by most of the particularly affectionate friends I have in the world. Which I do not think of much, any more than of Italy. You will be mad, and I shall be bad .. and *that* will be the effect of being poets! 'Till when, where are you?' – why in the very deepest of my soul – wherever in it is the fountain head of loving! beloved, *there* you are! - - -

Your

BA

R.B. TO E.B.B.

Tuesday Morning
(Post-mark, March 10, 1846)

Dear, dear Ba, if you were here I should not much *speak* to you, not at first – nor, indeed, at last, – but as it is, sitting alone, only words can be spoken, or (worse) written, and, oh how different to look into the eyes and imagine what *might* be said, what ought to be said, though it never can be – and to sit and say and write, and only imagine who looks above me, looks down, understanding and pardoning all! My love, my Ba, the fault you found once with some expressions of mine about the amount of imperishable pleasures already hoarded in my mind, the indestructible memories of you; that fault, which I refused to acquiesce under the imputation of, at first, you remember – well, *what* a fault it was, by this better light! If all stopped here and now; horrible! complete oblivion were the thing to be prayed for, rather! As it is, *now*, I must go on, must live the life out, and die yours. And you are doing your utmost to advance the event of events, – the exercise, and consequently (is it not?) necessarily improved sleep, and the projects for the fine days, the walking .. a pure bliss to think of! Well, now – I think I shall show seamanship of a sort, and 'try another tack' – do not be over bold, my sweetest; the cold *is* considerable, – taken into account the previous mildness. One ill-advised (I, the *adviser*, I should remember!) too early, or too late descent to the drawing-room,[1] and all might be ruined, – thrown back so far .. seeing that our flight is to be prayed for 'not in the winter' – and one would be called on to wait, wait – in this world where nothing waits, rests, as can be counted on. Now think of this, too, dearest, and never mind the slowness, for the sureness' sake! How perfectly happy I am as you stand by me, as yesterday you stood, as you seem to stand now - - -

God bless you, my dearest, dearest Ba!

E.B.B. TO R.B.

Tuesday Evening
(Post-mark, March 11, 1846)

- - - You would laugh to see me at my dinner – Flush and me – Flush placing in me such an heroic confidence, that, after he has cast one discriminating glance on the plate, and, in the case of 'chicken', wagged his tail with an emphasis, .. he goes off to the sofa, shuts his eyes and allows a full quarter of an hour to pass before he returns to take his share. Did you ever hear of a dog before who did not persecute one with beseeching eyes at mealtimes? And remember, this is not the effect of *discipline*.

[1] Such a 'descent' had been proposed by E.B.B. in her last letter.

Also if another than myself happens to take coffee or break bread in the room here, he teazes straightway with eyes and paws, .. teazes like a common dog and is put out of the door before he can be quieted by scolding. But with *me* he is sublime! Moreover he has been a very useful dog in his time (in the point of capacity), causing to disappear supererogatory dinners and impossible breakfasts which, to do him justice, is a feat accomplished without an objection on his side, always.

So, when you write me such a letter, I write back to you about Flush. Dearest beloved, but I have read the letter and felt it in my heart, through and through! and it is as wise to talk of Flush foolishly, as to fancy that I *could say how* it is felt .. this letter! - - - You mean, you say, to run all risks with me, and I don't mean to draw back from my particular risk of .. what am I to do to you hereafter to make you vexed with me? What is there in marriage to make all these people on every side of us, (who all began, I suppose, by talking of love,) look askance at one another from under the silken mask .. and virtually hate one another through the tyranny of the stronger and the hypocrisy of the weaker party. It never could be so with *us* – *I know that.* But you grow awful to me sometimes with the very excess of your goodness and tenderness, and still, I think to myself, if you do not keep lifting me up quite off the ground by the strong faculty of love in you, I shall not help falling short of the hope you have placed in me – it must be 'supernatural' of you, to the end! or I fall short and disappoint you. Consider this, beloved. Now if I could put my soul out of my body, just to stand up before you and make it clear - - -

Your own –

E.B.B. TO R.B.

Wednesday evening
(Post-mark, March 26, 1846)

- - - I had a visitor today – Mrs. Jameson;[1] and when she went

[1] Anna Brownell Jameson, 1794–1860; writer of many well-known books, including *Characteristics of Shakespeare's Women* and *Sacred and Legendary Art*; a close friend of E.B.B.'s.

away she left me ashamed of myself – I felt like a hypocrite – *I*, who was not born for one, I think. She began to talk of you .. talked like a wise woman, which she is .. led me on to say just what I might have said if I had not known you, (she, thoroughly impressed with the notion that we two are strangers!) and made me quite leap in my chair with a sudden consciousness, by ex-claiming at last .. 'I am really glad to hear you speak so. Such appreciation' &c. &c. .. imagine what she went on to say. Dearest – I believe she rather gives me a sort of credit for *appreciating you* without the jealousy 'de métier'. Good Heavens .. how humiliat-ing some conditions of praise are! She *approved* me with her eye – indeed she did. And this, while we were agreeing that you were the best .. 'none better .. none so good ..' of your country and age. Do you know, while we were talking, I felt inclined both to laugh and to cry, and if I had 'given way' the least, she would have been considerably astounded. As it was, my hands were so marble-cold when she took leave of me, that she observed it and began making apologies for exhausting me. Now here is a strip of the 'world', .. see what colour it will turn to presently! We had better, I think, go farther than to your siren's island – into the desert .. shall we say? Such stories there will be! For certain, .. I shall have seen you just once out of the window! Shall you not be afraid? Well – and she talked of Italy too – it was before she talked of *you* – and she hoped I had not given up the thoughts of going there. To which I said that 'I had not .. but that it seemed like scheming to travel in the moon'. She talked of a difference, and set down the moon-travelling as simple lunacy. 'And simply lunatical', .. I said, .. 'my thoughts, if chronicled, would be taken to be, perhaps' – 'No, no, no,' .. she insisted .. 'as long as I kept to the earth, everything was to be permitted to me.'

How people talk at cross-purposes in this world .. and act so too! It's the very spirit of worldly communion. Souls are gre-garious in a sense, but no soul touches another, as a general rule. I like Mrs. Jameson nevertheless – I like her *more*. She appreciates you – and it is *my* turn to praise for that, now - - -

Friday
(Post-mark, April 3, 1846)

Dearest, your flowers make the whole room look like April, they are so full of colours .. growing fuller and fuller as we get nearer to the sun. The wind was melancholy too, all last night – oh, *I* think the wind melancholy, just as *you* do, – or *more* than you do perhaps for having spent so many restless days and nights close on the seashore in Devonshire. I seem now always to hear the sea *in* the wind, voice within voice! But I like a sudden wind, not too loud, – a wind which you hear the rain in rather than the sea – and I like the half cloudy half sunny April weather, such as we have it here in England, with a west or south wind – I like and enjoy *that;* and remember vividly how I used to like to walk or wade nearly up to my waist in the wet grass or weeds, with the sun overhead, and the wind darkening or lightening the verdure all round.

But none of it was happiness, dearest dearest. Happiness does not come with the sun or the rain. Since my illness, when the door of the future seemed shut and locked before my face, and I did not tire myself with knocking any more, I thought I was happier, happy, I thought, just because I was tranquil *unto death.* Now I know life from death, .. and the unsorrowful life for the first time since I was a woman; though I sit here on the edge of a precipice in a position full of anxiety and danger. What matter, .. if one shuts one's eyes, and listens to the birds singing? Do you know, I am glad – I could almost thank God – that Papa keeps so far from me .. that he has given up coming in the evening .. I could almost thank God. If he were affectionate, and made me, or *let* me, feel myself necessary to him, .. how should I bear (even with my reason on my side) to prepare to give him pain? So that the Pisa business last year, by sounding the waters, was good in its way .. and the pang that came with it to me, was also good. He feels! – he loves me .. but it is not (this, I mean to say) to the *trying* degrees of feeling and love .. trying to *me*. Ah, well! In any case, I should have ended probably, in giving up all for you – I do not profess otherwise. I used to think I should, if ever I loved anyone – and if the love of you is different from, it is greater than, anything preconceived .. divined - - -

May God bless you, my own dearest – Think of me *a little* – as you say!

Your
B A

Thursday Evening
(Post-mark, April 10, 1846)

- - - Mrs. Jameson was here today, and in the room before, almost, I heard of her being on the stairs. It is goodnatured of her to remember me in her brief visits to London – and she brought me two or three St. Sebastians with the arrows through them, etched by herself, to look at – very goodnatured! Once she spoke of you – 'Oh', she said, 'you saw Mr. Browning's last number! yes, I remember how you spoke of it. I suppose Mr. Kenyon lent you his copy' .. And before I could speak, she was on another subject. But I should not have had heart to say what I meant and predetermined to say, even if the opportunity today had been achieved. As if you could not be read except in Mr. Kenyon's copy! I might have confessed to my own copy, even if not to my own original .. do you not think?

Before she came, I went down to the drawing-room, I and Flush, and found no one there .. and walked drearily up and down the rooms, and, so, came back to mine. May you have spent your day better. There was sunshine for you, as I could see. God bless you and keep you - - -

I think of you, bless, love you – but it would have been better for you never to have seen my face perhaps, though Mr. Kenyon gave the first leave. *Perhaps*!! I 'flatter' *myself* tonight, in change for *you*.

Best beloved I am your
B A

Friday Morning
(Post-mark, April 10, 1846)

- - - Your note arrives here – Ba; – it would have been 'better for me', *that?* Oh, dearest, let us marry soon, very soon, and end all this! If I could begin taking exceptions again, I might charge you with such wild conventionalism, such wondrous perversity of sight or blindness rather! *Can* you, now, by this time, tell me or yourself that you could believe me happy with any other woman that ever breathed? I tell *you*, without affectation, that I lay the whole blame to myself .. that I feel that if I had spoken my love out *sufficiently*, all this doubt could never have been possible. You quite believe I am in earnest, know my own mind and speak as I feel, on these points we disputed about – yet *I am* far from being sure of it, or so it seems now – but, as for loving you, – *there* I mistake, or may be wrong, or may, or might or or –

Now kiss me, my best-dearest beloved! It seems I am always understood *so* – the words are words, and faulty, and inexpressive, or wrongly expressive, – but when I live under your eyes, and die, you will never mistake, – you *do not now*, thank God, say to me – 'you want to go elsewhere for all you say the visit seems too brief' – and, 'you would change me for another, for all you possess' – never do you *say* such things – but when I am away, all the mistaking begins – let it end soon, come, dearest life of my life, light of my soul, heart's joy of my heart! - - -

Your own R.

Sunday
(Post-mark, April 13, 1846)

- - - You know the subject you wanted to discuss, on Saturday. Now whenever the time shall come for discussing that subject, let this be a point agreed upon by both of us. The peculiarity of our circumstances will enable us to be free of the world .. of our friends even .. of all observation and examination, in certain respects: now let us use the advantage which falls to us from our misfortune, – and, since we must act for ourselves at last, let us resist the curiosity of the whole race of third persons .. even the affectionate interest of such friends as dear Mr. Kenyon, .. and put it into the power of nobody to say to himself or to another, .. 'she had so much, and he, so much, in worldly possessions – or she had not so much and he had not so much'. Try to understand what I mean. As it is not of the least importance to either of us, as long as we can live, whether the sixpence, we live by, came most from you or from me .. and as it will be as much mine as yours, and yours as mine when we are together .. why let us join in throwing a little dust in all the winking eyes round – oh, it is nonsense and weakness, I know – but I would rather, rather, see winking eyes than staring eyes. What has anybody to do with us? Even my own family .. why should they *ever* see the farthest figure of *our* affairs, as to mere money? There now – it is said .. what I have had in my head so long to say. And one other word resumes my meditations on 'the subject' which will not be ripe for discussion for ever so many months .. and that other word is .. that if ever I am to wrong you so much as to be yours *so*, it is on the condition of leaving England within the fewest possible half hours afterwards. I told you *that*, long ago – so bear it in mind. I should not dare breathe in this England. Think! – There is my father – and there is yours! Do you imagine that I am *not afraid of your family*? and should be still more, if it were not for the great agony of fear on the side of my own house. Ah – I must love you unspeakably .. even to dare think of the possibility of such things. So we will not talk of them now. I write what I write, to throw it off my mind and have done. Bear it in yours, but do not refer to it – *I ask you not to refer to it* - - -

Love me, beloved .. do not leave off to see if I deserve it. I am at least (which is at most)

Your very own

How are you now, dearest? If the worse for my visit .. No, there is no affectation in what I would say – you might be worse,

you know, through *excitement*, whether pleasurable or the reverse.
One comfort is, the walking, going down-stairs, &c. have not
occasioned it. I expect everything from your going out of doors,
that is to be – what a joy to write it, think of it, expect it! Oh,
why are you not here – where I sit writing; whence, in a moment, I
could get to know why the lambs are bleating so, in the field
behind – I do not see it from either window in this room – but I
see a beautiful sunshine (2½ p.m.) and a chestnut tree leafy all over,
in a faint trembling chilly way, to be sure – and a holly hedge I
see, and shrubs, and blossomed trees over the garden wall, –
were you but here, dearest, dearest, – how we would go out,
with Flush on before, for with a key I have, I lock out the world,
and then look down on it; for there is a vast view from our
greatest hill – did I ever tell you that Wordsworth was shown
that hill or its neighbour; someone saying 'R.B. lives over *there*
by that HILL' – 'Hill?' interposed Wordsworth – '*we* call that,
such as that, a *rise*'! I must have told you, I think. (While I
write, the sun gets ever brighter – you must be down-stairs, I
feel sure –) - - -

Bless you my very dearest, sweetest Ba – I am your own,
heart and soul –

E.B.B. TO R.B.

Friday
(Post-mark, May 2, 1846)

How you write to me! Is there any word to answer to these
words .. which, when I have read, I shut my eyes as one bewildered, and think blindly .. or do not think – some feelings
are deeper than the thoughts touch. My only beloved, it is thus
with me .. I stand by a miracle in your love, and because I stand
in it and it covers me, just for *that*, you cannot see me! May God
grant that you *never see me* – for then we two shall be 'happy'
as you say, and I, in the only possible manner, be very sure.
Meanwhile, you do quite well not to speculate about making
me happy .. your instinct knows, if *you* do not know, that it is
implied in your own happiness .. or rather (not to assume a

magnanimity) in my sense of your being happy, not apart from me. As God sees me, and as I know at all the motions of my own soul, I may assert to you that from the first moment of our being to each other anything, I never conceived of happiness otherwise .. never thought of being happy through you or by you or in you, even – your good was all my idea of good, and *is*. I hear women say sometimes of men whom they love .. 'such a one will make me happy, I am sure', or 'I shall be happy with *him*, I think' – or again .. 'He is so good and affectionate that nobody need be afraid for my happiness'. Now, whether you like or dislike it, I will tell you that I never had such thoughts of *you*, nor ever, for a moment, gave you that sort of praise. I do not know why .. or perhaps I do .. but I could not so think of you .. I have not time nor breath .. I could as soon play on the guitar when it is thundering. So be happy, my own dearest .. and if it should be worth a thought that you *cannot* be *alone, so,* you may think *that* too. You have so deep and intense a nature, that it were impossible for you to love after the fashion of other men, weakly and imperfectly, and your love, which comes out like your genius, may glorify enough to make you happy, perhaps. Which is my dream, my calculation rather, when I am happiest now. May God bless you. - - -

Say how you are I beseech you, and honestly! I was downstairs today, since the wind changed, and am the better for it. What writing for a postman! – or for *you* even!

R.B. TO E.B.B.
Saturday
(Post-mark, May 2, 1846)

No, my Ba, your letter came as it ought last night, – and the promise it contained of another made me restless all the morning – to no purpose, – nothing more comes – yet – for there is a 'peradventure' yet unwithdrawn. When I do not hear from you, as now, I always fancy there was some signal reason why I ought to have heard .. that 'tomorrow', I could better bear the not hearing .. though never, never do yesterday's letters slip by a hair's breadth from the place in my affection they once take, – *they* could not have been dispensed with, – but the imaginary letter of tomorrow could, by contrast with today's exigencies .. till tomorrow really comes and is found preferring such claims of its own – such claims.

This letter I have got, and will try and love enough for two .. I can do no harm by trying .. *this* I do not mean to say that I expected. May I say 'in heart-playing', .. now, Ba, it will be a fancy, which you can pounce on and poke your humming-bird bill through, like a needle, in a very 'twinkling', and so shall my flower's eye be ruined for ever, and when it turns black and shrivels up as dead flowers do, you can triumph and ask 'are these your best flowers, best feelings for me?' But now, after this deprecation, you will be generous and only hover above, using the diamond eye rather than the needle-bill, – and I will go on and dare say that I should like, for one half second, *not to love you*, and then feel all the love lit up in a flame to the topmost height, at the falling of such a letter on my heart. Don't you know that foolish boys sometimes play at hanging themselves – suspend themselves by the neck actually for such a half second as this of my fancying – that they may taste the luxury of catching back at existence, and being cut down again? There is a notable exemplification, a worthy simile! – – –

So now, at 2½ p.m., I must (– *here is the Post* .. from you? *Yes* – the letter is here at last – I was waiting: – now to read; no, kissing it comes first).

And now .. I will not say a word, my love of loves, my dearest, dearest Ba, – not one word – but I will go out and walk where I can be alone, and think out all my thought of you, and bless you and love you with nothing to intercept the blessing and the love. I will look in the direction of London and send my heart there .. Dear, dear love, I kiss you and commend you to God. Your very own –

I am very well – quite well, dearest.

But my own only beloved, I surely did not speak too 'insist-ingly' yesterday. I shrank from your question as you put it, because you put it wrong. If you had asked me instead, whether I meant to keep my promise to you, I would have answered 'yes' without hesitation: but the form you chose, referred to *you* more than to *me*, and was indeed and indeed a foolish form of a ques-tion, my own dearest! For the rest .. ah, you do not see my inner-most nature, .. *you* are happily too high, and cannot see into it .. cannot perceive how the once elastic spring is broken with the long weights! .. you wonder that it should drop, when you, who lifted it up, do not hold it up! you cannot understand! .. you wonder! And *I* wonder too .. on the other side! *I* wonder how I can feel happy and alive .. as I can, *through you*! how I can turn my face toward life again .. as I can, *for you*! .. and chiefly of all, how I can ever imagine .. as I do, sometimes .. that such a one as you, may be happy perhaps with such a one as *I*! .. happy!

Do not judge me severely, you, to whom I have given *both* hands, for your own uses and ends! – you, who are more to me than I can be to you, even by your own statement – better to me than life .. or than death even, as death seemed to me before I knew you.

Certainly I love you enough, and trust you enough, if you knew what God knows. Yet, .. 'now hear me'. I shall not be able to please you, I think, by a firm continued belief of this engagement's being justifiable, until the event wholly *has* justified it .. I mean, .. until I shall see you not less happy for having lived near me for six months or a year – should God's mercy permit such justification. Do not blame me. I cannot help it .. I would, if I could, help it. Every time you say, as in this dearest letter, ever dearest, that you have been happy on such a day through being with me, I have a new astonishment – it runs through me from head to feet .. I open my eyes astonished, whenever my sun rises in the morning, as if I saw an angel in the sun. And I *do* see him, in a sense. Ah – if you make a crime to me of my *astonishments*, it is all over indeed! can I help it, indeed? So forgive me! let it not be too great a wrong to be covered by a pardon. Think that we are different, you and I – and do not think that I would send you to 'money and worldly advancement' .. do not think so meanly of my ambition for you.

Dearest dearest! – do you ever think that I could fail to you? Do you doubt for a moment, ever .. ever, .. that my hand might peradventure 'shake less' in being loosed from yours? Why, it might – and would! *Dead* hands do not shake at all, – and only *so*, could my hand be loosed from yours through a failing on my part. It is your hand, while you hold it: while you choose to hold it, and while it is a living hand.

Do you know what you are to me, .. *you*? We talk of the mild weather doing me good .. of the sun doing me good .. of going into the air as a means of good! Have you done me no good, do you fancy, in loving me and lifting me up?[1] Has the unaccustomed divine love and tenderness been nothing to me? Think! Mrs. Jameson says earnestly .. said to *me* the other day .. that 'love was only magnetism'. And I say in my heart, that, magnet or no magnet, I have been drawn back into life[2] by your means and for you .. that I see the dancing mystical lights which are seen through the eyelids .. and I think of you with an unspeakable gratitude always–always! No other could have done this for me – it was not possible, except by you - - -

Wholly and ever yours I am

E.B.B. TO R.B.

May 7th, 1846

- - - Miss Bayley[3] is what is called *strong-minded*, and with all her feeling for art and Beauty, talks of utility like a Utilitarian of the highest, and professes to receive nothing without *proof*, like a reasoner of the lowest. She told me with a frankness for

[1] Cf. *Sonnets from the Portuguese*, No. XXVII.
[2] Cf. *Sonnets from the Portuguese*, No. I.
[3] Sarah Bayley (d. 1868), a friend of John Kenyon's and a recent acquaintance of E.B.B.'s.

which I did not like her less, that she was a materialist of the strictest order, and believed in no soul and no future state. In the face of those conclusions, she said, she was calm and resigned. It is more than *I* could be, as I confessed. My whole nature would cry aloud against that most pitiful result of the struggle here – a wrestling only for the dust, and not for the crown. What a resistless melancholy would fall upon me if I had such thoughts! – and what a dreadful indifference. All grief, to have itself to end in! – all joy, to be based upon nothingness! – all love, to feel eternal separation under and over it! Dreary and ghastly, it would be! I should not have strength to love you, I think, if I had such a miserable creed. And for life itself, .. would it be worth holding on such terms, – with our blind Ideals making mocks and mows at us wherever we turned? A game to throw up, this life would be, as not worth playing to an end! - - -

E.B.B. TO R.B.

Monday
(Post-mark, May 12, 1846)

- - - Look what is inside of this letter – look! I gathered it for you today when I was walking in the Regent's Park. Are you surprised? Arabel and Flush and I were in the carriage – and the sun was shining with that green light through the trees, as if he carried down with him the very essence of the leaves, to the ground, .. and I wished so much to walk through a half open gate along a shaded path, that we stopped the carriage and got out and walked, and I put both my feet on the grass, .. which was the strangest feeling! .. and gathered this laburnum for you. It hung quite high up on the tree, the little blossom did, and Arabel said that certainly I could not reach it – but you see! It is a too generous return for all your flowers: or, to speak seriously, a proof that I thought of you and wished for you – which it was natural to do, for I never enjoyed any of my excursions as I did today's – the standing under the trees and on the grass, was so delightful. It was like a bit of that Dreamland which is your especial dominion, – and I felt joyful enough for the moment, to look round for you, as for the cause. It seemed *illogical*, not to see you close by. And you were not far after all, if thoughts count as bringers near. Dearest, we shall walk together under the trees some day! - - -

Love me, my only beloved; since you *can*. May God bless you!

I am ever and wholly your

BA

R.B. TO E.B.B.

Tuesday
(Post-mark, May 12, 1846)

My Ba, your flower is the one flower I have seen, or see, or shall see – when it fades 'I will bless it till it shine', and when I can bless you no longer it shall fade with me and my letters and .. perhaps .. my ring. Ba, if .. I was going to say, *if* you meant to make me most exquisitely happy .. and you *did* surely mean it .. well, you succeed, as you know! And I see you on the grass, and am with you as you properly acknowledge. And by this letter's presence and testimony, I may judge you to be not much the worse, – not fatigued .. is it so? Oh, it was a good inspiration that led you through the half-opened gate and under the laburnum, and, better still, that made you see us 'one day walking by the trees together' – when all I shall say is, – I hope, in spite of that felicity to remember and feel *this*, as vividly as now - - -

E.B.B. TO R.B.

Tuesday
(Post-mark, May 13, 1846)

- - - Today Mrs. Jameson has been here, and having left with me a proof about Titian, she comes again tomorrow to take it. I think her quite a lovable person now – I like her more and more. How she talked of you today, and called you the most charming companion in the world, setting you too on your right throne as 'poet of the age'. Wouldn't it have been an *'effect'* in the midst of all, if I had burst out crying? And what with being flurried, frightened, and a little nervous from not sleeping well last night, I assure you it was quite possible – but happily, on every account, I escaped that 'dramatic situation'. I wish .. no, I can't wish that she wouldn't talk of you as she does whenever she comes here. And then, to make it better, she told me how you had recited 'in a voice and manner as good as singing', my 'Catarina'.[1] How are such things to be borne, do you think, when people are not made of marble? But I took a long breath, and held my mask on with both hands - - -

Exactly at eight tomorrow, and exactly at three the next day, I shall be with you – being at any hour

Your very own

Friday
(Post-mark, May 15, 1846)

- - - Papa brought me some flowers yesterday when he came home .. and they went a little to my heart as I took them. I put them into glasses near yours, and they look faded this morning nevertheless, while your roses, for all your cruelty to them, are luxuriant in beauty as if they had just finished steeping themselves in garden-dew. I look gravely from one set of flowers to the other – I cannot draw a glad omen – I wish he had not given me these. Dearest, there seems little kindness in teazing you with such thoughts .. but they come and I write them: and let them come ever so sadly, I do not for a moment doubt .. hesitate. One may falter, where one does not fail. And for the rest, .. it is my fault, and not my sorrow rather, that we act so? It is by choice that we act so? If he had let me I should have loved him out of a heart altogether open to him. It is not my fault that he would not let me. Now it is too late – I am not his nor my own, any more - - -

Your own BA

[1] 'Catarina to Camoens', one of E.B.B.'s 1844 *Poems.*

Tuesday
(Post-mark, May 19, 1846)

With this day expires the first year since you have been yourself to me[1] – putting aside the anticipations, and prognostications, and even assurances from all reasons short of absolute sight and hearing, – excluding the five or six months of these, there remains a year of this intimacy. You accuse me of talking extravagantly sometimes. I will be quiet here, – is the tone *too* subdued if I say, such a life – made up of such years – I would deliberately take rather than any other imaginable one in which fame and worldly prosperity and the love of the whole human race should combine, excluding 'that of yours – to which I hearken' – only wishing the rest were there for a moment that you might see and know that I did turn from them to you. My dearest, inexpressibly dearest. How can I thank you? I feel sure you *need* not have been so kind to me, so perfectly kind and good, – I should have remained your own, gratefully, entirely your own, through the bare permission to love you, or even without it – seeing that I never dreamed of stipulating at the beginning for 'a return', and 'reward', – but I also believe, joyfully, that no course but the course you have taken would have raised me above my very self, as I feel on looking back. I began by loving you in comparison with all the world, – now, I love you, my Ba, in the face of your past self, as I remember it.

All words are foolish – but I kiss your feet and offer you my heart and soul, dearest, dearest Ba.

I left you last evening without the usual privilege – you did not rise, Ba! But, – I don't know why, – I got nervous of a sudden, it seemed late and I remembered the Drawing-room and its occupants.

[1] i.e. since his first visit to her.

Do you remember how, when poor Abou Hassan, in the
Arabian story, awakens from sleep in the Sultan's chamber, to
the sound of instruments of music, he is presently complimented
by the grand vizier on the royal wisdom displayed throughout his
reign .. do you remember? Because just as he listened, do *I*
listen, when you talk to me about 'the course I have taken' ..
I, who have just had the wit to sit still in my chair with my eyes
half shut, and dream .. dream! – Ah, whether I am asleep or
awake, what do I know .. even now? As to the 'course I have
taken', it has been somewhere among the stars .. or under the
trees of the Hesperides, at lowest ..

Why how can I write to you such foolishness? Rather I should
be serious, grave, and keep away from myths and images, and
speak the truth plainly. And speaking the truth plainly, I, when
I look back, dearest beloved, see that you have done for me everything, instead of my doing anything for you – that you have
lifted me .. Can I speak? Heavens! – how I had different thoughts
of you and of myself and of the world and of life, last year at
this hour! The spirits who look backward over the grave, cannot
feel much otherwise from my feeling as I look back.[1] As to
your thanking *me, that* is monstrous, it seems to me. It is the action
of your own heart alone, which has appeared to do you any good.
For myself, if I do not spoil your life, it is nearest to deserving
thanks that I can come. Think what I was when you saw me
first .. laid there on the sofa as an object of the merest compas-
sion! and of a sadder spirit than even the face showed! and then
think of all your generosity and persistence in goodness. Think
of it! – shall I ever cease? Not while the heart beats, which beats
for you.

And now as the year has rounded itself to 'the perfect round',
I will speak of that first letter,[2] about which so many words
were, .. just to say, this time, that I am glad now, yes, glad, .. as

[1] Cf. *Sonnets from the Portuguese*, Nos. VII, XX, XXVII.
[2] See p. 19.

we were to have a miracle, .. to have it *so*, a born-miracle from the beginning. I feel glad, now, that nothing was *between* the knowing and the loving .. and that the beloved eyes were never cold discerners and analyzers of me at any time. I am glad and grateful to you, my own altogether dearest! Yet the letter was read in pain and agitation, and you have scarcely guessed how much. I could not sleep night after night, – could not, – and my fear was at nights, lest the feverishness should make me talk deliriously and tell the secret aloud. Judge if the deeps of my heart were not shaken. From the first you had that power over me, notwithstanding those convictions which I also had and which you know.

For it was not the character of the letter apart from you, which shook me, – I could prove that to you – I received and answered very calmly, with most absolute calmness, a letter of the kind last summer .. knowing in respect to the writer of it, (just as I thought of *you*), that a moment's enthusiasm had carried him a good way past his discretion. I am sure that he was perfectly satisfied with my way of answering his letter .. as I was myself. But *you* .. *you* .. I could not escape so from *you*.[1] You were stronger than I, from the beginning, and I felt the mastery in you by the first word and first look.

Dearest and most generous. No man was ever like you, I know! May God keep me from laying a blot on one day of yours! – on one hour! and rather blot out mine!

For my life, it is yours, as this year has been yours. But how can it make you happy, such a thing as my life? *There*, I wonder still. It never made *me* happy, without you! –

Your very own
B A

E.B.B. TO R.B.

Thursday
(Post-mark, May 22, 1846)

- - - The sonnet[2] was purely manuscript, and for the good of

[1] Cf. *Life in a Love*, p. 226.

[2] A sonnet by an American admirer, beginning 'Daughter of Graecian Genius!' R.B. had asked to see it.

the world should remain so. Oh – you cannot care for all this trash – such trash! Why I had a manuscript sonnet sent to me last autumn by 'person or persons unknown,' .. 'To EBB on her departure from England *to Pisa*'. Can you fancy that melodious piece of gossiping? Then a lady of the city, famous, I believe, for haberdashery, used to address *all* her poems to me – which really was original .. for she would write five or six 'poems' on an evening, and sweep them up and send them to me once a fortnight, upon faith, hope and charity, seaweed and moonshine, cornlaws and the immortality of the soul, and take me for her standing muse, properly *thou*'d and *thee*'d all through. What a good vengeance it would be upon your unjust charges, if I set you to read a volume or two of those 'poems' .. which all went into the fire – so you need not be frightened.

And today I had a rose-tree sent to me by somebody who has laid close siege to me this long while, and whom I have escaped hitherto .. but who has encamped, she says 'till July' in *16* Wimpole Street. She writes too on her card .. 'When are you going to Italy?'

Ah! you, who blame me (half blame me) for 'seeing women', do not know how difficult it is to help it sometimes, without being in appearance ungrateful and almost brutal. Just because I am unwell, they teaze me more, I believe - - - Once I had this proposition – 'If we mayn't come in, *will you stand up at the window that we may see?*' Now! – And there's the essence of at least ten MS sonnets! – so don't complain any more - - -

May God bless you – Think of me. I am ever and ever,

Your own

BA

Monday Morning
(Post-mark, May 26, 1846)

- - - You are very strange in what you say about my reading your poetry – as if it were not my peculiar gladness and glory! – my own, which no man can take from me. And not *you*, indeed! Yet I am not likely to mistake your poetry for the flower of your nature, knowing what that flower is, knowing something of what that flower is without a name, and feeling something of the mystical perfume of it. When I said, or when others said for me, that my poetry was the flower of me, was it praise, did you think, or blame? might it not stand for a sarcasm? It might, – if it were not true, miserably true after a fashion.

Yet something of the sort is true, of course, with all poets who write directly from their personal experience and emotions – their ideal rises to the surface and floats like the bell of the waterlily. The roots and the muddy water are subaudita, you know – as surely there as the flower.

But *you* .. you have the superabundant mental life and individuality which admits of shifting a personality and speaking the truth still. *That* is the highest faculty, the strongest and rarest, which exercises itself in Art, – we are all agreed there is none so great faculty as the dramatic. Several times you have hinted to me that I made you care less for the drama, and it has puzzled me to fancy how it could be, when I understand myself so clearly both the difficulty and the glory of dramatic art. Yet I am conscious of wishing you to take the other crown besides – and after having made your own creatures speak in clear human voices, to speak yourself out of that personality which God made, and with the voice which He tuned into such power and sweetness of speech. I do not think that, with all that music in you, only your own personality should be dumb, nor that having thought so much and deeply on life and its ends, you should not teach what you have learnt, in the directest and most impressive way, the mask thrown off however moist with the breath. And it is not, I believe, by the dramatic medium, that poets teach most impressively – I have seemed to observe *that*! .. it is too difficult for the common reader to analyse, and to discern between the vivid and the earnest. Also he is apt to understand better always when he sees the lips move. Now, here is yourself, with your wonderful faculty! – it is wondered at and recognised on all sides where there are eyes to see – it is called wonderful and admirable! Yet, with an inferior power, you might have taken yourself closer to the hearts and lives of men, and made yourself dearer, though being less great. Therefore I do want you to do this with your surpassing power – it will be so easy to you to speak, and so noble, when spoken.

Not that I usen't to fancy I could see you and know you, in a reflex image, in your creations! I used, you remember. How these broken lights and forms look strange and unlike to me, when I stand by the complete idea. Yes, *now* I feel that no one can know you worthily by those poems. Only .. I guessed a little. *Now* let us have your own voice speaking of yourself – if the voice may not hurt the speaker – which is my fear - - -

Wholly and ever your

BA

E.B.B. TO R.B.   *Tuesday*
                                   (Post-mark, June 2, 1846)

- - - I am going to ask you a question, dearest of mine, and you will consider it carefully and examine your own wishes in respect to it, before I have any answer. In fact it is not necessary to treat of the subject of it at all at this moment – we have a great deal of time before us. Still, I want to know whether, upon reflection, you see it to be wise and better for me to go to Italy with Miss Bayley, or with any other person who may be willing to take me (supposing I should find such a plan possible) and that you should follow with Mr. Chorley or alone, .. leaving other thoughts for another year. Or if I find this scheme, as far as I am concerned, impossible, shall we gain anything, do you think, on any side of the question that you can see, by remaining quietly as we are, you at New Cross, and I here, until next year's summer or autumn? Shall we be wiser, more prudent, for any reason, or in any degree, by such a delay?

It is the question I ask you – it is no proposal of mine, understand – nor shall I tell you my own impression about it. I have told you that I would do as you should decide, and I will do that and no other. Only on that very account it is the more necessary that you should decide well, and according to the best lights of your own judgment and reason - - -

Your own

BA

Wednesday Morning
(Post-mark, June 3, 1846)

I will tell you, dearest: your good is my good, and your will mine; if you were convinced *that* good would be promoted by our remaining as we are for twenty years instead of one, I should endeavour to submit in the end .. after the natural attempts to find out and remove the imagined obstacle. If, as you seem to do here, you turn and ask about *my* good – yours being supposed to be uninfluenced by what I answer .. then, here is my TRUTH on that subject, in that view, – my good for myself. Every day that passes before *that day* is one the more of hardly endurable anxiety and irritation, to say the least; and the thought of another year's intervention of hope deferred – altogether intolerable! Is there anything I can do in that year – or that you can do – to forward our object? Anything impossible to be done sooner? If not –

You may misunderstand me now at first, dear, dearest Ba; at first I sate quietly, you thought; do I live quietly now, do you think? Ought I to show the evidence of the unselfishness I *strive*, at least, to associate with my love, by coolly informing you 'what would please me'.

But I will not say more, you must know .. and *I* seem to know that this question was one of Ba's old questions .. a branch-licence, perhaps, of the original inestimable one, that charter of my liberties, by which I am empowered to 'hold myself unengaged, unbound' &c. &c.

Good Heaven; I would not, – even to save the being asked such questions, – have played the horseleech that cries 'give, give', in Solomon's phrase – 'Do you let me see you once a week? Give me a sight once a day! – May I dare kiss you? Let me marry you tomorrow!'

But to the end, the very end, I am yours: God knows I would not do you harm for worlds – worlds! I may easily mistake what *is* harm or not. I will ask your leave to speak – at your foot, my Ba: I would not have dared to take the blessing of kissing your hand, much less your lip, but that it seemed as if I was leading you into a mistake – as did happen – and that you might fancy I only felt a dreamy, abstract passion for a phantom of my own creating out of your books and letters, and which only took your name .. *That* once understood, the rest you shall give me. In every event, I am your own - - -

R.

Wednesday Evening
(Post-mark, June 4, 1846)

Nothing at all had it to do with your Magna Charta, beloved, that question of mine. After you were gone the other day and I began turning your words over and over, .. (*so*, I make hay of them to feed the horses of the sun!) it struck me that you had perhaps an instinct of common sense, which, with a hand I did not see and a voice I could not hear, drew you perhaps. So I thought I would ask. For after all, this is rather a serious matter we are upon, and if you think that you are not to have your share of responsibility .. that you are not to consider and arrange and decide, and perform your own part, .. you are as much mistaken as ever *I* was. 'Judge what I say.' For my part, I have done, it seems to me, nearly as much as I can do. I do not, at least, seem to myself to have any power to *doubt* even, of the path to choose for the future. If for any reason you had seen wisdom in delay, it would have been a different thing – and the seeing was a *possible* thing, you will admit. I did not ask you if you *desired* a delay, but if you saw a reason for it. In the meantime I was absolutely yours, I remembered thoroughly, .. and the question went simply to enquire what you thought it best to do with your own. For me I agree with your view – I never once thought of proposing a delay on my own account. We are standing on hot scythes, and because we do not burn in the feet, by a miracle, we have no right to count on the miracle's prolongation. Then nothing is to be gained – and everything may be lost – and the sense of mask-wearing for another year would be suffocating. This for *me*. And for yourself, I shall not be much younger or better otherwise, I suppose, next year. I make no motion, then, for a delay, further than we have talked of, .. to the summer's end.

My good .. happiness! Have I any that did not come from you, that is not *in* you, that you should talk of my good apart from yours? I shudder to look back to the days when you were not for me. Was ever life so like death before? My face was so close against the tombstones, that there seemed no room even for the tears. And it is unexampled generosity of yours, that, having done all for me, you should write as you always do, about *my giving* .. giving! Among the sons of men there is none like you as I believe and know, .. and every now and then declare to my sisters - - -

E.B.B. TO R.B.

(Post-mark, June 9, 1846)

- - - Mrs. Jameson - - - brought me the engravings of Xanthian marbles, and also her new essays .. and was very kind as usual, and proposed to come some day next week with a carriage to take me out, – and all this time, how we treat her! Will she not have a right to complain of being denied the degree of confidence we gave (.. Mr. Kenyon gave for me ..) to Miss Bayley? Will she not think hereafter 'There was no need of their deceiving *me*'? And yet I doubt how to retreat now. Could I possibly say to her the next time she speaks of you .. or could I not? it would set her on suspecting perhaps. She talked a little today of Italy, and plainly asked me what thoughts I had of it, – to which I could answer truthfully 'No thoughts, but dreams'. Then she insisted, 'But whenever you have thoughts, you will let me know them? You will not be in Italy when I am there, without my knowing it? And where will you go –? to Pisa? .. to Sienna? to Naples?' And she advised .. 'Don't go where the English are, in any case'. And encouraged like an oracle, .. 'Remember that where there's a will there's a way' – knowing no more what she spoke, than a Pythian on the serpent's skin - - -

I am your own

BA

Tuesday
(Post-mark, June 9, 1846)

- - - Always remember, my Ba, that the secret is *your* secret and not mine .. that I keep it while you bid me, but that you may communicate it to whom you please, *when* you please, without waiting to apprize me. I should, I think, have preferred telling Mrs. Jameson from the beginning about the mere visits .. or, I don't know .. by one such piece of frankness you only expose yourself to fifty new – whatever they are! For there would be so much the more talk about you, – and either the quick woman's wit and discernment are to be eluded, or they are not, – foiled or not – and how manage without .. without those *particular* evasions which seem to degrade most of all? - - - In short I think the best way in such a case is to tell *all* or none. I believe you might tell all to Mrs. Jameson with perfect safety, but for *her* sake, I doubt the propriety .. for it would be to introduce her forthwith to exactly our own annoyances with respect to Mr. Kenyon, Chorley, &c. Once knowing, she cannot *un*-know. In any case, I promise my conscience to give her, – and anybody else that may have a right to it, – a full explanation at the earliest safe moment .. may *that* be at no great distance! My own feeling is for telling Mr. Kenyon .. though you would considerably startle me if you answered 'well, *do*!' But, of the whole world, I seem only to care for *his* not feeling aggrieved: oh, he will understand! – and *can*, because he knows the circumstances at your house. Come what will, I am sure of you; 'if you live, and are well' – even this last clause I might exclude; it has often been in my thought to tell you .. only, dearest, there is always, when I plan never so dreamily and vaguely, always an understood submission the most absolute to your own desire .. but I fancied, that, in the case of any *real* obstacle arising so as to necessitate the 'postponement', &c., I should have *stipulated* .. in the right yourself have given me .. I should have said – 'we will postpone it, if you will marry me *now* .. merely as to the form .. but so as to enable me, if difficulties should thicken, to be by your bed*side* at least'. You see, what you want 'to relieve' me of, is just what my life should be thrice paid down for and cheaply. How could you ever be so truly mine as *so*? Even the poor service does not 'part us' before 'death' – 'till *sickness* do us part!'

But there will be no sickness and all happiness, I trust in God! Dear, dear Ba, I love you wholly and for ever – true as I kiss your rose, and will keep it for ever. Bless you - - -

E.B.B. TO R.B.

Tuesday Evening
(Post-mark, June 10, 1846)

Best, dearest beloved, .. would it not be strange if you were not so to me? How do you think I feel, hearing you say such things .. finding such thoughts in your mind? If it is not worthy of you to have a burden set on your shoulders and to be forced into the shadow of disquietudes not your own, yet this divine tenderness is worthy of you .. worthy of your nature; as I know and recognise! May God help me to thank you, for I have not a word.

Practically however, see how your proposal would work. It could not work *at all*, unless circumstances were known – and if they were known, at the very moment of their being known you would be saved, dearest, all the trouble of coming upstairs to me, by my being thrown out of the window to you .. upon which, you might certainly pick up the pieces of me and put them into a bag and set off for Nova Zembla. *That* would be the event of the working of your proposition. Yet remember that I will accede to whatever you shall choose – so *think for us both*. You know more of the world and have more practical sense than I – and if you did not, had not, you may *do what you like with your own*, as surely as the Duke of Newcastle might.

For Mrs. Jameson, I never should think of telling her '*all*' – I should not, could not, would not! and the gods forefend that you should think of telling Mr. Kenyon any more. Now, listen. Perfectly I understand your reasons, your scruples .. what are they to be called? But I promise to take the blame of it. I will tell dear Mr. Kenyon hereafter that you would have spoken, but that I *would not let you* – won't *that* do? won't it stop the pricking of the conscience? Because, you see, I know Mr. Kenyon, .. and I know perfectly that either he would be unhappy himself, or he would make us so. He never could bear the sense of responsibility. Then, as he told me today, and as long ago I knew, .. he is 'irresolute', timid in deciding. Then he shrinks before the daemon of the world – and 'what may be said' is louder to him than thunder. And then again, and worst of all, he sees afar off casualty within casualty, and a marriage without lawyers would be an abomination in his sight. Moreover, to discover ourselves to him, and *not submit to his counsels*, would be a real offence .. would it not? As it is, it may seem natural and excusable that we two of ourselves should poetically rush into a foolishness – but if we heard counsel, and rejected it!! Do you see? - - -

May God bless you, you who bless me!

I am wholly your own.

E.B.B. TO R.B.

Thursday Evening
(Post-mark, June 19, 1846)

- - - When everybody was at dinner I remembered that I had not been out – it was nearly eight .. there was no companion for me unless I called one from the dinner-table; and Wilson,[1] whom I thought of, had taken holiday. Therefore I put on my bonnet, as a knight of old took his sword, – aspiring to the pure heroic, – and called Flush, and walked downstairs and into the street, all alone – *that* was something great! And, with just Flush, I walked there, up and down in glorious independence. Belgium might have felt so in casting off the yoke. As to Flush, he frightened me a little and spoilt my vain-glory – for Flush has a very good, stout vain-glory of his own, and, although perfectly fond of me, has no idea whatever of being ruled over by me! – (he looks beautiful scorn out of his golden eyes, when I order him to do this or this) .. and *Flush* chose to walk on the opposite side of the street, – he *would*, – he insisted on it! and every moment I

[1] E.B.B.'s maid.

expected him to disappear into some bag of the dogstealers, as an end to *his* glory, à lui. Happily, however, I have no moral with which to point my tale – it's a very immoral story, and shows neither Flush nor myself punished for our sins. Often, I am not punished for my sins, .. am I? *You* know *that* .. dearest, dearest! - - -

It is my last letter perhaps till I see you. May God bless you, I lift up my heart to say. How happy I ought to be .. and am, .. with your thoughts all round me, *so*, as you describe! Let them call me your very own

BA

R.B. TO E.B.B.

Tuesday Morning
(Post-mark, June 23, 1846)

I was just on the point of answering your dear letter, in all the good spirits it might be expected to wake in me, when the sad news of poor Haydon's[1] death stopped all; much I feel it, for the light words of my own about his extravagance, as I had been told of it, but very much more on your account, who were so lately in communication with him. I earnestly hope, – I will trust – you have not been rudely apprised of this – I am happy to remember that you do not see the newspaper in the morning, – others will see it first; perhaps there may be no notice in the *Chronicle* at all, or on the other hand, a more circumstantial one than this in *The Times* which barely says – 'that B.R.H. died suddenly at his residence – yesterday morning. He was in his usual health on the previous evening, and it is believed that his decease was hastened by pecuniary embarrassment' – and he is called 'the unfortunate gentleman' – which with the rest implies the very worst, I fear. If by any chance *this* should be the first intimation you receive of it .. do not think me stupid nor brutal, – for I thought again and again as to the right course to take .. whether it would not be best to be silent altogether and wait and see .. but in that case I should have surprised you more by my

[1] The painter, Benjamin Robert Haydon (1786–1846). Disappointed in his ambitions, and beset by financial troubles, he had committed suicide.

cold letter, – such an one as I could bring myself to write, – for how were it possible to speak of pictures and indifferent matters when you perhaps have been shocked, made ill by this news? If I have done wrong, forgive me, my own best, dearest Ba – I would give the world to know how you are. The storm, too, and lightning may have made you even more than ordinarily unfit to be startled and grieved. God knows and must help you! I am but your devoted –

How glad I am you told me you had never seen him. And perhaps he may be after all a mere acquaintance .. anything I will fancy that is likely to relieve you of pain! Dearest dearest!

E.B.B. TO R.B.

Tuesday
(Post-mark, June 24, 1846)

Ever tenderest, kindest and most beloved, I thank you from the quick of my heart, where the thought of you lives constantly! In this world full of sadness, of which I have had my part .. full of sadness and bitterness and wrong .. full of most ghastly contrasts of life and death, strength and weakness side by side .. it is too much, to have *you* to hold by, as the river rushes on .. too much good, too much grace for such as I, .. as I feel always, and cannot cease to feel!

Oh yes – it has shocked me, this dreadful news of poor Mr. Haydon – it chilled the blood in my veins - - - For, *this I* cannot help thinking. Could anyone – *could my own hand even .. have averted what has happened?* My head and heart have ached today over the inactive hand! But, for the moment, it was out of my power, without an application where it would have been useless – and then, I never fancied this case to be more than a piece of a continuous case .. of a habit fixed. Two years ago he sent me boxes and pictures precisely so,[1] and took them back again – poor, poor Haydon! – as he will not this time. And he said last

---

[1] Just before his death, he had again entrusted some of his paintings and pictures to E.B.B. for safe keeping. He had been one of her correspondents, but they had never met.

week that Peel had sent him fifty pounds .. adding .. 'I do not however want *charity*, but employment'. Also, I have been told again and again (oh, never by *you* my beloved!) that to give money *there*, was to drop it into a hole of the ground.

But if to have dropped it so, dust to dust, would have saved a living man – what then?

Yet of the three notes I had from him last week, the first was written so lightly, that the second came to desire me not to attribute to him a 'want of feeling'. And who could think .. contemplate .. this calamity? May God have mercy on the strongest of us, for we are weak. Oh, that a man so high hearted and highly endowed .. a bold man, who has thrown down gauntlet after gauntlet after gauntlet in the face of the world – that such a man should go mad for a few paltry pounds! For he was *mad* if he killed himself! of that I am as sure as if I knew it. If he killed himself, he was mad first.

Some day, when I have the heart to look for it, you shall see his last note. I understand now that there are touches in it of a desperate pathos – but never could he have meditated self-destruction while writing that note. He said he should write six sets of lectures more .. six more volumes. He said he was painting a new background to a picture, which made him 'feel as if his soul had wings'. And then he hoped his brain would not turn. And he 'gloried' in the naval dangers of his son at sea. And he repeated an old phrase of his, which I had heard from him often before, and which now rings hollowly to the ears of my memory .. that he *couldn't and wouldn't die.* Strange and dreadful!

It is nearly two years since we had a correspondence of some few months – from which at last I receded, notwithstanding the individuality and spirit of his letters, and my admiration for a certain fervour and magnanimity of genius, no one could deny to him. His very faults partook of that nobleness. But for a year and a half or more perhaps, I scarcely have written or heard from him – until last week when he wrote to ask for a shelter for his boxes and pictures. If you had enquired of me the week before I might have answered that I did not *wish to renew the intercourse* – yet who could help being shocked and saddened? *Would* it have availed, to have dropped something into that 'hole in the ground'? Oh, to imagine *that*! Yet a little would have been but as nothing! – and he did not ask even for a little – and I should have been ashamed to have offered but a little. Yet I cannot turn the thought away – *that I did not offer* - - -

Friday Morning
(Post-mark, June 26, 1846)

I drew the table to the fire before I wrote this. Here is cool weather, grateful to those overcome by last week's heat, I suppose! – much as one conceives of a day's starvation being grateful to people who were overfeasted some time back. But the coolness (that is, piercing cold as the north wind can make) sets me to ponder on what you said yesterday, – of considering summer as beginning next Wednesday, or there about, and ending by consequence with September. Our time is 'at the Summer's end': and it does strike me that there may be but too many interpositions beside that of 'my own will' .. far too many. If those equinoctial winds disturb the sea, the cold weather adds to the difficulties of the land-journey .. then the will may interpose or stand aloof .. I cannot take you and kill you .. really, inevitably kill you! - - - Therefore if any September weather shall happen in September .. let us understand and wait .. another year! and another, and another.

Now, have I ever, with all those askings, asked you once too often, that is, unnecessarily – 'if this should be', – or 'when this should be?' What is my 'will' to do with it? Can I keep the winds away, alas? My own will has all along been annihilated before you, – with respect to you – I should never be able to say 'she shall dine on fish, or fruit', 'She shall wear silk gloves or thread gloves' – even to exercise in fancy that much 'will over *you*' is revolting – I *will this*, never to be 'over you' if I could!

So, you decide here as elsewhere – but *do* decide, Ba, my own only Ba – do *think*, to decide. I *can* know nothing here as to what is gained or lost by delay or anticipation – I only refer to the few obvious points of the advantage of our 'flight not being in the winter' – and the consideration that the difficulty in another quarter will never be less nor more, – therefore is out of the question.

I will tell you something I meant to speak of yesterday. Mrs. Jameson said Mr. Kenyon had assured her, with the kindest intentions, that it was quite vain to make those offers of company to Pisa or elsewhere, for your Father would never give his consent, and the very rationality of the plan, and probability of the utmost benefit following the adoption of it, would be the harder to forego the more they were entertained – whereupon, 'having the passions of his kind he spoke some certain things' – bitter and unavoidable. Then Mrs. J. spoke too, as you may imagine; apparently from better knowledge than even I possess. Now I repeat this to your *common-sense*, my Ba – it is not hard to see that *you* must be silent and suffering, where no other can or will be either – so that if a verdict needs must be pronounced on our conduct, it will be 'the world's' and not an individual's – and for once a fair one. Mrs. Jameson's very words were .. (writing from what *has been*, observe – what is irrevocably past, and not what *may* be) – 'I feel unhappy when in her presence .. impelled to do her some service, and impeded. *Can* nothing be done to rescue her from this? *ought* it to continue?' So speaks – not your lover! – who, as he told you, *did* long to answer 'someone will attempt, at least!' But it was best, for Mrs. Jameson would be blamed afterward, as Mr. K. might be abused, as ourselves will be vituperated, as my family must be calumniated .. by *whom*?

Do you feel me kiss your feet while I write this? I think you must, Ba! There is surely, – I trust, surely no impatience here, in this as in the other letter – if there is, I will endeavour to repress it .. but it will be difficult – for I love you, and am not a stock nor a stone.

And as we are now, – another year!

Well, kissing the feet answers everything, declares everything – and I kiss yours, my own Ba.

Friday Morning
(Post-mark, June 26, 1846)

- - - I have not had the heart to look at the newspapers, but hear that Sir Robert Peel has provided liberally for the present necessities of the poor Haydons. And do you know, the more I think the more I am inclined to conclude that the money-distress was merely an additional irritation, and that the despair leading to the revolt against life, had its root in disappointed ambition. The world did not recognize his genius, and he punished the world by withdrawing the light - - - All the audacity and bravery and self-exultation which drew on him so much ridicule were an agony in disguise – he could not live without reputation, and he wrestled for it, struggled for it, *kicked* for it, forgetting grace of attitude in the pang. When all was vain, he went mad and died. Poor Haydon! He measures things differently now! and let *us* now be right and just in our admeasurement of what he was – for, with all his weaknesses, he was not certainly *far* from being a great man - - -

May God bless you – très bon! – très cher, pour cause.
Toute à toi – pour toujours.

Saturday
(Post-mark, June 27, 1846)

I said I would answer your letter today, my beloved, but how shall I say more than I have said and you know? *Do* you not know, you who will not will 'over' me, that I *cannot* will against you, and that if you set yourself seriously to take September for October, and August for September, it is all at an end with me and the calendar? Still, seriously .. there is time for deciding, is there not? .. even if I grant to you, which I do at once, that the road does not grow smoother for us by prolonged delays. The single advantage perhaps of delay is, that in the summer I get stronger every week and fitter to travel – and then, it never was thought of before (that I have heard) to precede September *so*. Last year, was I not ordered to leave England in October, and *permitted* to leave it in November? Yet I agree, November and perhaps October might be late – might be running a risk through lingering .. in our case; and you will believe me when I say I should be loth to run the risk of being forced to the further delay of a year – the position being scarcely tenable. Now for September, it generally passes for a hot month – it ripens the peaches – it is the figtime in Italy. Well – nobody decides for September nevertheless. The end of August is nearer – and at any rate we can consider, and observe the signs of the heavens and earth in the meanwhile – there is so much to think of first; and the end, remember, is only too frightfully easy. Also you shall not have it on your conscience to have killed me, let ever so much snow fall in September. If the sea should be frozen over, almost we might go by the land – might we not? and apart from fabulous ports, there are the rivers – the Seine, the Soane [sic], the Rhone which might be cheaper than the sea and the steamers; and *would*, I almost should fancy. These are things among the multitude, to think of, and you shall think of them, dearest, in your wisdom. Oh – there is time – full time - - -

May God bless you. I shall see you on Monday. I am better for Highgate – I walked longer today than usual. How strong you make me, you who make me happy!

I am your own.

E.B.B. TO R.B.

Thursday Evening
(Post-mark, July 3, 1846)

- - - Dear Miss Mitford[1] came at two today and stayed until seven, and all those hours you were not once mentioned – *I* had not courage – and she perhaps avoided an old subject of controversy .. I do not know. It is singular that for this year past you are not mentioned between us, while other names come up like grass in the rain. No single person will be more utterly confounded

---

[1] Mary Russell Mitford (1787–1855), novelist and playwright; author of *Our Village*. An intimate friend and correspondent of E.B.B.'s.

than she, when she comes to be aware of what you are to me now – and *that* I was thinking today, while she talked to never a listener. She will be confounded, and angry perhaps – it will be beyond her sympathies – or if they reach so far, the effort to make them do so will prove a more lively affection for me, than, with all my trust in her goodness, I dare count on. Yet very good and kind and tender, she was to me today. And very variously intelligent and agreeable. Do you know, I should say that her *natural* faculties were stronger than Mrs. Jameson's – though the latter has a higher aspiration and, in some ways a finer sensibility of intellect. You would certainly call her superior to her own books – certainly you would. She walks strongly on her two feet in this world – but nobody shall see her (not even *you*) fly out of a window. Too closely she keeps to the ground, I always feel. Now Mrs. Jameson can 'aspire' like Paracelsus; and believes enough in her own soul, to know a poet when she sees one. Ah – but all cannot be all.

Miss Mitford wrung a promise from me – that 'if I were well enough and in England next summer, I would go to see *her*'. So remember. Isn't it a promise for two?

Only we shall be mule-riding in those days – unless I shall have tired you. *Shall* you be tired of me in one winter, I wonder? My programme is, to let you try me for one winter, and if you are tired (as I shall know without any confession on your side) why then I shall set the mule on a canter and leave you in La Cava,[1] and go and live in Greece somewhere all alone, taking enough with me for bread and salt. Is it a jest, do you think? Indeed it is not. It is very grave earnest, be sure. I believe that I never could quarrel with you; but the same cause would absolutely hinder my living with you if you did not love me. We could not lead the abominable lives of 'married people' all round – you *know* we could not – *I* at least know that *I* could not, and just because I love you so entirely. Then, you know, you could come to England by yourself – and .. 'Where's Ba?' – 'Oh, she's somewhere in the world, I suppose. How can *I* tell?' And then Mrs. Jameson would shake her head, and observe that the prob-

[1] In southern Italy. She and R.B. had discussed the possibility of living there after their marriage.

lem was solved exactly as she expected, and that artistical natures smelt of sulphur and brimstone, without any exceptions.

Am I laughing? am I crying? who can tell. But I am not *teazing*, .. Robert! .. because, my Robert, if gravely I distrusted your affection, I could not use such light-sounding words on the whole – now could I? It is only the supposition of a *possible* future .. just possible .. (as the end of human affections passes for a possible thing) – which made me say what I would do in such a case.

But I am yours – your own: and it is impossible, in my *belief*, that I can ever fail to you so as to be less yours, on this side the grave or across it. *So*, I think of *im*possibilities – whatever I may, of possibilities!

Will it be possible to see you tomorrow, I wonder! I ask myself and not you.

And if you love me only nearly as much (instead of the prodigal 'more') *afterward*, I shall be satisfied, and shall not run from you further than to the bottom of the page.

Where you see me as your own

BA

R.B. TO E.B.B.
Friday
(Post-mark, July 3, 1846)

- - - Ba, there is nothing in your letter that shocks me, – nothing: if you choose to imagine *that* 'possibility', you are consistent in imagining the proper step to take .. it is all imagining. But I feel altogether as you feel about the horribleness of married friends, mutual esteemers, &c. – when your name sounds in my ear like any other name, your voice like other voices, – when we wisely cease to interfere with each other's pursuits, – respect differences of taste &c. &c., all will be over *then*!

I cannot myself conceive of one respect in which I shall ever fall from this feeling for you .. there never has been one word, one gesture unprompted by the living, immediate love beneath – but there have been many, many, *so* many that the same love has suppressed, refused to be represented by! I say this, because I can suppose a man taking up a service of looks and words, which service is only to last for a time, and so may be endured, – after which the 'real affection', 'honest attachment' &c. &c. means to go to its ends by a shorter road, saving useless ceremony and phrases .. do you know what I mean? I hardly do .. except that it is, whatever it is, opposed, as heaven to earth, to what I feel is. I count confidently on being more and more able to find the true words and ways (which may not be *spoken* words perhaps), the true rites by which you should be worshipped, you dear, dear Ba, my entire blessing now and ever – and *ever*; if God shall save me also.

Let me kiss you now, and long for tomorrow – I shall bring you the poorest flowers – all is brown, dry, autumnal. The sun shines and reproves me .. After all, there would have been some rocks in the pleasant water of today's meeting .. 'Oh, hardness to dissemble'!

Here is no dissembling .. I kiss you, my very own!

E.B.B. TO R.B.

Sunday
(Post-mark, July 6, 1846)

– – – My aunt's presence here has seemed to throw me back suddenly and painfully into real life out of my dream-life with you – into the old dreary flats of real life. She does not know your name even – she sees in me just *Ba* who is not your Ba – and when she talks to me .. seeing me so .. I catch the reflection of the cold abstraction as *she* apprehends it, and feel myself for a moment a Ba who is not your Ba .. sliding back into the melancholy of it! Do you understand the curious process, I talk of so mistily? Do you understand that she makes me sorrowful with not talking of *you* while she talks to *me*? Everything, in fact, that divides us, I must suffer from – so I need not treat metaphysically of causes and causes .. splitting the thinner straws.

Once she looked to the table where the remains of your flowers are, .. and said, 'I suppose Miss Mitford brought you those flowers.' 'No,' I answered, 'she did not.' 'Oh no,' began Arabel with a more suggestive voice, 'not Miss Mitford's flowers.' But I turned the subject quickly.

Robert! – how did you manage to write me the dear note from Mrs. Jameson's? how could you dare write and direct it before her eyes? What an audacity that was of yours. Oh – and how I regretted the missing you, as you proved it was a missing, by the letter! Twice to miss you on one day, seemed too much ill-luck .. even for *me*, I was going to write .. but *that* would have been a word of my old life, before I knew that I was born to the best fortune and happiest, which any woman could have, .. in being loved by *you* - - -

I am your own

BA

E.B.B. TO R.B.

Thursday
(Post-mark, July 9, 1846)

- - - Ah Flush, Flush! – he did not hurt you really? You will forgive him for me? The truth is that he hates all unpetticoated people, and that though he does not hate *you*, he has a certain distrust of you, which any outward sign, such as the umbrella, reawakens. But if you had seen how sorry and ashamed he was yesterday! I slapped his ears and told him that he never should be loved again: and he sate on the sofa (sitting, not lying) with his eyes fixed on me all the time I did the flowers, with an expression of quite despair in his face. At last I said, 'If you are good, Flush, you may come and say that you are sorry' .. on which he dashed across the room and, trembling all over, kissed first one of my hands and then another, and put up his paws to be shaken, and looked into my face with such great beseeching eyes that you would certainly have forgiven him just as I did. It is not savageness. If he once loved you, you might pull his ears and his tail, and take a bone out of his mouth even, and he would not bite you. He has no savage caprices like other dogs and men I have known - - -

Your own BA

Thursday Evening
(Post-mark, July 10, 1846)

- - - Poor Haydon! Think what an agony, life was to him, so constituted! – his own genius a clinging curse! the fire and clay in him seething and quenching one another! – the man seeing maniacally in all men the assassins of his fame! and, with the whole world against him, struggling for the thing which was his life, through night and day, in thoughts and in dreams .. struggling, stifling, breaking the hearts of the creatures dearest to him, in the conflict for which there was no victory, though he could not choose but fight it. Tell me if Laocoon's anguish was not as an infant's sleep, compared to this? And could a man, suffering *so*, stop to calculate very nicely the consideration due to A, and the delicacy which should be observed toward B? Was he scrupulously to ask himself whether this or that cry of his might not give C a headache? Indeed no, no. It is for *us* rather to look back and consider! Poor Haydon.

As to grief as grief – of course he had no killing grief. But he *suffered*.

Often it has struck me as a curious thing (yet it is not perhaps curious) that suicides are occasioned nearly always by a mortified self-love .. by losses in money, which force a man into painful positions .. and scarcely ever by bereavement through death .. scarcely ever. The wound on the vanity is more irritating than the wound on the affections – and the word *Death* if it does not make us recoil (which it does I think sometimes, .. even from the graves of beloved beings!), yet keeps us humble .. casts us down from our heights. We may despond, but we do not rebel – we feel God over us.

Your own, very own BA

Sunday, 6 p.m.
(Post-mark, July 13, 1846)

Ever, ever dearest, I have to *feel* for you all through Sunday, and I hear no sound and see no light. How are you? how did you get home yesterday? I thought of you more than usual after you went, if I did not love you as much as usual — What could *that* doubt have been made of? - - -

When you had gone Arabel came to persuade me to go to the park in a cab, notwithstanding my too lively recollections of the last we chanced upon, – and I was persuaded, and so we tumbled one over another (yet not all those cabs are so rough!) to the nearest gate opening on the grass, and got out and walked a little. A lovely evening it was, but I wished somehow rather to be at home, and Flush had his foot pinched in shutting the cab-door, . . and altogether there was not much gain: – only, as for Flush's foot, though he cried piteously and held it up, looking straight to me for sympathy, no sooner had he touched the grass than he began to run without a thought of it. Flush always makes the most of his misfortunes – he is of the Byronic school – *il se pose en victime* - - -

I loved you yesterday — I love you today .. I shall love you tomorrow.

Every day I am yours.

BA

E.B.B. TO R.B.

Wednesday Morning
(Post-mark, July 15, 1846)

And is it true of today as you said it would be, ever dearest, that you wish to be with me? Let me have the comfort, or luxury rather, of the thought of it, before tomorrow takes you a step farther off.

At dinner my aunt said to Papa .. 'I have not seen Ba all day – and when I went to her room, to my astonishment a gentleman was sitting there.' 'Who was *that*?' said Papa's eyes to Arabel – 'Mr. Browning called here today,' she answered – 'And Ba bowed her head,' continued my aunt, 'as if she meant to signify to me that I was not to come in' – 'Oh,' cried Henrietta, '*that* must have been a mistake of yours. Perhaps she meant just the contrary.' 'You should have gone in,' Papa said, 'and seen the *poet*.' Now if she really were to do that the next time! – Yet I did not, you know,

143

make the expelling gesture she thought she saw. Simply I was startled. As to Saturday we must try whether we cannot defend the position .. set the guns against the approaches to right and left .. we must try.

In speaking too of your visit this morning, Stormy said to her .. 'Oh Mr. Browning is a *great* friend of Ba's! He comes here twice a week – is it twice a week or once, Arabel?'

While I write, the Hedleys come – and Mrs. Hedley is beseeching me into seeing Mr. Bevan,[1] whom perhaps I must see notwithstanding Flush's wrongs.

By the way, I made quite clear to Flush that you left the cakes, and they were very graciously received indeed.

Dearest, since the last word was written, Mrs. Hedley came back leading Mr. Bevan, and Papa who had just entered the room found the door shut upon him .. I was nervous .. oh, so nervous! and the six feet, and something more, of Mr. Bevan seemed to me as if they never would end, so tall the man is. Well – and he sate down by me according to my aunt's arrangement; and I, who began to talk a thousand miles from any such subject, with a good reason for the precaution, found myself thrown headforemost into ecclesiastical architecture at the close of about three minutes – how he got there all his saints know best! It's his subject .. par excellence. He talks to Arabella about arches and mullions – he can't talk of anything else, I suspect. And because the Trinity is expressed in *such* a form of church-building, the altar at the east, and the baptistery at the door, .. there's no other lawful form of a church, none at all! Not that he has an opinion! he 'adopts opinions', but would not think for himself for the world at the risk of ultimate damnation! Which was the amount of his talk today .. and really it does not strike me as wisdom, now that I set it down so. Yet the man expressed himself well and has a sensible face – he is a clever third-class man, I think – better than the mass for sense, but commonplace essentially. Only, inasmuch as ecclesiastical architecture is not *my* subject, I may think otherwise of him when I know him otherwise. I do not dislike him now. And then I am conscious how you spoil me for common men, dearest! It is scarcely fair on them.

[1] He was engaged to marry E.B.B.'s cousin Arabella Hedley.

My aunt (Mrs. Hedley) said when she introduced him: 'You are to understand this to be a great honour – for she never lets anybody come here except Mr. Kenyon, .. and a few other gentlemen' .. (laughing). Said Papa – 'Only *one* other gentleman, indeed. Only Mr. Browning, the poet – the man of the pome-granates'. Was *that* likely to calm me, do you think? How late it is – I must break off. Tonight I shall write again. Dearest beloved,

I am your own always.

R.B. TO E.B.B.

Thursday
(Post-mark, July 16, 1846)

- - - I think your Father's words on those two occasions, very kind, – very! They confuse, – perhaps humble me .. that is not the expression, but it may stay. I dare say he is infinitely kind at bottom – I think so, that is, on my own account, – because, come what will or may, I shall never see otherwise than with your sight. If he could know me, I think he would soon reconcile himself to all of it, – know my heart's purposes toward you. But that is impossible – and with the sincere will to please him by any exertion or sacrifice in my power, I shall very likely never have the opportunity of picking up a glove he might drop. In old novels, the implacable father is not seldom set upon by a round dozen of ruffians with blacked faces from behind a hedge, – and just as the odds prove too many, suddenly a stranger (to all save the reader) leaps over an adjacent ditch, &c. 'Sir, under Providence, I owe you my life!' &c. &c. How does Dumas improve on this in 'Monte Cristo' – are there 'new effects'? Absurdity! Yet I would fain .. fain! you understand - - -

E.B.B. TO R.B.

Thursday
(Post-mark, July 17, 1846)

Dearest, if *you* feel *that*, must I not feel it more deeply? Twice or three times lately he has said to me 'my love' and even 'my

145

puss', his old words before he was angry last year, .. and I quite quailed before them as if they were so many knife-strokes. Anything but his *kindness*, I can bear now.

Yet I am glad that you feel *that* .. The difficulty, (almost the despair!) has been with me, to make you understand the two ends of truth .. both that he is *not* stone .. and that he *is* immovable *as* stone. Perhaps only a very peculiar nature could have held so long the position he holds in his family. His hand would not lie so heavily, without a pulse in it. Then he is upright – faithful to his conscience. You would respect him, .. and love him perhaps in the end. For me, he might have been king and father over me *to* the end, if he had thought it worth while to love me openly enough – yet, even *so*, he should not have let you come too near. And you could not (so) have come too near – for he would have had my confidence from the beginning, and no opportunity would have been permitted to you of proving your affection for me, and I should have thought always what I thought at first. So the nightshade and the eglantine are twisted, twined, one in the other, .. and the little pink roses lean up against the pale poison of the berries – we cannot tear this from that, let us think of it ever so much!

We must be humble and beseeching *afterwards* at least, and try to get forgiven – Poor Papa! I have turned it over and over in my mind, whether it would be less offensive, less *shocking* to him, if an application were made first. If I were strong, I think I should incline to it at all risks – but as it is, .. it might .. would, probably, .. take away the power of action from me altogether. We should be separated, you see, from *that moment*, .. hindered from writing .. hindered from meeting .. and I could evade nothing, as I am – not to say that I should have fainting fits at every lifting of his voice, through that inconvenient nervous temperament of mine which has so often made me ashamed of myself. Then .. the positive disobedience might be a greater offence than the unauthorised act. I shut my eyes in terror sometimes. May God direct us to the best - - -

Ever and ever I am your own

BA

- - - If ever I mistake you, Robert, doing you an injustice, .. you ought to be angry, I think, *rather* and *more* with me than with another – I should have far less excuse it appears to me, for making such a mistake, than any other person in the world. I thought so yesterday when you were speaking, and now upon consideration I think so with an increasing certainty. Is it your opinion that the members of our family, .. those who live with us always, .. know us best? They know us on the side we offer to them .. a bare profile .. or the head turned round to the ear – yes! – they do not, except by the merest chance, look into our eyes. They know us in a conventional way .. as far from God's way of knowing us, as from the world's – mid-way, it is – and the truest and most cordial and tender affection will not hinder this from being so partial a knowledge. Love! I love those who at the present moment, .. who love me (and tenderly on both sides) .. but who are so far from *understanding* me, that I never think of speaking myself into their ears .. of trying to speak myself. It is wonderful, it is among the great mysteries of life, to observe how people can love one another in the dark, blindly .. loving without knowing. And, as a matter of general observation, if I sought to have a man or woman revealed to me in his or her innermost nature, I would not go to the *family* of the person in question – though I should learn there best, of course, about personal habits, and the social bearing of him or her. George Sand delights me in one of her late works, where she says that the souls of blood relations seldom *touch* except at one or two points. Perfectly true, *that* is, I think – perfectly.

Remember how you used to say that I did not know you .. which was true in a measure .. yet I felt I knew you, and I did actually know you, in another larger measure. And if *now* you are not known to me altogether, it is my dulness which makes me unknowing.

But I know you – and I should be without excuse if ever I wronged you with a moment's injustice. I do not think I ever could depreciate you for a moment, – *that* would not be possible. There are other sins against you (*are* they against you?) which bring their own punishment! You shall never be angry with me for those - - -

I am your very own BA

Tuesday
(Post-mark, July 22, 1846)

- - - Will you let me write something, and forgive me? Because it is, I know, quite unnecessary to be written, and beside, may almost seem an interference with your own delicacy, – teaching it its duty! However, I will venture to go on, with your hand before my two eyes. Then, – you remember what we were speaking of yesterday, – house-rents and styles of living? You will never overlook, through its very obviousness, that to consult my feelings on the only point in which they are sensitive to the world you must endeavour to live as simply and cheaply as possible, down to my own habitual simplicity and cheapness - - - You see, Ba, if you have more money than you want, you shall save it or spend it in pictures or parrots or what you please .. you avoid all offence to *me* who never either saved money nor spent it – but the large house, I should be forced to stay in, – the carriage, to enter, I suppose. And you see too, Ba, that the one point on which I desire the world to be informed concerning our future life, will be that it is ordered *so* – I wish they could hear we lived in one room like George Sand in 'that happy year –'

No, there I have put down an absurdity – because, I shall have to confess a weakness, at some time or other, which is hardly reconcilable to that method of being happy – why may I not tell you now, my adored Ba, to whom I tell everything as it rises to me? Now put the hand on my eyes again – now that I have kissed it. I shall begin by begging a separate room from yours – I could never brush my hair and wash my face, I do think, before my own father – I could not, I am sure, take off my coat before you *now* – why should I ever? The kitchen is an unknown horror to me, – I come to the dining-room for whatever repast there may be, – nor willingly stay too long there, – and on the day on which poor Countess Peppa taught me how maccaroni is made, – *then* began a quiet revolution, (indeed a rapid one) against 'tagliolini', 'fettucce', 'lasagne', etc. etc. etc. – typical, typical!

What foolishness .. spare me, my own Ba, and don't answer one word, – do not even laugh, – for I *know* the exceeding unnecessary foolishness of it!

- - - Bless you, ever dearest, dearest, as yesterday, and always you bless me – I love you with all my heart and soul – *yes* Ba!

Your own, very own.

E.B.B. TO R.B.

Wednesday Morning
(Post-mark, July 22, 1846)

I did not go out yesterday, and was very glad not to have a command laid on me to go out, the wind blew so full of damp and dreariness. Then it was pleasanter to lie on the sofa and think of you, which I did, till at last I actually dreamed of you, falling asleep for that purpose. As to Flush, he came upstairs with a good deal of shame in the bearing of his ears, and straight to me – no indeed! I would not speak to him – then he went up to Arabel .. 'naughty Flush, go away' .. and Wilson, .. who had whipped him before, 'because it was right', she said .. in a fit of poetical justice, .. did not give him any consolation. So he lay down on the floor at my feet looking from under his eyebrows at me. I did not forgive him till nearly eight o'clock however. And I have not yet given him your cakes. Almost I am inclined to think now that he has not *a soul*. To behave so to you! It is nearly as bad as if I had thrown the coffee-cup! Wicked Flush! – Do you imagine that I scolded Wilson when she confessed to having whipped him? I did not. It was done with her hand, and not very hardly perhaps, though 'he cried', she averred to me – and if people, like Flush, choose to behave like dogs savagely, they must take the consequences indeed, as dogs usually do! And *you*, so good and gentle to him! Anyone but *you*, would have said 'hasty words' at least. I think I shall have a muzzle for him, to make him harmless while he learns to know you. Would it not be a good plan?

But nobody heard yesterday of either your visit or of Flush's misdoings .. so Wilson was discreet, I suppose, as she usually is, by the instinct of her vocation. Of all the persons who are *not* in our confidence, she has the most certain knowledge of the truth. Dearest, we shall be able to have Saturday. There will be no danger in it - - -

You shall see some day at Pisa what I will not show you now.[1] Does not Solomon say that 'there is a time to read what is written'. If he doesn't, he *ought*.

Your very own BA

Wednesday
(Post-mark, July 23, 1846)

Dearest, what you say is unnecessary for you to say – it is in everything *so* of course and obvious! You must have an eccentric idea of *me* if you can suppose for a moment such things to be necessary to say. If they had been *unsaid*, it would have been precisely the same, believe me, in the event.

As to the way of living – now you shall arrange *that* for yourself. You shall choose your own lodging, order your own dinner .. and if you choose to live on locusts and wild honey, I promise not to complain .. I shall not indeed be *inclined* to complain .. having no manner of ambition about carriages and large houses, even if they were within our possibilities, – which they may not be, according to Mr. Surtees's calculation or experience. The more simply we live, the better for *me*! So you shall arrange it for yourself, lest I should make a mistake! .. which, in *that* question, is a just possible thing.

One extravagance I had intended to propose to you .. but it shall be exactly as you like, and I hesitate a little as I begin to speak of it. I have thought of taking Wilson with me, .. for a year, say, if we returned then – if not, we might send her home alone .. and by that time, I should be stronger perhaps and wiser .. rather less sublimely helpless and impotent than I am now. My

[1] Probably *Sonnets from the Portuguese*; see note on p. 98 and p. 204 ff.

sisters have urged me a good deal in this matter – but if you would rather it were otherwise, be honest and say so, and let me alter my thoughts at once. There is one consideration which I submit to yours, .. that I cannot leave this house with the necessary number of shoes and pocket handkerchiefs, without help from somebody. Now whoever helps me, will suffer through me. If I left her behind she would be turned into the street before sunset. Would it be right and just of me, to permit it? Consider! I must manage a sheltering ignorance for my poor sisters, at the last, .. and for all our sakes. And in order to *that*, again, I must have some one else in my confidence. Whom, again, I would unwillingly single out for an absolute *victim*.

Wilson is attached to me, I believe – and, in all the discussions about Italy she has professed herself willing 'to go anywhere in the world with me'. Indeed I rather fancy that she was disappointed bitterly last year, and that it would not be a pure devotion. She is an expensive servant – she has sixteen pounds a year, .. but she has her utilities besides, and is very amiable and easily satisfied, and would not add to the expenses, or diminish from the economies, even in the matter of room – *I* would manage *that* for her. Then she would lighten your responsibilities .. as the Archbishop of Canterbury and company do Mr. Bevan's. Well – you have only to consider your own wishes. I shall not care many straws, if you decide this way or that way. Let it be as may seem to you wisest - - -

I am your Ba, always!

R.B. TO E.B.B.

Wednesday
(Post-mark, July 23, 1846)

- - - My dearest – dearest, – you might go to Pisa without shoes, – or feet to wear them, for aught I know, since you may have wings, only folded away from me – but without your Wilson, or some one in her capacity, you .. no, I will not undertake to speak of *you*; then, *I*, should be simply, exactly, INSANE to move a step; I would rather propose, let us live on bread and water, and sail in the hold of a merchant-ship; THIS CANNOT

151

be dispensed with! It is most fortunate, most providential, that Wilson is inclined to go – I am *very* happy; for a new servant, with even the best dispositions, would never be able to anticipate your wants and wishes during the voyage, at the very beginning. Yet you write of this to me *so,* my Ba! I think I will, in policy, begin the anger at a good place. Yes, all the anger I am capable of descends on the head – (not in kisses, whatever you may fancy).

And so poor Flush suffered after all! Dogs that are dog-like would be at no such pains to tell you they would not see you with comfort approached by a stranger who might be –! A 'muzzle'? oh, no, – but suppose you have him removed next time, and perhaps the next, till the whole occurrence is out of his mind as the fly bite of last week – because, if he sees me and begins his barking and valiant snapping, and gets more and heavier vengeance down-stairs, perhaps, – his transient suspicion of me will confirm itself into absolute dislike, hatred, whereas, after an interval, we can renew acquaintance on a better footing. Dogs have such memories! - - -

Ever your own R.

E.B.B. TO R.B.

Tuesday Evening
(Post-mark, July 29, 1846)

Dearest, as I lost nearly an hour of you today, I make amends to myself by beginning to write to you as if I had not seen you at all. A large sheet of paper, too, has flown into my hands – the Fates giving ample room and verge enough, my characters .. not 'of *Hell*' .. to trace, *as* I am not going to swear at Mr. Kenyon, whatever the provocation! Dear Mr. Kenyon!

It appears that he talked to my sisters some time before he let himself be announced to me – he said to them 'I want to talk to you .. sit down by me and listen'. Then he began to tell them of Mrs. Jameson, repeating what *you* told me, of her desire to take me to Italy, .. and of her earnestness about it. To which, he added, he had replied by every representation likely to defeat those thoughts – that only a relative would be a fit companion for me, and that no person out of my family could be justified in accepting such a responsibility, on other grounds, entering on the occurrences of last year, and reasoning on from them to the possibility that if I offended by an act of disobedience, I might be 'cast off' as for a crime. Oh – poor Papa was not spared at all – not to Mrs. Jameson, not to my sisters. Mr. Kenyon said .. 'It is painful to you perhaps to hear me talk so, but it is a sore subject with me, and I cannot restrain the expression of my opinions.' He 'had told Mrs. Jameson everything – it was due to her to have a full knowledge, he thought .. and he had tried to set before her the impossibility she was under, of doing any good'. Then he asked my sisters .. if I ever spoke of Italy .. if they thought I dwelt on the idea of it. 'Yes,' they answered 'in *their* opinion, I had made up my mind to go.' 'But *how?* what is the practical side of the question? She can't go alone – and which of you will go with her? You know, last year, she properly rejected the means which involved you in danger.' Henrietta advised that nothing should be said or done. 'Ba must do everything for herself. Her friends cannot help her. She must help herself.' 'But she must not go to Italy by herself. Then, *how?*' 'She has determination of character,' continued Henrietta – 'She will surprise everybody some day.'

'*But how?*' Mr. Kenyon repeated .. looking uneasy. (And how imprudent of Henrietta to say *that*! I have been scolding her a little.)

The discussion ended by his instructing them to tell *me* of Mrs. Jameson's proposal; 'because it was only right that I should have the knowledge of her generous kindness, though for his part, he did not like to agitate me by conversing on the subject.'

Yes, one thing more was said. He mentioned having had some conversation with my uncle Hedley, who was 'very angry' – and he asked if my aunt Hedley had no influence with the highest authority. My sisters answered in the negative. And this is all. He appears to have no 'plan' of his particular own.

What do you say, Robert, to all this? Since I am officially *informed* of Mrs. Jameson's goodness, I must thank her certainly – and in what words! '*How*'! – as Mr. Kenyon asks. Half I have felt inclined to write and thank her gratefully, and confide to her, not the secret itself, but the secret of *there being a secret* with the weight of which I am unwilling to oppress her at this time. Could it be done, I wonder? Perhaps not. Yet how hard, how very difficult, it seems to me, to thank her worthily, and be silent wholly on my motives in rejecting her companionship! And a *whole confidence* NOW is dangerous .. would torment her with a sense of responsibility. Think which way it should be - - -

May God bless you, my own! – are you my own? and not rather, yes, rather, far rather, *I* am your own, your very own.

BA

Wednesday Morning
(Post-mark, July 29, 1846)

- - - Oh, how *can* you, blessing me so, speak as you spoke yesterday – for the *first* time! I thought you would only write such suppositions, such desires – (for it was a desire) .. and that along with you I was safe from them, – yet you are adorable amid it all – only I *do* feel such speaking, Ba, lightly as it fell – no, not *now* I feel it, – this letter is before my heart like the hand on my eyes. I feel this letter, only – how good, good, good of you to write it! - - -

Whatever you decide on writing to Mrs. Jameson will be rightly written – it seems to me *nearly* immaterial; (putting out of the question the confiding the whole secret, which, from its responsibility, as you feel, must not be done) whether you decline her kindness for untold reasons which two months (Ba?) will make abundantly plain, – or whether you farther inform her that there *is* a special secret – of which she must bear the burthen, even in that mitigated form, for the same two months, – as I say, it seems immaterial – but it is most material that you should see how the ground is crumbling from beneath our feet, with its chances and opportunities – do not talk about 'four months', – till December, that is – unless you mean what *must* follow as a consequence. The next thing will be Mr. Kenyon's application to me – *he certainly knows everything* .. how else, after such a speech from your sister? But his wisdom as well as his habits incline him to use the force that is in kindness, patience, gentleness: your father might have entered the room suddenly yesterday and given vent to all the passionate indignation in the world. I dare say we should have been married today: but I shall have the quietest, most considerate of expositions made me (with one arm on my shoulder), of how I am sure to be about to kill you, to ruin you, your social reputation, your public estimation, destroy the peace of this member of your family, the prospects of that other, – and the end will be?

Because I *can* not only die for you but live without you *for you* – once sure it IS for you: I know what you once bade me promise – but I do not know what assurances on assurance, all on the ground of a presumed knowledge of your good above your own possible knowledge, – might not effect! *I do not know*!

This is through you! You *ought* to know now that 'it would *not* be better for me to leave you'! That after this devotion of myself to you I cannot undo it all, and devote myself to objects so utterly insignificant that yourself do not venture to specify them – 'it would be better – people will say such things' .. I will never *force* you to know this, however – if your admirable senses do not instruct you, I shall never seem to, as it were, threaten you, by prophecies of what my life would probably be, disengaged from you – it should certainly not be passed where the 'people' are, nor where their 'sayings' influenced me any more – but I ask you to look into my heart, and into your own belief in what is worthy and durable and *the better* – and then *decide*: – for instance, to speak of waiting for four months will be a decision - - -

I believe in you, or what shall I believe in? I wish I could take my life, my affections, my ambitions, all my very self, and fold over them your little hand, and leave them there – then you would see what belief is mine! But if you had *not* seen it, would you have uttered one word, written one line, given one kiss to me? May God bless you, Ba –

R.B.

'Such desires – (for it was a desire –)'

Well put into a parenthesis *that* is! – ashamed and hiding itself between the brackets!

Because – my own dearest – it was *not* a 'desire' – it was the farthest possible from being a 'desire' .. the word I spoke to you on Tuesday .. yesterday!

And if I spoke it for the first time instead of writing it – what did *that* prove, but that I *was able* to speak it, and that just it was so much less earnest and painfully felt? Why it was not a proposition even –. I said only 'You had better give me up!' It was only the reflection, in the still water, of what *had been* a proposition. 'Better' perhaps! – 'Better' for you, that you should desire to give me up and do it – my 'Idée fixe' you know. But *said* with such different feelings from those which have again and again made the tears run down my cheeks while I wrote to you the vexatious letter .. that I smile at you seeing no difference. You, blind! – Which is wrong of me again. I will not smile for having vexed you .. teazed you. Which is wrong of *you*, though .. the being vexed for so little! because 'you *ought* to know by this time' .. (now I will use your reproachful words) – you ought certainly to know that I am your own, and ready to go through with the matter we are upon, and willing to leave the times and the seasons in your hand! Four months! meant nothing at all. Take September, if you please. All I thought of answering to you, was, that there was no need yet of specifying the exact time. And yet –

Ah – yes! – I feel as *you* feel, the risks and the difficulties which close around us. And *you* feel *that* about Mr. Kenyon? Is it by an instinct that I tremble to think of *him*, more than to think of others? The hazel-rod turns round in my hand when I stand *here*. And as you show him speaking and reasoning .. his arm laid on your shoulder .. oh, what a vision, *that* is! before *that*, I cannot stand any longer! – it takes away my breath – the likelihood of it is so awful that it seems to *promise* to realise itself, one day!

But *you promised*. I have your solemn promise, Robert! If ever you should be moved by a single one of those vain reasons, it will be an unfaithful cruelty in you. You will have trusted *another*, against *me*. You would not do it, my beloved.

For I have none in the world who will hold me to make me live in it, except only you. I have come back for you alone .. at your voice and because you have use for me! I have come back to live a little for you – I see *you*. My fault is .. not that I think too much of what people will say. I see you and hear you. 'People' did not make me live for *them*. I am not theirs, but yours. I deserve that you should believe in me, beloved, because my love for you is *'Me'* - - -

May God bless you, dearest, dearest! – I owe all to you, and love you wholly – I am your very own –

E.B.B. TO R.B.

Thursday Evening
(Post-mark, July 31, 1846)

- - - Where did you guess that I was today? In Westminster Abbey! But we were there at the wrong hour, as the service was near to begin .. and I was so frightened of the organ, that I hurried and besought my companions out of the door after a moment or two. Frightened of the organ! – yes, just exactly *that* – and you may laugh a little as they did. Through being so disused to music, it affects me quite absurdly. Again the other day, in the drawing room, because my cousin sang a song from the 'Puritani', of no such great melancholy, I had to go away to finish my sobbing by myself. Which is all foolish and absurd, I know – but people cannot help their nerves – and I was ready to cry today, only to *think* of the organ, without hearing it – I, who do not cry easily, either! and all Arabel's jests about how I was sure of my life even if I *should* hear one note, .. did not reassure me in the least. We talked within the chapel .. merely within .. and looked up and looked down! How grand – how solemn! Time itself seemed turned to stone there! Then we stood where the poets were laid – oh, it is very fine – it is better than Laureateships and pensions. Do you remember what is written on Spenser's monument – 'Here lyeth, in expectation of the second coming of Jesus Christ, .. Edmond Spenser, having given proof of his divine spirit in his poems' – something to that effect; and it struck me as being earnest and beautiful, and as if the writer believed in him. We should not dare, nowadays, to put such words on a poet's monument. We should say .. the author of such a book .. at most! Michael Drayton's inscription has crept back into the brown heart of the stone .. all but the name and a date, which somebody has renewed with black lines .. black as ink - - -

E.B.B. TO R.B.

Sunday Morning and Evening
(Post-mark, August 3, 1846)

- - - I seem to be with you, Robert, at this moment, more than yesterday I was .. though if I look up now, I do not see you sitting there! – but when you sate there yesterday, I was looking at Papa's face as I saw it through the floor, and now I see only yours.

Dearest, he came into the room at about seven, before he went to dinner – I was lying on the sofa and had on a white dressing gown, to get rid of the strings .. so oppressive the air was, for all the purifications of lightning. He looked a little as if the thunder had passed into him, and said, 'Has this been your costume since the morning, pray?'

'Oh no' – I answered – 'Only just now, because of the heat.'

'Well,' he resumed, with a still graver aspect .. (so displeased he looked, dearest!) 'it appears, Ba, that *that man* has spent the whole day with you.' To which I replied as quietly as I could, that you had several times meant to go away, but that the rain would not let you, – and there the colloquy ended. Brief enough – but it took my breath away .. or what was left by the previous fear. And think how it must have been a terrible day, when the lightning of it made the least terror - - -

Before yesterday's triple storms, I had a presentiment which oppressed me during two days .. a presentiment that it would all end *ill*, through some sudden accident or misery of some kind. What is the use of telling you this? I do not know. I will tell you besides, that it cannot .. shall not .. be, by my fault or failing. I may be broken indeed, but never bent.

If things should go smoothly, however, I want to say one word, once for all, in relation to them. Once or twice you have talked as if a change were to take place in your life through marrying – whereas I do beg you to keep in mind that not a pebble in the path changes, nor is pushed aside because of me. If you should make me feel myself in the way, should I like it, do you think? And how could I disturb a single habit or manner of yours .. as an unmarried man .. though being within call – I? The best of me is, that I am really very quiet and not difficult to content – having not been spoilt by an excess of prosperity even in little things. It will be prosperity in the greatest, if you seem to be happy – believe that, and leave all the rest. You will go out just as you do now .. when you choose, and as a matter of course, and without need of a word – you will be precisely as you are now in everything, – lord of the house-door-key, and of your own ways – so that when I shall go to Greece, you shall not feel yourself much better off than before I went. That shall be a reserved vengeance, Robert - - -

May God bless you! Do say how you are after that rain. The storm is calm,

and ever and ever I am your own BA

R.B. TO E.B.B.

Monday Morning
(Post-mark, August 3, 1846)

- - - How you have mistaken my words, whatever they may have been, about the 'change' to be expected in my life! I have, most sincerely I tell you, no one habit nor manner to change or persevere in, – if you once accept the general constitution of me as accordant to yours in a sufficient degree, – my incompleteness with your completeness, dearest, – there is no further difficulty. I want to be a Poet – to read books which make wise in their various ways, to see just so much of nature and the ways of men as seems necessary – and having done this already in some degree,

I can easily and cheerfully afford to go without any or all of it for the future, if called upon, – and so live on, and 'use up', my past acquisitions such as they are. I will go to Pisa and learn, – or stay here and learn in another way – putting, as I always have done, my whole pride, if that is the proper name, in the being able to work with the least possible materials. There is my scheme of life *without* you, *before* you existed for me; prosecuted hitherto with every sort of weakness, but always kept in view and believed in. Now then, please to introduce Ba, and say what is the habit she changes? But do not try to say what divinest confirmation she brings to 'whatever is good and holy and true' in this scheme, because even She cannot say that! All the liberty and forbearance .. most graceful, most characteristic of you, sweet! - - -

May God bless you, infinitely bless you, ever dearest, dearest, prays ever your very own –

R.

Thursday
(Post-mark, August 7, 1846)

I told you nothing yesterday; but the interruption left me no time, and the house was half asleep before I had done writing what I was able to write. Otherwise I wanted to tell you that Mrs. Jameson had been here .. that she came yesterday, and without having received my note. So I was thrown from my resources. I was obliged to thank her with my voice .. so much weaker than my hand. If you knew how frightened I was! The thunder, the morning before, (which I did not hear holding *your* hand!) shook me less, upon the whole. I thanked her at least .. I could do *that*. And then I said it was in vain .. impossible.

'Mr. Kenyon threw cold water on the whole scheme. But *you*! Have *you* given up going to Italy?'

I said 'no, that I have not certainly'. I said 'I felt deeply how her great kindness demanded every sort of frankness and openness from me towards her, – and yet, that at that moment I could not be frank – there were reasons which prevented it. Would she promise not to renew the subject to Mr. Kenyon? not to repeat to him what I said? and to wait until the whole should be explained to herself?'

She promised. She was kind beyond imagination – at least, far beyond expectation. She looked at me a little curiously, but asked no more questions until she rose to go away. And then –

'But you will go?' 'Perhaps – if something unforeseen does not happen.' 'And you will let me know, and when you can, – when everything is settled?' 'Yes.' 'And you think you shall go?' 'Yes.' 'And with efficient companionship?' 'Yes.' 'And happily and quietly?' .. 'Ye ..' I could not say the full 'Yes', to *that* – if it had been utterable, the idea of 'quiet' would have been something peculiar. She loosened her grasp of her catechumen, therefore – nothing was to be done with me.

I forgot, however, to tell you that in the earlier part of the discussion she spoke of having half given up her plan of going herself. In her infinite goodness she said, 'she seemed to want an object, and it was in the merest selfishness, she had proposed taking *me* as an object' – 'And if you even go without me, would it not be possible to meet you on the road? I shall go to Paris in any case. *If* you go, *how* do you go?'

'Perhaps across France – by the rivers.'

'Precisely. That is as it should be. Mr. Kenyon talked of a long sea-voyage.'

Now I have recited the whole dialogue to you, I think, except where my gratitude grew rhetorical, as well it might. She is the kindest, most affectionate woman in the world! and you shall let me love her for you and for me - - -

R.B. TO E.B.B.

Wednesday Morning
(Post-mark, August 12, 1846)

I have been putting all the letters into rings – twenty together – and they look now as they should – 'infinite treasure in a little room' – note, that they were so united and so ranged from the beginning, at least since I began to count by twenties – but the white tape I used (no red tape, thank you!) was vile in its operation,

– the untying and retying (so as to preserve a proper *cross*) hard for clumsy fingers like mine: – these rings are perfect. How strange it will be to have no more letters! Of all the foolishnesses that ever were uttered that speech of mine, – about your letters strewing the house, – was the most thoroughly perfect! yet you have nothing to forgive in me, you say! - - -

Bless you, Ba, my dearest, perfect love – now I will begin thinking of you again – let me kiss you, my own!

E.B.B. TO R.B.

Wednesday Morning
(Post-mark, August 12, 1846)

- - - Here is a letter from a lady in a remote district called Swineshead, who sends me lyrical specimens, and desires to know if *this be Genius*. She does not desire to publish; at any rate not for an indefinite number of years; but for her private and personal satisfaction, she would be glad to be informed whether she is a Sappho or George Sand or anything of that kind. What in the world is to be answered, now, to an application of *that* kind! To meddle with a person's opinion of himself or herself (quite a private opinion) seems like meddling with his way of dressing, with her fashion of putting in pins – like saying you *shall* put your feet on a stool, or you *shan't* eat pork. It is an interference with private rights, from which I really do shrink. Unfortunately too it is impossible to say what she wants to hear – I am in despair about it. When we are at Pisa we shall not hear these black stones crying after us any more perhaps - - -

Not only I loved you yesterday, but even today I love you; which is remarkable. Tomorrow and tomorrow and tomorrow, what will *you* do? Is *that* an 'offence'? Nay, but it is rather reasonable that when the hour strikes the fairy-gold should turn back into leaves, and poor Cinderella find herself sitting in her old place among the ashes, just as she had touched the hand of the king's son.

Don't think I mean anything by *that*, ever dearest – not so much as to teaze you – Robert!

I only love you today – that is, I love you and do nothing more. And the Fairy Tales are on the whole, I feel, the most available literature for illustration, whenever I think of loving you.

Your own BA

E.B.B. TO R.B.

Saturday Morning
(August 15, 1846)

- - - Dearest, when I told you yesterday, after speaking of the many coloured theologies of the house, that it was hard to answer for what *I* was, .. I meant that I felt unwilling, for my own part, to put on any of the liveries of the sects. The truth, as God sees it, must be something so different from these opinions about truth – these systems which fit different classes of men like their coats, and wear brown at the elbows always! I believe in what is divine and floats at highest, in all these different theologies – and because the really Divine draws together souls, and tends so to a unity, I could pray anywhere and with all sorts of worshippers, from the Sistine Chapel to Mr. Fox's,[1] those kneeling and those standing. Wherever you go, in all religious societies, there is a little to revolt, and a good deal to bear with – but it is not otherwise in the world without; and, *within*, you are especially reminded that God has to be more patient than yourself after all. Still you go quickest there, where your sympathies are least ruffled and disturbed – and I like, beyond comparison best, the simplicity of the dissenters .. the unwritten prayer, .. the sacraments administered quietly and without charlatanism! and the principle of a church, as they hold it, *I* hold it too, .. quite apart from state-necessities .. pure from the law. Well – there is enough to dissent from among the dissenters – the Formula is rampant among them as among others – you hear things like the buzzing of flies in proof of a corruption – and see every now and then something divine set up like a post for men of irritable minds and passions to rub themselves against, calling it a holy deed – you feel moreover bigotry and ignorance pressing on you on all

[1] William Johnson Fox (1786–1864), a Unitarian minister, and celebrated preacher and philanthropist; early friend and patron of R.B.

sides, till you gasp for breath like one strangled. But better this, even, than what is elsewhere – *this* being elsewhere too in different degrees, besides the evil of the place. Public and social prayer is right and desirable – and I would prefer, as a matter of custom, to pray in one of those chapels, where the minister is simple-minded and not controversial – certainly would prefer it. Not exactly in the Socinian chapels, nor yet in Mr. Fox's – not by preference. The Unitarians seem to me to throw over what is most beautiful in the Christian Doctrine; but the Formulists, on the other side stir up a dust, in which it appears excusable not to see. When the veil of the body falls, how we shall look into each other's faces, astonished, . . after one glance at God's! - - -

Your very own BA

E.B.B. TO R.B.

Saturday Evening
(Post-mark, August 17, 1846)

- - - You were made perfectly to be loved – and surely I have loved you, in the idea of you, my whole life long. Did I tell you *that* before, so often as I have thought it? It is *that* which makes me take it all as visionary good – for when one's Ideal comes down to one, and walks beside one suddenly, what is it possible to do but to cry out . . 'a dream'? You are the best . . best. And if you loved me only and altogether for pity, (and I think that, more than *you* think, the sentiment operated upon your generous chivalrous nature), and if you confessed it to me and proved it, and I knew it absolutely – what then? As long as it was *love*, should I accept it less gladly, do you imagine, because of the root? Should I think it less a gift? should I be less grateful, . . or *more*? Ah – I have my 'theory of causation' about it all – but we need not dispute, and will not, on any such metaphysics. Your *loving* me is enough to satisfy me – and if you did it because I sate rather on a green chair than a yellow one, it would be enough still for me: – only it would not, for *you* – because your motives are as worthy always as your acts. – Dearest!

So let us talk of the great conference in Mr. Kenyon's carriage in which joined himself, Arabel, Flush and I. First he said . . 'Did

Browning stay much longer with you?' 'Yes – some time.' This was as we were going on our way towards some bridge, whence to look at the Birmingham train. As we came back, he said, with an epical leap *in medias res* . . 'What an extraordinary memory our friend Browning has.' 'Very extraordinary' – said I – 'and how it is raining.' I give you Arabel's report of my reply, for I did not myself exactly remember the full happiness of it – and she assured me besides that he looked . . looked at me . . as a man may look . . And this was everything spoken of you throughout the excursion.

But he spoke of *me* and observed how well I was – on which Arabel said 'Yes – she considered me quite well; and that nothing was the matter now but *sham*.' Then the railroads were discussed in relation to me . . and she asked him – 'Shouldn't she try them a little, before she undertakes this great journey to Italy?' 'Oh' . . he replied – '*she* is going on no great journey.' 'Yes, she will, perhaps – Ba is inclined to be a great deal too wild, and now that she is getting well, I do assure you, Mr. Kenyon.'

To sit upon thorns, would express rather a 'velvet cushion' than where I was sitting, while she talked this foolishness. I have been upbraiding her since, very seriously; and I can only hope that the words were taken for mere jest – *du bout des lèvres*.

Moreover Mr. Kenyon is *not* going away on Thursday – he has changed his plans: he has put off Cambridge till the 'spring' – he meets Miss Bayley nowhere – he holds his police-station in London. 'When *are* you going,' I asked in my despair, trying to look satisfied. He did not know – 'not directly, at any rate' – 'I need not hope to get rid of him,' he said aside perhaps.

But we saw the great roaring, grinding Thing . . a great blind mole, it looked for blackness. We got out of the carriage to see closer – and Flush was so frightened at the roar of it, that he leapt upon the coach-box. Also it rained, – and I had ever so many raindrops on my gown and in my face even, . . which pleased me nearly as much as the railroad sight. It is something new for me to be rained upon, you know.

As for happiness – the words which you use so tenderly are in my heart already, making me happy, . . I am happy by you. Also I may say solemnly, that the greatest proof of love I could give you, is to be happy because of you – and even *you* cannot judge and see how great a proof *that* is. You have lifted my very soul up into the light of your soul, and I am not ever likely to mistake it for the common daylight. May God bless you, ever ever dearest!

I am your own –

R.B. TO E.B.B.

Sunday
(Post-mark, August 17, 1846)

- - - I told you on Friday I loved you more at that instant than at any previous time – I will show you why, because I *can* show you, I think – though it seems at first an irrational word .. for always having loved you wholly, how can I, still *only* loving you wholly, speak of 'more' or 'less'? – This is why – I used to see you once a week, to sit with you for an hour and a half – to receive a letter, or two, or three, during the week – and I loved you, Ba, wholly, as I say, and reckoned time for no time in the intervals of seeing you and hearing from you. Now I see you twice in the week, and stay with you the three hours, and have letter on dear letter, – and the distance is, at least, the *same*, between the days, and between the letters – I will only affirm it is the *same* – so I must love you more – because if you were to bring me back to the old allowance of you, – the one short visit, the two or three letters, – I should be starved with what once feasted me! (If you do not understand Flush does!) - - -

Dearest, I know your very meaning, in what you said of religion, and responded to it with my whole soul – what you express now, is for us both .. those are my own feelings, my convictions beside – instinct confirmed by reason. Look at that injunction to 'love God with all the heart, and soul, and strength' – and then imagine yourself bidding any faculty, that arises towards the love of him, be still! If in a meeting house, with the blank white walls, and a simple doctrinal exposition, – all the senses should turn (from where they lie neglected) to all that sunshine in the Sistine with its music and painting, which would lift them at once to Heaven, – why should you not go forth? – to return just as quickly, when they are nourished into a luxuriance that extinguishes, what is called, Reason's pale wavering light, lamp or whatever it is – for I have got into a confusion with thinking of our convolvuluses that climb and tangle round the rose-trees – which might be lamps or tapers! See the levity! No – this sort of levity only exists because of the strong conviction, I do believe! There seems no longer need of earnestness in assertion, or proof .. so it runs lightly over, like foam on the top of a wave - - -

Now goodbye, my own Ba – 'goodbye'. Be prepared for all fantasticalness that may happen! Perhaps some day I shall shake hands with you, simply, and go .. just to remember the more exquisitely where I once was, and where you let me stay now, you dearest, dearest heart of my heart, soul of my soul! But the shaking-hands, at a very distant time! *Now* – let me kiss you, beloved – and so I do kiss you –

Ever your own.

E.B.B. TO R.B.

Saturday
(Post-mark, August 22, 1846)

- - - I have had a visitor. Guess whom – Mrs. Jameson. So I am on a 'narrow neck of land' .. such as Wesley wrote hymns about; .. and *stans in pede uno* on it – can make for you but a hurried letter.

She came in with a questioning face, and after wondering to find me visible so soon, plunged into the centre of the question and asked 'what was settled .. what I was doing about Italy. – '

'Just nothing,' I told her. 'She found me as she left me, able to say no word.'

'But what *are* you going to do –' throwing herself back in the chair with a sudden – 'but oh, I must not enquire'.

I went on to say that 'in the first place my going would not take place till quite the end of September if so soon, – that I had determined to make no premature fuss, – and that, for the actual present, nothing was either to be done or said.'

'Very sudden then, it is to be. In fact, there is only an *elopement* for you –' she observed laughing.

So I was obliged to laugh.

(But, dearest, nobody will use such a word surely to the *event*. We shall be in such an obvious exercise of Right by Daylight – surely nobody will use such a word.)

I talked of Mr. Kenyon, – how he had been with me yesterday and brought the mountains of the Earth into my room – 'which was almost too much,' I said, 'for a prisoner.' 'Yes – but if you go to Italy . .'

'But Mr. Kenyon thinks I shall not. In his opinion, my case is desperate.'

'But I tell you that it is not. Nobody's case is desperate when the will is not at fault. And a woman's will when she wills thoroughly as I hope you do, is strong enough to overcome. When I hear people say that *circumstances are against them*, I always retort, . . you mean *that your will is not with you*! I believe in the will – I have faith in it.'

There is an oracle for us, to remember for good! - - -

On Monday morning she comes to see me again. It is all painful, or rather unpleasant. One should not use strong words out of place, and there will remain too much use for this. How I teaze you now!

Believe me, through it all, that when I think of the very worst of the future, I love you the best, and feel most certain of never hesitating. As long as you choose to have me, my beloved, I have chosen – I am yours already –

and your own always –

BA

E.B.B. TO R.B.

Sunday Morning
(Post-mark, August 24, 1846)

- - - While I am writing, comes in Arabel with such a face. My brother had been talking, talking of me. Stormie suddenly touched her and said – 'Is it true that there is an engagement between Mr. Browning and Ba –?' She was taken unaware, but had just power to say 'You had better ask them, if you want to know. What nonsense, Storm.' 'Well,' he resumed, 'I'll ask Ba when I go up-stairs.' George was by, looking as grave as if antedating his judgeship. Think how frightened I was, Robert .. expecting them up-stairs every minute, – for all my brothers come here on Sunday, all together. But they came, and not a single word was said – not on that subject, and I talked on every other in a sort of hurried way – I was so frightened - - -

Since I began this letter, I have been to the Scotch Church in our neighbourhood – and it has all been in vain – I could not stay. We heard that a French minister, a M. Alphonse Monod of Montauban, was to preach at three o'clock, in French – and counting on a small congregation, and Arabel (through a knowledge of the localities) encouraging me with the prospect of sitting close to the door, and retiring back into the entrance-hall when the singing began, so as to escape that excitement – I agreed to make the trial, and she and I set out in a cab from the cab-stand hard by .. to which we walked. But the church was filling, obviously filling, as we arrived .. and grew fuller and fuller. We went in and came out again, and I sate down on the stairs – and the people came faster and faster, and I could not keep the tears out of my eyes to begin with. One gets nervous among all these people if a straw stirs. So Arabel after due observations on every side, decided that it would be too much of a congregation for me, and that I had better go home to Flush – (poor Flush having been left at home in a state of absolute despair). She therefore put me into a cab and sent me to Wimpole Street, and stayed behind herself to hear M. Monod – there's my adventure today. When I opened my door on my return, Flush threw himself upon me with a most ecstatical agony, and for full ten minutes did not cease jumping and kissing my hands – he thought he had lost me for certain, this time. Oh! and you warn me against the danger of losing *him*. Indeed I take care and take thought too – those 'organised banditti'[1] are not merely banditti de comedie – they are a dreadful reality. Did I not tell you once that they had announced to me that I should not have Flush back the *next time*, for less than ten guineas? But you will let him come with us to Italy, instead – will you not, dear, dearest? in good earnest, will you not? Because, if I leave him behind, he will be teazed for my sins in this house – or I could not

[1] Gangs of dog-stealers.

be sure of the reverse of it. And even if he escaped that fate, consider how he would break his heart about me. Dogs pine to death sometimes – and if ever a dog loved a man, or a woman, Flush loves me. But you say that he shall keep the house at Pisa – and you mean it, I hope and I think? – you are in earnest. May God bless you, – *so*, I say in my prayers, though I missed the Church. Tomorrow, comes my letter .. come my two letters! the happy Monday! The happier Tuesday, if on Tuesday comes the writer of the letters!

His very own BA

R.B. TO E.B.B.

Monday Morning
(Post-mark, August 24, 1846)

My own dearest, let me say the most urgent thing first. You hear these suspicions of your brothers. Will you consider if, during this next month, we do not risk too much in seeing each other as usual? We risk everything .. and what do we gain, in the face of that? I can learn no more about you, be taught no new belief in your absolute peerlessness – I have taken my place at your feet for ever: all my use of the visits is, therefore, the perfect delight of them .. and to hazard a whole life of such delight for the want of self-denial during a little month, – that would be horrible. I altogether sympathise with your brothers' impatience, or curiosity, or anxiety, or 'graveness' – and am prepared for their increasing and growing to heights difficult or impossible to be borne. But do you not think we may avoid compelling any premature crisis of this kind? I am guided by your feelings, as I seem to perceive them, in this matter; the harm to be apprehended is *through* the harm to *them* – to your brothers. If they determine on avowedly *knowing* what we intend, I do not see which to fear most; the tacit acquiescence in our scheme which may draw down a vengeance on them without doing us the least good, – or the open opposition which would bring about just so much additional misfortune. I *know*, now, your perfect adequacy to any pain and danger you will incur for our love's sake – I believe in you as you would have me believe: but give yourself to me, dearest dearest Ba, the entire creature you are, and not a lacerated thing only reaching

my arms to sink there. Perhaps this is all a sudden fancy, not justified by circumstances, arising from my ignorance of the characters
of those I talk about; that is for you to decide – your least word
reassures me, as always. But I fear much for *you*, to make up, perhaps, for there being nothing else in the world fit to fear: I exclude
direct visitations of God, which cannot be feared, after all –
dreadful dooms to which we should bow. But the 'fear' *proper*,
means with me an apprehension that, with all my best effort, it
may be unable to avert some misfortune .. the effort going on all
the time: and *this* is a real effort, dearest Ba, this letter: consider it
thus. I will (if possible) send it to town, so as to reach you earlier
and allow you to write *one line* in reply. You have heard all I can
say .. say you, *shall I come tomorrow?* If you think it advisable,
I will come and be most happy.

Another thing: you see your excitement about the church and
the crowd .. My own love, are you able, – with all that great,
wonderful heart of yours, – to bear the railway fatigues, and the
entering and departure from Paris and Orleans and the other
cities and towns? Would not the long sea-voyage be infinitely
better, if a little dearer? Or what can be *dear* if it prevents all that
risk, or rather certainty, of excitement and fatigue? You see, the
packet sails on the 30th September and the *15th October*. As three
of us go, they would probably make some reduction in price.
Ah, even here, I must smile .. will you affirm that ever *an approxi-
mation to a doubt* crossed your mind about Flush? - - -

I shall give this letter to be put in the post – I have *all* to say,
but the *very* essential is said – understand me, my best, only love,
and forgive my undue alarm, for the sake of the love that prompts
it. Write the one line .. do not let me do myself wrong by my
anxiety – if I *may* come, *let me*! Bless you, Ba.

E.B.B. TO R.B.

Monday Evening
(Post-mark, August 25, 1846)

- - - Dearest you are, and best in the world, .. it all comes
to *that*, .. and considerate for me always: and at once I agree

171

with you that for this interval it will be wise for us to set the visits, .. 'our days' .. far apart, .. nearly a week apart, perhaps, so as to escape the dismal evils we apprehend. I agree in all you say – in all. At the same time, the cloud has passed for the present – nothing has been said more, and not a word to me; and nobody appears out of humour with me. They will be displeased of course, in the first movement .. we must expect *that* .. they will be vexed at the occasion given to conversation and so on. But it will be a passing feeling, and their hearts and their knowledge of circumstances may be trusted to justify me thoroughly. I do not fear offending them – there is no room for fear. At this point of the business too, you place the alternative rightly – their approbation or their disapprobation is equally to be escaped from. Also, we may be certain that they would press the applying for permission – and I might perhaps, in the storm excited, among so many opinions and feelings, fail to myself and you, through weakness of the body. Not of the *Will*! And for my affections and my conscience, they turn to you – and untremblingly turn - - -

Your own

R.B. TO E.B.B.

Friday
(Post-mark, August 28, 1846)

- - - I altogether agree with you – it is best to keep away – we cannot be too cautious now at the 'end of things'. I am prepared for difficulties enough, without needing to cause them by any rashness or wilfulness of my own. I really expect, for example, that out of the various plans of these sympathising friends and relations some one will mature itself sufficiently to be directly proposed to you, for your acceptance or refusal contingent on your father's approbation: the shortness of the remaining travelling season serving to compel a speedy development. Or what if your father, who was the first to propose, or at least talk about, a voyage to Malta or elsewhere, when you took no interest in the matter comparatively, and who perhaps chiefly found fault with last year's scheme from its not originating with himself .. what if he should again determine on some such voyage now that you are apparently as obedient to his wishes as can be desired? Would it be strange, not to say improbable, if he tells you some fine morning that your passage is taken to Madeira, or Palermo? Because, all the attempts in the world cannot hide the truth from the mind, any more than all five fingers before the eyes keep out the sun at noon-day: you see a red through them all – and your father must see your improved health and strength, and divine the opinion of everybody round him as to the simple proper course for the complete restoration of them. Therefore be prepared, my own Ba! - - -

E.B.B. TO R.B.

Friday Evening
(Post-mark, August 29, 1846)

- - - Dearest, I have had all your thoughts by turns, or most of them .. and each one has withered away without coming to bear fruit. Papa seems to have no more idea of my living beyond these four walls, than of a journey to Lapland. I confess that I thought it possible he might propose the country for the summer, or even Italy for the winter, in a 'late remark' – but no, 'nothing' and there is not a possibility of either word, as I see things. My brothers 'wish that something could be arranged' – a wish which I put away quietly as often as they bring it to me. And for my uncle and aunt, they have been talking to me today – and she with her usual acuteness in such matters, observing my evasion, said, 'Ah, Ba, you have arranged your plans more than you would have us believe. But you are right not to tell us – indeed I would rather not hear. Only *don't be rash* – *that* is my only advice to you' - - -

While we were talking, Papa came into the room. My aunt said, 'How well she is looking' – 'Do you think so?' he said. 'Why, do not *you* think so? Do you pretend to say that you see no surprising difference in her?' – 'Oh, I don't know,' he went on to say. 'She is mumpish, I think.' Mumpish!

'She does not talk,' resumed he –

'Perhaps she is nervous' – my aunt apologised – I said not one word .. When birds have their eyes out, they are apt to be mumpish.

Mumpish! The expression proved a displeasure. Yet I am sure that I have shown as little sullenness as was possible. To be very talkative and vivacious under such circumstances as those of mine, would argue insensibility, and was certainly beyond my power.

I told her gently afterwards that she had been wrong in speaking of me at all – a wrong with a right intention, – as all her wrongness must be. She was very sorry to have done it, she said, and looked sorry.

Poor Papa! – Presently I shall be worse to him than 'mumpish' even. But *then*, he will try to forgive me, as I have forgiven him, long ago - - -

E.B.B. TO R.B.

Sunday
(Post-mark, August 31, 1846)

- - - And I said what you 'would not have believed of me'! Have you forgiven me, beloved – for saying what you would not have believed of me – understanding that I did not mean it very seriously, though I proved to be capable of saying it? Seriously, I don't want to make unnecessary delays. It is a horrible position, however I may cover it with your roses and the thoughts of you – and far worse to myself than to you, inasmuch that what is painful to you once a week, is to me so continually. To hear the voice of my father and meet his eye makes me shrink back – to talk to my brothers leaves my nerves all trembling .. and even to receive the sympathy of my sisters turns into sorrow and fear, lest they should suffer through their affection for me. How I can look and sleep as well as I do, is a miracle exactly like the rest – or would be, if the love were not the deepest and strongest thing of all, and did not hold and possess me overcomingly. I feel myself to be yours notwithstanding every other influence, and being yours, cannot but be happy by you. Ah – let people talk as they please of the happiness of early youth! Mrs. Jameson did, the other day, when she wished kindly to take her young niece with her to the Continent, that she might enjoy what in a few years she could not so much enjoy. There is a sort of blind joy common perhaps to such times – a blind joy which blunts itself with its own leaps and bounds; peculiar to a time of comparative ignorance and inexperience of evil: – but I for my part, with all the capacity for happiness which I had from the beginning, I look back and listen to my whole life, and feel sure of what I have already told you, .. that I am *happier now than I ever was before*.. infinitely happier now, through you .. infinitely happier; even now in this position I have just called 'horrible'. When I hear you say for instance, that you 'love me *perceptibly* more' .. why I cannot, cannot be more happy than when I hear you say *that* – going to Italy seems nothing! a vulgar walk to Primrose Hill after being caught up to the third Heaven! I think nothing of Italy now, though I shall enjoy it of course when the time comes. I think only that you love me, that you are the angel of my life, – and for the despair and desolation behind me, they serve to mark the hour of your coming, – and they *are* behind, as Italy is *before*. Never can you feel for me, Robert, as I feel for you .. it is not possible of course. I am yours in a way and degree which the tenderest of other women could not be at her will. Which you know. Why should I repeat it to you? Why, except that is a reason to prove that we cannot, as you say, 'ever be a common wife and husband'. But I don't think I was intending to give proofs of *that* – no, indeed - - -

Your very own BA

R.B. TO E.B.B.

Sunday Morning
(Post-mark, August 31, 1846)

I wonder what I shall write to you, Ba – I could suppress my feelings here, as I do on other points, and say nothing of the hatefulness of this state of things which is prolonged so uselessly. There is the point – show me one good reason, or show of reason, why we gain anything by deferring our departure till next week instead of tomorrow, and I will bear to perform yesterday's part for the amusement of Mr. Kenyon a dozen times over without complaint. But if the cold plunge *must* be taken, all this shivering delay on the bank is hurtful as well as fruitless. I *do* understand your anxieties, dearest – I take your fears and make them mine, while I put my own natural feeling of quite another kind away from us both, succeeding in *that* beyond all expectation. There is no amount of patience or suffering I would not undergo to relieve you from these apprehensions. But if, on the whole, you really determine to act as we propose in spite of them, – why, a new leaf is turned over in our journal, an old part of our adventure done with, and a new one entered upon, altogether distinct from the other. Having once decided to go to Italy with me, the next thing to decide is on the best means of going – or rather, there is just this connection between the two measures, that by the success or failure of the last, the first will have to be justified or condemned. You tell me you have decided to go – then, dearest, you will be prepared to go earlier than you promised yesterday – by the end of September at very latest. In proportion to the too probable excitement and painful circumstances of the departure, the greater amount of advantages should be secured for the departure itself. How can I take you away even in the beginning of October? We shall be a fortnight on the journey – with the year, as everybody sees and says, a full month in advance .. cold mornings and dark evenings already. Everybody would cry out on such folly when it was found that we let the favourable weather escape, in full assurance that the Autumn would come to us unattended by any one beneficial circumstance.

My own dearest, I am wholly your own, for ever, and under every determination of yours. If you find yourself unable, or unwilling to make this effort, tell me so and plainly and at once – I will not offer a word in objection, – I will continue our present life, if you please, so far as may be desirable, and wait till next autumn, and the next and the next, till providence end our waiting. It is clearly not for me to pretend to instruct you in your duties to God and yourself; .. enough, that I have long ago chosen to accept your decision. If, on the other hand, you make up your mind to leave England now, you will be prepared by the end of September.

I should think myself the most unworthy of human beings if I could employ any arguments with the remotest show of a tendency to *frighten* you into a compliance with any scheme of mine. Those methods are for people in another relation to you. But you love me, and, at lowest, shall I say, wish me well – and the fact is too obvious for me to commit any indelicacy in reminding you, that in any dreadful event to our journey of which I could accuse myself as the cause, – as of this undertaking to travel with you in the worst time of year when I could have taken the best, – in the case of your health being irretrievably shaken, for instance .. the happiest fate I should pray for would be to live and die in some corner where I might never hear a word of the English language, much less a comment in it on my own wretched imbecility, – to disappear and be forgotten.

So that must not be, for all our sakes. My family will give me to you that we may be both of us happy .. but for such an end – no! - - -

At all events, God knows I have said this in the deepest, truest love of you. I will say no more, praying you to forgive whatever you shall judge to need forgiveness here, – dearest Ba! I will also say, if that may help me, – and what otherwise I might not have said, – that I am not too well this morning, and write with an aching head - - -

Your own R.

E.B.B. TO R.B.

Monday Night
(Post-mark, September 1, 1846)

You are better, dearest, – and so I will confess to having felt a little inclined to reproach you gently for the earlier letter, except that you were not well when you wrote it. That you should endure painfully and impatiently a position unworthy of you, is the natural consequence of the unworthiness – and I do hold that you would be justified at this moment, on the barest motives of self-respect, in abandoning the whole ground and leaving me to Mr. Kenyon and others. What I might complain of, is another thing – what I might complain of is, that I have not given you reason to *doubt me* or my inclination to accede to any serious wish of yours relating to the step before us. On the contrary I told you in so many words in July, that, if you really wished to go in August rather than in September, I would make no difficulty – to which you answered, remember, that *October or November would do as well*. Now *is* it fair, ever dearest, that you should turn round on me so quickly, and call in question my willingness to keep my engagement for years, if ever? Can I help it, if the circumstances around us are painful to both of us? Did I not keep repeating, from the beginning, that they *must* be painful? Only you could not believe, you see, until you felt the pricks. And when all is done, and the doing shall be the occasion of new affronts, sarcasms, every form of injustice, will you be any happier then, than you are now that you only imagine the possibility of them? I tremble to answer that question – even to myself –! As for myself, though I cannot help feeling pain and fear, in encountering what is to be encountered, and though I sometimes fear, in addition, for *you*, lest you should overtask your serenity in bearing your own part in it, .. yet certainly I have never wavered for a moment from the decision on which all depends - - - So if September shall be possible, let it be September. I do not object nor hold back. To sail from the Thames has not the feasibility – and listen why! All the sailing or rather steaming from London begins *early*; and I told you how out of the question it was, for me to leave this house early. I could not, without involving my sisters. Arabel sleeps in my room, on the sofa, and is seldom out of the room before nine in the morning– and for me to draw her into a ruinous confidence, or to escape without a confidence at that hour, would be equally impossible. Now see if it is my fancy, my whim! And for the expenses, *they* are as nearly equal as a shilling and two sixpences can be – the expense of the sea-voyage from London to Havre, and of the land and sea voyage, through Southampton .. *or* Brighton. But of course what you say of Brighton, keeps us to Southampton, of those two routes. We can go to Southampton and meet the packet .. take the river-steamer to Rouen, and proceed as rapidly as your programme shows. You are not angry with me, dearest, dearest? I did not mean any harm.

May God bless you always. *I* am not angry either, understand, though I did think this morning that you were a little hard on me, just when I felt myself ready to give up the whole world for you at the holding up of a finger. And now say nothing of this. I kiss the end of the dear finger; and when *it* is ready, *I* am ready; I will not be reproached again. Being too much your own, very own

BA

Tell me that you keep better. And your mother?

E.B.B. TO R.B.

Tuesday
(Post-mark, September 2, 1846)

Here is a distress for me, dearest! I have lost my poor Flush – *lost* him! You were a prophet when you said 'Take care'.

This morning Arabel and I, and he with us, went in a cab to Vere Street where we had a little business, and he followed us as usual into a shop and out of it again, and was at my heels when I stepped up into the carriage. Having turned, I said 'Flush', and Arabel looked round for Flush – there was no Flush! He had been caught up in that moment, from *under* the wheels, do you understand? and the thief must have run with him and thrown him into a bag perhaps. It was such a shock to me – think of it! losing him in a moment, *so*! No wonder if I looked white, as Arabel said! So she began to comfort me by showing how certain it was that I should recover him for ten pounds at most, and we came home ever so drearily. Because *Flush* doesn't know that we can recover him, and he is in the extremest despair all this while, poor darling Flush, with his fretful fears, and pretty whims, and his fancy of being near me. All this night he will howl and lament, I know perfectly, – for I fear we shall not ransom him tonight. Henry went down for me directly to the captain of the banditti, who evidently knew all about it, said Henry, – and after a little form of consideration and enquiry, promised to let us hear something this evening, but has not come yet. In the morning perhaps he will come. Henry told him that I was resolved not to give much – but of course they will make me give what they choose – I am not going to leave Flush at their mercy, and they know that as well as I do. My poor Flush! - - -

If we go to Southampton, we go straight from the railroad to the packet, without entering any hotel – and if we do *so, no* greater expense is incurred than by the long water-passage from London. Also, we reach Havre alike in the morning, and have the day before us for Rouen, Paris and Orleans. Thereupon nothing is lost by losing the early hour for the departure. Then, if I accede to your idée fixe about the marriage! Only do not let us put a long time between that and the setting out, and do not you come here afterwards – let us go away as soon as possible afterwards at least. You are afraid for me of my suffering, from the autumnal cold when it is yet far off – while *I* (observe this!) while *I* am afraid for myself, of breaking down under quite a different set of causes, in nervous excitement and exhaustion. I belong to that pitiful order of weak women who cannot command their bodies with their souls at every moment, and who sink down in hysterical disorder when they ought to act and resist. Now I think and believe that I shall take strength from my attachment to you, and so go through to the end what is before us; but at the same time, knowing myself and fearing myself, I do desire to provoke the 'demon' as little as possible, and to be as quiet as the situation will permit. Still, where things *ought* to be done, they of course *must* be done. Only we should consider whether they really *ought* to be done – not for the sake of the inconvenience to me, but of the consequence to both of us.

Do I frighten you, ever dearest? Oh no – I shall go through it, if I keep a breath of soul in me to live with. I shall go through it, as certainly as that I love you. I speak only of the accessory circumstances, that they may be kept as smooth as is practicable - - -

More, tomorrow! But I cannot be more tomorrow, your very own –

R.B. TO E.B.B.

Wednesday Morning
(Post-mark, September 2, 1846)

Poor Flush – how sorry I am for you, my Ba! But you will recover him, I dare say .. not, perhaps directly; the delay seems to justify their charge at the end: poor fellow – was he no better than the rest of us, and did all that barking and fanciful valour spend itself on such enemies as Mr. Kenyon and myself, leaving only blandness and waggings of the tail for the man with the bag? I am sure you are grieved and frightened for our friend and follower, that was to be, at Pisa – will you not write a special note to tell me when you get him again?

For the rest – I will urge you no more by a single word – you shall arrange everything henceforward without a desire on my part, – an expressed one at least. Do not let our happiness be caught up from us, after poor Flush's fashion – there may be no redemption from *that* peril - - -

Bless you once again, my Ba.

E.B.B. TO R.B.

Wednesday Evening
(Post-mark, September 3, 1846)

'Our friend and follower, that *was* to be' – is *that*, then, your opinion of my poor darling Flush's destiny – Ah, – I should not have been so quiet if I had not known differently and better. I 'shall not recover him directly', you think? But, dearest, I am *sure* that I *shall*. I am learned in the ways of the Philistines – I knew from the beginning where to apply and how to persuade. The worst is poor Flush's fright and suffering. And then, it is inconvenient just now to pay the ransom for him. But we shall have time tomorrow if not tonight. Two hours ago the chief of the Confederacy came to call on Henry and to tell him that the 'Society had the dog', having done us the honour of tracking us into Bond Street and out of Bond Street into Vere Street where he was kidnapped. Now he is in Whitechapel (poor Flush). And the great man was going down there at half past seven to meet other great men in council and hear the decision as to the ransom exacted, and would return with their *ultimatum*. Oh, the villainy of it is excellent, and then the humiliation of having to pay for your own vexations and anxieties! *Will* they have the insolence, now, to make me pay ten pounds, as they said they would? But I must have Flush, you know – I can't run any risk, and bargain and haggle. There is a dreadful tradition in this neighbourhood, of a lady who did *so* having her dog's head sent to her in a parcel. So I say to Henry – 'Get Flush back, whatever you do' – for Henry is angry as he may well be, and as *I* should be if I was not too afraid .. and talks police-officers against thieves, and finds it very hard to attend to my instructions and be civil and respectful to their captain. There he found him, smoking a cigar in a room with pictures! They make some three or four thousand a year by their honourable employment. As to Flush's following anyone 'blandly', never think it. He was caught up and gagged .. depend upon that. If he could have bitten, he would have bitten – if he could have yelled, he would have yelled. Indeed on a former occasion the ingenuous thief observed, that he 'was a difficult dog to get, he was so distrustful'. They had to drag him with a string, put him into a cab, they said, before. Poor Flush! - - -

R.B. TO E.B.B.

Thursday
(Post-mark, September 3, 1846)

I am rejoiced that poor Flush is found again, dearest – altogether rejoiced.

And now that you probably have him by your side, I will tell you what I should have done in such a case, because it explains our two ways of seeing and meeting oppression lesser or greater. I would not have given five shillings on that fellow's application. I would have said, – and in entire earnestness '*You* are responsible for the proceedings of your gang, and *you* I mark – don't talk nonsense to me about cutting off heads or paws. Be as sure as that I stand here and tell you, I will spend my whole life in putting you down, the nuisance you declare yourself – and by every imaginable means I will be the death of you and as many of your accomplices as I can discover – but *you* I have discovered and will never lose sight of – now try my sincerity, by delaying to produce the dog by tomorrow. And for the ten pounds – see!' Whereupon I would give them to the first beggar in the street. You think I should receive Flush's head? Perhaps – *so* God allows matters to happen! on purpose, it may be, that I should vindicate him by the punishment I would exact.

Observe, Ba, this course ought not to be yours, because it *could* not be – it would not suit your other qualities. But all religion, right and justice, with me, seem implied in such a resistance to wickedness and refusal to multiply it a hundredfold – for from this prompt payment of ten pounds for a few minutes' act of the easiest villainy, there will be encouragement to – how many similar acts in the course of next month? And how will the poor owners fare who have not money enough for their dogs' redemption? I suppose the gentleman, properly disgusted with such obstinacy, will threaten roasting at a slow fire to test the sincerity of attachment! No – the world would grow too detestable a den of thieves and oppressors that way! And this is too great a piece of indignation to be expressed when one has the sick vile headache that oppresses me this morning. Dearest, I am not inclined to be even as tolerant as usual. Will you be tolerant, my Ba, and forgive me – till tomorrow at least – when, what with physic, what with impatience, I shall be better one way or another?

Ever your own R.

E.B.B. TO R.B.

Thursday Evening
(Post-mark, September 4, 1846)

Ever dearest, you are not well – that is the first thing! – And that is the thing I saw first, when, opening your letter, my eyes fell on the ending sentence of it, – which disenchanted me in a moment from the hope of the day - - - How everything goes against me this week! I cannot see you. I cannot comfort myself by knowing that you are well. And then poor Flush! You must let him pass as one of the evils, and you *will*, I know; for I have not got him back yet – no, indeed.

I should have done it. The archfiend, Taylor, the man whom you are going to spend your life in persecuting (the life that belongs to me, too!), came last night to say that they would accept six pounds, six guineas, with half a guinea for himself, considering the trouble of the mediation; and Papa desired Henry to refuse to pay, and not to tell me a word about it – all which I did not find out till this morning. Now it is less, as the money goes, than I had expected, and I was very vexed and angry, and wanted Henry to go at once and conclude the business – only he wouldn't, talked of Papa, and persuaded me that Taylor would come today with a lower charge. He has not come – I knew he would not come, – and if people won't do as I choose, I shall go down tomorrow morning myself and bring Flush back with me. All this time he is suffering and I am suffering. It may be very foolish – I do not say it is not - - - but I cannot endure to run cruel hazards about my poor Flush for the sake of a few guineas, or even for the sake of abstract principles of justice – I cannot. *You* say that *I* cannot, .. but that *you would*. You would! – Ah dearest – most pattern of citizens, but you *would not* – I know you better. Your theory is far too good not to fall to pieces in practice. A man may love justice intensely; but the love of an abstract principle is not the strongest love – now is it? Let us consider a little, putting poor Flush out of the question. (You would bear, you say, to receive his head in a parcel – it would satisfy you to cut off Taylor's in return.) Do you mean to say that if the banditti came down on us in Italy and carried me off to the mountains, and, sending to you one of my ears, to show you my probable fate if you did not let them have .. how much may I venture to say I am worth? .. five or six scudi, – (is *that* reasonable at all?) .. would your answer be 'Not so many crazie'; and would you wait, poised upon abstract principles, for the other ear, and the catastrophe, – as was done in Spain not long ago? Would you, dearest? Because it is as well to know beforehand, perhaps - - -

May God bless you. I love you always and am your own - - -

E.B.B. TO R.B.

Sunday
(Post-mark, September 7, 1846)

- - - I shall see you with my own eyes soon after you read what I write today; so I shall not write much. Only a few words to tell you that Flush is found, and lying on the sofa, with one paw and both ears hanging over the edge of it. Still my visit to Taylor was not the successful one. My hero was not at home.

I went you know, .. did I tell you? .. with Wilson in the cab. We got into obscure streets; and our cabman stopped at a public house to ask his way. Out came two or three men, .. 'Oh, you want to find Mr. Taylor, I dare say!' (mark that no name had been mentioned!) and instantly an unsolicited philanthropist ran before us to the house, and out again to tell me that the great man 'wasn't at home! but wouldn't I get out?' Wilson, in an aside of terror, entreated me not to think of such a thing – she believed devoutly in the robbing and murdering, and was not reassured by the gang of benevolent men and boys who 'lived but to oblige us' all round the cab. 'Then wouldn't I see Mrs. Taylor,' suggested the philanthropist, – and, notwithstanding my negatives, he had run back again and brought an immense feminine bandit, .. fat enough to have had an easy conscience all her life, .. who informed me that 'her husband might be in in a few minutes, or in so many hours – wouldn't I like to get out and wait' (Wilson pulling at my gown, the philanthropist echoing the invitation of the feminine Taylor.) – 'No, I thanked them all – it was not necessary that I should get out, but it *was*, that Mr. Taylor should keep his promise about the restoration of a dog which he had agreed to restore – and I begged her to induce him to go to Wimpole Street in the course of the day, and not defer it any longer.' To which, replied the lady, with the most gracious of smiles – 'Oh yes certainly' – and indeed she *did* believe Taylor had left home precisely on that business – poising her head to the right and left with the most easy grace – 'She was sure that Taylor would give his very best attention' ..

So, in the midst of the politeness, we drove away, and Wilson seemed to be of opinion that we had escaped with our lives barely. Plain enough it was, that the gang was strong there. The society .. the 'Fancy' .. had their roots in the ground. The faces of those men! –

I had not been at home long, when Mr. Taylor did actually come – desiring to have six guineas confided to his honour!! ..

and promising to bring back the dog. I sent down the money, and told them to trust the gentleman's honour, as there seemed no other way for it – and while the business was being concluded, in came Alfred,[1] and straightway called our 'honourable friend' (meeting him in the passage) a swindler and a liar and a thief. Which no gentleman could bear, of course. Therefore with reiterated oaths he swore, 'as he hoped to be saved, we should never see our dog again' – and rushed out of the house. Followed a great storm. I was very angry with Alfred, who had no business to risk Flush's life for the sake of the satisfaction of trying on names which fitted. Angry I was with Alfred, and terrified for Flush, – seeing at a glance the probability of his head being cut off as the proper vengeance! and downstairs I went with the resolution of going again myself to Mr. Taylor's in Manning Street, or Shoreditch [or] wherever it was, and saving the victim at any price. It was the evening, getting dusk – and everybody was crying out against me for being 'quite mad' and obstinate, and wilful – I was called as many names as Mr. Taylor. At last, Sette[2] said that *he* would do it, promised to be as civil as I could wish, and got me to be 'in a good humour and go up to my room again'. And he went instead of me, and took the money and fair words, and induced the 'man of honour' to forfeit his vengeance and go and fetch the dog. Flush arrived here at eight o'clock (at the very moment with your letter, dearest!), and the first thing he did was to dash up to this door, and then to drink his purple cup full of water, filled three times over. He was not so enthusiastic about seeing me, as I expected – he seemed bewildered and frightened – and whenever anyone said to him 'Poor Flush, did the naughty men take you away?' he put up his head and moaned and yelled. He has been very unhappy certainly. Dirty he is, and much thinner, and continually he is drinking. Six guineas, was his ransom – and now I have paid twenty for him to the dog-stealers.

Arabel says that I wanted *you* yesterday, she thought, to manage me a little. She thought I was suddenly seized with madness, to prepare to walk out of the house in that state of excitement and

[1] E.B.B.'s sixth brother.
[2] E.B.B.'s brother Septimus.

that hour of the evening. But now – *was* I to let them cut off Flush's head? –

There! I have told you the whole history of yesterday's adventures – and tomorrow I shall see you, my own dear, dear! – Only remember for my sake, *not* to come if you are not fit to come. Dearest, remember not to run any hazards! - - - So I expect you tomorrow *conditionally* .. if you are well enough! – and I thank you for the kind dear letter, welcome next to you, .. being ever and ever your own

BA

Wednesday Night
(Post-mark, September 10, 1846)

Dearest, you are a prophet, I suppose – there can be no denying it. This night, an edict has gone out, and George is tomorrow to be on his way to take a house for a month either at Dover, Reigate, Tunbridge, .. Papa did 'not mind which', he said, and 'you may settle it among you!!' but he 'must have this house empty for a month in order to its cleaning' – we are to go therefore and not delay.

Now! – what *can* be done? It is possible that the absence may be longer than for a month, indeed it is probable – for there is much to do in painting and repairing, here in Wimpole Street, more than a month's work they say. Decide, after thinking. I am embarrassed to the utmost degree, as to the best path to take. If we are taken away on Monday .. what then?

Of course I decline to give any opinion and express any preference, – as to places, I mean. It is not for my sake that we go: – if *I* had been considered at all, indeed, we should have been taken away earlier, .. and not certainly now, when the cold season is at hand. And so much the better it is for me, that I have not, obviously, been thought of.

Therefore decide! It seems quite too soon and too sudden for us to set out on our Italian adventure now – and perhaps even we could not compass –

Well – but you must think for both of us. It is past twelve and

I have just a moment to seal this and entrust it to Henrietta for the morning's post.

More than ever beloved, I am

Your own BA

I will do as you wish – understand.

Thursday Morning
(Post-mark, September 10, 1846)

What do you expect this letter will be about, my own dearest? Those which I write on the mornings after our days seem naturally to *answer* any strong point brought out in the previous discourse, and not then completely disposed of .. so they generally run in the vile fashion of a disputatious 'last word'; 'one word yet' – do not they? Ah, but you should remember that never does it feel so intolerable, – the barest fancy of a possibility of losing you – as when I have just seen you and heard you and, alas – left you for a time; on these occasions, it seems so horrible – that if the least recollection of a fear of yours, or a doubt .. anything which might be nursed, or let grow quietly into a serious obstacle to what we desire – if *that* rises up threateningly, – do you wonder that I begin by attacking *it*? There are always a hundred deepest reasons for gratitude and love which I could write about, but which my after life shall prove I never have forgotten .. still, that very after-life depends perhaps on the letter of the morning reasoning with you, teazing, contradicting. Dearest Ba, I do not tell you that I am justified in plaguing you thus, at any time .. only to get your pardon, if I can, on the grounds – the true grounds.

And this pardon, if you grant it, shall be for the past offences, not for any fresh one I mean to commit now. I will not add one word to those spoken yesterday about the extreme perilousness of delay. You *give* me yourself. Hitherto, from the very first till this moment, the giving hand has been advancing steadily – it is not for me to grasp it lest it stop within an inch or two of my forehead with its crown.

I am going to Town this morning, and will leave off now.

What a glorious dream; through nearly two years – without a single interval of blankness, – much less, bitter waking!

I may say *that*, I suppose, safely through whatever befalls!

Also I will ever say, God bless you, my dearest dearest, – my perfect angel you have been! While I am only your R.

My mother is deeply gratified at your present.

12 o'clock. On returning I find your note,

'I will do as you wish – understand' – then I understand you are in earnest. If you *do* go on Monday, our marriage will be impossible for another year – the misery! You see what we have gained by waiting. We must be *married directly* and go to Italy. I will go for a licence today and we can be married on Saturday. I will call tomorrow at 3 and arrange everything with you. We can leave from Dover &c., *after* that, – but otherwise, impossible! Inclose the ring, or a substitute – I have not a minute to spare for the post.

Ever your own R.

R.B. TO E.B.B.

4 p.m. Thursday
(Post-mark, September 10, 1846)

I broke open your sealed letter and added the postscript just now. The post being thus saved, I can say a few words more leisurely.

I will go tomorrow, I think, and not today for the licence – there are fixed hours I fancy at the office – and I might be too late. I will also make the arrangement with my friend for Saturday, if we should want him, – as we shall, in all probability – it would look suspiciously to be unaccompanied. We can arrange tomorrow.

Your words, first and last, have been that you 'would not fail me' – you will not.

And the marriage over, you can take advantage of circumstances and go early or late in the week, as may be practicable. There will be facilities in the general packing &c. – your own measures may be taken unobserved. Write short notes to the proper persons, – promising longer ones, if necessary.

See the *tone* I take, the way I write to *you* .. but it is all through you, in the little brief authority you give me, – and in the perfect belief of your truth and firmness – indeed, I do not consider this an extraordinary occasion for proving those qualities – this conduct of your father's is quite characteristic.

Otherwise, too, the departure with its bustle is not unfavourable. If you hesitated, it would be before a little hurried shopping and letter-writing! I expected it, and therefore spoke as you heard yesterday. *Now your* part must begin. It may as well begin and end, both, *now* as at any other time. I will bring you every information possible tomorrow.

It seems as if I should insult you if I spoke a word to confirm you, to beseech you, to relieve you from your promise, if you claim it.

God bless you, prays your own R.

E.B.B. TO R.B.[1]

Thursday
(Post-mark, September 11, 1846)

Dearest, I write one word, and have one will which is yours. At the same time, do not be precipitate – we shall not be taken away on Monday, no, nor for several days afterward. George has simply gone to look for houses – going to Reigate first.

Oh yes – come tomorrow. And then, you shall have the ring . . soon enough and safer.

Not a word of how you are! – *you* so good as to write me that letter beyond compact, yet not good enough, to say how you are! Dear, dearest . . take care, and keep yourself unhurt and calm. I shall not fail to you – I do not, I will not. I will act by your decision, and I wish you to decide. I was yours long ago, and though you give me back my promise at this eleventh hour, . . you generous, dear unkind! . . you know very well that you can do as well without it. So take it again for my sake and not your own.

I cannot write, I am so tired, having been long out. Will not

[1] The envelope of this letter is endorsed by R.B. 'Saturday, Septr. 12, 1846, ¼ 11–11 ¼ A.M. (91).' This is the record of his marriage with E.B.B. in St. Marylebone Parish Church. The number 91 indicates that it was the ninety-first of their meetings.

this dream break on a sudden? Now is the moment for the breaking of it, surely.

But come tomorrow, come. Almost everybody is to be away at Richmond, at a picnic, and we shall be free on all sides.

Ever and ever your BA.

R.B. TO E.B.B.

1 p.m. Saturday
(Post-mark, September 12, 1846)

You will only expect a few words – what will those be? When the heart is full it may run over, but the real fulness stays within.

You asked me yesterday 'if I should repent?' Yes – my own Ba, – I could wish all the past were to do over again, that in it I might somewhat more, – never so little more, conform in the outward homage to the inward feeling. What I have professed .. (for I have performed nothing) seems to fall short of what my first love required even – and when I think of *this* moment's love .. I could repent, as I say.

Words can never tell you, however, – form them, transform them anyway, – how perfectly dear you are to me – perfectly dear to my heart and soul.

I look back, and in every one point, every word and gesture, every letter, every *silence* – you have been entirely perfect to me – I would not change one word, one look.

My hope and aim are to preserve this love, not to fall from it – for which I trust to God who procured it for me, and doubtlessly can preserve it.

Enough now, my dearest, dearest, own Ba! You have given me the highest, completest proof of love that ever one human being gave another. I am all gratitude – and all pride (under the proper feeling which ascribes pride to the right source) all pride that my life has been so crowned by you.

God bless you prays your very own R.

I will write tomorrow of course. Take every care of *my life* which is in that dearest little hand; try and be composed, my beloved.

Remember to thank Wilson for me.

Saturday, Sept. 12–4½ p.m.
(Post-mark, September 12, 1846)

Ever dearest, I write a word that you may read it and know how all is safe so far, and that I am not slain downright with the day – oh, *such a day*! I went to Mr. Boyd's[1] directly, so as to send Wilson home the faster – and was able to lie quietly on the sofa in his sitting room downstairs, before he was ready to see me, being happily engaged with a medical councillor. Then I was made to talk and take Cyprus wine, – and, my sisters delaying to come, I had some bread and butter for dinner, to keep me from looking too pale in their eyes. At last they came, and with such grave faces! Missing me and Wilson, they had taken fright, – and Arabel had forgotten at first what I told her last night about the fly. I kept saying, 'What nonsense, .. what fancies you do have to be sure,' .. trembling in my heart with every look they cast at me. And so, to complete the bravery, I went on with them in the carriage to Hampstead .. as far as the heath, – and talked and looked – now you shall praise me for courage – or rather you shall love me for the love which was the root of it all. How necessity makes heroes – or heroines at least! For I did not sleep all last night, and when I first went out with Wilson to get to the fly-stand[2] in Marylebone Street I staggered so, that we both were afraid for the fear's sake, – but we called at a chemist's for sal volatile and were thus enabled to go on. I spoke to her last night, and she was very kind, very affectionate, and never shrank for a moment. I told her that always I should be grateful to her.

You – how are you? how is your head, ever dearest?

It seems all like a dream! When we drove past that church again, I and my sisters, there was a cloud before my eyes. Ask your mother to forgive me, Robert. If *I* had not been there, *she* would have been there, perhaps.

And for the rest, if either of us two is to suffer injury and sorrow for what happened there today – I pray that it may all fall upon

---

[1] Hugh Stuart Boyd (1781–1848), the blind Greek scholar; one of E.B.B.'s earliest friends.
[2] Cab-rank.

me! Nor should I suffer the most pain *that* way, as I know, and God knows.

Your own
B A

E.B.B. TO R.B.

Sunday
(Post-mark, September 14, 1846)

My own beloved, if ever you should have reason to complain of me in things voluntary and possible, all other women would have a right to tread me underfoot, I should be so vile and utterly unworthy. There is my answer to what you wrote yesterday of wishing to be better to me .. you! What could be better than lifting me from the ground and carrying me into life and the sunshine? I was yours rather by right than by gift (yet by gift also, my beloved!); for what you have saved and renewed is surely yours. All that I am , I owe you – if I enjoy anything now and henceforth, it is through you. You know this well. Even as *I*, from the beginning, knew that I had no power against you or, .. that, if I *had*, it was for your sake.

Dearest, in the emotion and confusion of yesterday morning, there was yet room in me for one thought which was not a feeling – for I thought that, of the many, many women who have stood where I stood, and to the same end, not one of them all perhaps, not one perhaps, since that building was a church, has had reasons strong as mine, for an absolute trust and devotion towards the man she married, – not one! And then I both thought and felt that it was only just, for them, .. those women who were less happy, .. to have that affectionate sympathy and support and presence of their nearest relations, parent or sister .. which failed to *me*, .. needing it less through being happier!

All my brothers have been here this morning, laughing and talking, and discussing this matter of the leaving town, – and in the room, at the same time, were two or three female friends of ours, from Herefordshire – and I did not *dare* to cry out against the noise, though my head seemed splitting in two (one half for each shoulder), I had such a morbid fear of exciting a suspicion - - -

193

And all in the midst, the bells began to ring. 'What bells are those?' asked one of the provincials. 'Marylebone Church bells' said Henrietta, standing behind my chair.

And now .. while I write, having escaped from the great din, and sit here quietly, – comes .. who do you think? – Mr. Kenyon.

He came with his spectacles, looking as if his eyes reached to their rim all the way round; and one of the first words was, '*When did you see Browning?*' And I think I shall make a pretension to presence of mind henceforward; for, though *certainly* I changed colour and he saw it, I yet answered with a tolerably quick evasion, .. 'He was here on Friday' – and leapt straight into another subject, and left him gazing fixedly on my face. Dearest, he saw something, but not all. So we talked, talked - - - On rising to go away, he mentioned your name a second time .. 'When do you see Browning again?' To which I answered that I did not know.

Is not *that* pleasant? The worst is that all these combinations of things make me feel so bewildered that I cannot make the necessary arrangements, as far as the letters go. But I must break from the dream-stupor which falls on me when left to myself a little, and set about what remains to be done.

A house near Watford is thought of now – but, as none is concluded on, the removal is not likely to take place in the middle of the week even, perhaps.

I sit in a dream, when left to myself. I cannot believe, or understand. Oh! but in all this difficult, embarrassing and painful situation, I look over the palms to Troy – I feel happy and exulting to belong to you, past every opposition, out of sight of every will of man – none can put us asunder, now, at least. I have a right now openly to love you, and to hear other people call it *a duty*, when I do, .. knowing that if it were a sin, it would be done equally. Ah – *I* shall not be first to leave off *that* – see if I shall! May God bless you, ever and ever dearest! Beseech for me the indulgence of your father and mother, and ask your sister to love me. I feel so as if I had slipped down over the wall into somebody's garden – I feel ashamed. To be grateful and affectionate to them all, while I live, is all that I can do, and it is too much a matter of course to need to be promised. Promise it however for your very own Ba whom you made so happy with the dear letter last night. But say in the next how you are – and how your mother is.

I did hate so, to have to take off the ring! You will have to take the trouble of putting it on again, some day.

R.B. TO E.B.B.

Monday Morning
(Post-mark, September 14, 1846)

You go on to comfort me, love – bless you for it. I collect from the letter that you are recovering from the pain and excitement; that is happy! I waited to hear from you, my own Ba, and will only write a word – then go out – I *think*.

Do you feel *so*, through the anxieties and trouble of this situation? You take my words from me – *I* 'exult' in the irrevocability of this precious bestowal of yourself on me – come what will my life has borne flower and fruit – it is a glorious, successful, felicitous life, I thank God and you - - -

My family all love you, dearest – you cannot conceive my father and mother's childlike faith in goodness – and my sister is very high-spirited, and quick of apprehension – so as to seize the true point of the case at once. I am in great hopes you will love them all, and understand them. Last night, I asked my father, who was absorbed over some old book, 'if he should not be glad to see his new daughter?' – to which he, starting, replied 'Indeed I *shall*!' with such a fervour as to make my mother laugh – not abated by his adding, 'And how I should be glad of her seeing Sis!' his other daughter, Sarianna, to wit – who was at church - - -

Goodbye, my own – very own Ba, from your R.

E.B.B. TO R.B.

Monday Evening
(Post-mark, September 15, 1846)

First, God is to be thanked for this great joy of hearing that you are better, my ever dearest – it is a joy that floats over all the other emotions. Dearest, I am so glad! I had feared that excitement's telling on you quite in another way. When the whole is done, and we have left England and the talkers thereof behind our backs, you will be well, steadfastly and satisfactorily, I do trust. In the meantime, there seems so much to do, that I am frightened to look towards the heaps of it. As to accoutrements, everything has been arranged as simply as possible that way – but still there are necessities – and the letters, the letters! I am paralysed when I think of having to write such words as .. 'Papa, I am married; I hope you will not be too displeased'. Ah, poor Papa! You are too sanguine if you expect any such calm from him as an assumption of indifference would imply. To the utmost, he will be angry, – he will cast me off as far from him. Well – there is no comfort in such thoughts. How I felt tonight when I saw him at seven o'clock for the first time since Friday, and the event of Saturday! He spoke kindly too, and asked me how I was. Once I heard of his saying of me that I was 'the purest woman he ever knew', – which made me smile at the moment, or laugh I believe, outright, because I understood perfectly what he meant by *that* – viz – that I had not troubled him with the iniquity of love affairs, or any impropriety of seeming to think about being married. But now the whole sex will go down with me to the perdition of faith in any of us. See the effect of my wickedness! – 'Those women!'

But we will submit, dearest. I will put myself under his feet, to be forgiven a little, .. enough to be taken up again into his arms. I love him – he is my father – he has good and high qualities after all: he is my father *above* all. And *you*, because you are so generous and tender to me, will let me, you say, and help me to try to win back the alienated affection – for which, I thank you and bless you, – I did not thank you enough this morning. Surely I may say to him, too, .. 'With the exception of this act, I have submitted to the least of your wishes all my life long. Set the life against the act, and forgive me, for the sake of the daughter you once loved.' Surely I may say *that*, and then remind him of the long suffering I have suffered, – and entreat him to pardon the happiness which has come at last.

And *he* will wish in return, that I had died years ago! For the storm will come and endure. And at last, perhaps, he will forgive us – it is my hope[1] - - -

Your very own BA

R.B. TO E.B.B.

Wednesday
(Post-mark, September 16, 1846)

- - - It is absolutely for yourself to decide on the day and the mode – if for no other reason, because I am quite ready, and shall have no kind of difficulty; while you have every kind. Make the arrangements that promise most comfort to yourself. Observe the packets and alter the route if necessary. There is one from Brighton to Dieppe every day, for instance .. but then the getting to Rouen! The Havre-boat leaves Southampton, *Wednesdays* and *Saturdays* – and Portsmouth, *Mondays* and *Thursdays*. The boat from London, Thursdays and Saturdays at 9 A.M. - - -

The business of the letters will grow less difficult when once begun – see if it will not! and in these four or five days whole epics might be written, much more letters. Have you arranged all with Wilson? Take, of course, the simplest possible wardrobe &c. – so as to reduce our luggage to the very narrowest compass. The expense – (beside the common sense of a little luggage) – is considerable – every ounce being paid for. Let us treat our journey as a mere journey – we can return for what else we want, or get it sent, or procure it abroad. I shall take just a portmanteau and carpet bag. I think the fewer books we take the better; they take up room – and the wise way always seemed to me to read in rooms at home, and open one's eyes and *see* abroad - - -

Be sure, dearest, I will do my utmost to conciliate your father: sometimes I could not but speak impatiently to you of him .. that was while you were in his direct power – now there is no *need* of a word in any case .. I shall be silent if the *worst imaginable* happens; and if anything better, most grateful. You do not need to remind me he is your father .. I shall be proud to say *mine* too. Then, he said *that* of you – for which I love him – love the

---

[1] The hope was not fulfilled. Mr. Barrett refused to see her again, and returned all her letters unopened.

full prompt justice of that ascription of 'perfect purity' – it is another voice responding to mine, confirming mine - - -

Kiss me as I kiss you, dearest Ba. I can bring you no flowers but I pluck this bud and send it with all affectionate devotion.

Your own

R.B.

E.B.B. TO R.B.

(Post-mark, September 17, 1846)

Dearest, the general depature from this house takes place on Monday – and the house at Little Bookham is six miles from the nearest railroad, and a mile and a half from Leatherhead where a coach runs. Now you are to judge. Certainly if I go with you on Saturday I shall not have half the letters written – you, who talk so largely of epic poems, have not the least imagination of my state of mind and spirits. I began to write a letter to Papa this morning, and could do nothing but cry, and looked so pale thereupon, that everybody wondered what could be the matter. Oh – quite well I am now, and I only speak of myself in that way to show you how the inspiration is by no means sufficient for epic poems. Still, I may certainly write the necessary letters, .. and do the others on the road .. could I, do you think? I would rather have waited – indeed rather – only it may be difficult to leave Bookham .. yet *possible* – so tell me what you would have me do.

Wilson and I have a light box and a carpet bag between us – and I will be docile about the books, dearest. Do you take a desk? Had I better not, I wonder?

Then for box and carpet bag .. Remember that we cannot take them out of the house with us. We must send them the evening before – Friday evening, if we went on Saturday .. and where? Have you a friend anywhere, to whose house they might be sent, or could they go direct to the railroad office – and what office? In that case they should have your name on them, should they not?

Now think for me, ever dearest – and tell me what you do not tell me .. that you continue better. Ah no – you are ill again – or you would not wait to be told to tell me. And the dear, dear little

bud! – I shall keep it to the end of my life, if you love me so long
.. or *not,* sir! I thank you, dearest - - -

No more tonight from your very own

BA

R.B. TO E.B.B.

(Post-mark, September 17, 1846)

My only sweetest, I will write just a word to catch the earlier
post, – time pressing. Bless you for all you suffer .. I *know* it
though it would be very needless to call your attention to the
difficulties. I know much, if not all, and can only love and admire
you, – not help, alas!

Surely these difficulties will multiply, if you go to Bookham –
the way will be to leave at once. The letters may easily be written
during the journey .. at Orléans, for example. But now, – you
propose *Saturday* .. nothing leaves Southampton according to
today's advertisement, till *Tuesday* .. the days seemed changed to
Tuesdays and *Fridays.* Tomorrow at $8\frac{1}{4}$ p.m. and Friday the 22,
$10\frac{1}{4}$. Provoking! I will go to town directly to the railway office
and enquire particularly – getting the time-table also. Under these
circumstances, we have only the choice of Dieppe (as needing the
shortest diligence-journey) – or the Sunday morning Havre-
packet, at 9 a.m. – which you do not consider practicable: though
it would, I think, take us the quickliest out of all the trouble. I
will let you know all particulars in a note tonight .. it shall reach
you tonight.

If we went from London only, the luggage could be sent here
or in any case, perhaps .. as one fly will carry them with me and
mine, and save possibility of delay - - -

Take no desk .. I will take a large one – take nothing you can
leave – but secure letters &c. I will take out a passport. Did you
not tell me roughly at how much you estimated our expenses for
the journey? Because I will take about *that* much, and get Roths-
child's letter of credit for Leghorn. One should avoid carrying
money about with one.

All this in such haste! Bless you, my dearest dearest Ba.

Your R.

R.B. TO E.B.B.

5 o'clock
(Post-mark, September 17, 1846)

My own Ba, I believe, or am sure the mistake has been mine – in the flurry I noted down the departures from *Havre*–instead of *Southampton*. You must either be at the Vauxhall Station by *four* o'clock – so as to arrive in 3 hours and a half at Southampton and leave by $8\frac{1}{4}$ p.m. – or must go by the Sunday Boat, – or *wait* till Tuesday. Dieppe is impossible, being too early. You must decide – and let me know directly. Tomorrow *is* too early – yet one .. that is, *I* – could manage.

Ever your own, in all haste

R.B.

R.B. TO E.B.B.

$7\frac{1}{2}$ – Thursday
(Post-mark, September 18, 1846)

My own Ba – forgive my mistaking! I had not enough confidence in my own correctness. The advertisement of the Tuesday and Friday Boats is of the South of England Steam Company. The Wednesday and Saturday is that of the *South Western*. There must be then *two* companies, because on the Southampton Railway Bill it is expressly stated that there are departures for Havre on all four days. Perhaps you have seen my blunder. In that case you can leave by $1–/2\frac{1}{2}$ as you may appoint –

Your R.

E.B.B. TO R.B.

(Post-mark, September 18, 1846)

Dearest take this word, as if it were many. I am so tired – and then it shall be the right word.

Sunday and Friday are impossible. On Saturday I will go to you, if you like – with half done, .. nothing done .. scarcely. Will you come for me to Hodgson's?[1] or shall I meet you at the

---

[1] A neighbouring bookshop.

station? At what o'clock should I set out, to be there at the hour you mention?

Also, for the boxes .. we cannot carry them out of the house, you know, Wilson and I. They must be sent on Friday evening to the Vauxhall station, 'to be taken care of'. Will the people keep them carefully? Ought someone to be spoken to beforehand? If we sent them to New Cross, they would not reach you in time.

Hold me my beloved – with your love. It is very hard – But Saturday seems the only day for us. Tell me if you think so indeed.

Your very own BA

E.B.B. TO R.B.

(Post-mark, September 18, 1846)

Dearest, here is the paper of addresses. I cannot remember, I am so confused, half of them.

Surely you say wrong in the hour for tomorrow. Also there is the express train. Would it not be better?

Your BA

R.B. TO E.B.B.

11½ Friday
(Post-mark, September 18, 1846)

My own best Ba. How thankful I am you have seen my blunder, – I took the other company's days for the South Western's changed. What I shall write now is with the tables before me (of the Railway) and a transcript from *today's* advertisement in *The Times*.

The packet will leave tomorrow evening, from the Royal Pier, Southampton at *nine*. We leave Nine Elms, Vauxhall, at *five* – to arrive at *eight*. Doors close *five* minutes before. I will be at Hodgson's *from* half-past three to *four precisely* when I shall hope you can be ready. I shall go to Vauxhall, apprise them that luggage is coming (yours) and send *mine* there – so that we both shall be unencumbered and we can take a cab or coach from H's.

Never mind your scanty preparations .. we can get everything at Leghorn, – and the new boats carry parcels to Leghorn on the 15th of every month, remember – so can bring what you may wish to send for.

I enclose a letter to go with yours. The cards as you choose – they are here – we can write about them from Paris or elsewhere. The advertisement, as you advise. All shall be cared for.

God bless and strengthen you, my ever dearest dearest – I will not trust myself to speak of my feelings for you – worship well belongs to such fortitude. One struggle more – if all the kindness on your part brought a strangely insufficient return, is it not possible that this step may produce all you can hope? Write to me one word more. Depend on me. I go to Town about business.

Your own, own R.

E.B.B. TO R.B.

Friday Night
(Post-mark, September 19, 1846)

At from half-past three to four, then – four will not, I suppose, be too late. I will not write more – I *cannot*. By tomorrow at this time, I shall have *you* only, to love me – my beloved!

You *only*! As if one said *God only*. And we shall have *Him* beside, I pray of Him.

I shall send to your address at New Cross your Hanmer's[1] poems – and the two dear books you gave me, which I do not like to leave here and am afraid of hurting by taking them with me. Will you ask *our* Sister to put the parcel into a drawer, so as to keep it for us?

Your letters to me I take with me, let the 'ounces' cry out aloud, ever so. I *tried* to leave them, and I could not. That is, they would not be left: it was not my fault – I will not be scolded. Is this my last letter to you, ever dearest? Oh – if I loved you less .. a little, little less.

Why I should tell you that our marriage was invalid, or ought to be; and that you should by no means come for me tomorrow.

[1] Sir John Hanmer (1809–1881), poet and politician.

It is dreadful .. dreadful .. to have to give pain here by a voluntary act – for the first time in my life.

Remind your mother and father of me affectionately and gratefully – and your Sister too! Would she think it too bold of me to say *our* Sister, if she had heard it on the last page?

Do you pray for me tonight, Robert? Pray for me, and love me, that I may have courage, feeling both –

Your own
BA

The boxes are *safely sent*. Wilson has been perfect to me. And I .. calling her 'timid', and afraid of her timidity! I begin to think that none are so bold as the timid, when they are fairly roused.

Sonnets from the Portuguese
by Elizabeth Barrett Browning

I

I thought once how Theocritus had sung
Of the sweet years, the dear and wished-for years,
Who each one in a gracious hand appears
To bear a gift for mortals, old or young:
And, as I mused it in his antique tongue,
I saw, in gradual vision through my tears,
The sweet, sad years, the melancholy years,
Those of my own life, who by turns had flung
A shadow across me. Straightway I was 'ware,
So weeping, how a mystic Shape did move
Behind me, and drew me backward by the hair;
And a voice said in mastery, while I strove, –
'Guess now who holds thee?' – 'Death,' I said.
                              But, there,
The silver answer rang, – 'Not Death, but Love'.

II

But only three in all God's universe
Have heard this word thou hast said, – Himself, beside
Thee speaking, and me listening! and replied
One of us ... *that* was God, ... and laid the curse
So darkly on my eyelids, as to amerce
My sight from seeing thee, – that if I had died,
The deathweights, placed there, would have signified
Less absolute exclusion. 'Nay' is worse
From God than from all others, O my friend!
Men could not part us with their worldly jars,
Nor the seas change us, nor the tempests bend;
Our hands would touch for all the mountain-bars:
And, heaven being rolled between us at the end,
We should but vow the faster for the stars.

III

Unlike are we, unlike, O princely Heart!
Unlike our uses and our destinies.
Our ministering two angels look surprise
On one another, as they strike athwart
Their wings in passing. Thou, bethink thee, art
A guest for queens to social pageantries,
With gages from a hundred brighter eyes
Than tears even can make mine, to play thy part
Of chief musician. What has *thou* to do
With looking from the lattice-lights at me,
A poor, tired, wandering singer, singing through
The dark, and leaning up a cypress tree?
The chrism is on thine head, – on mine, the dew, –
And Death must dig the level where these agree.

IV

Thou hast thy calling to some palace-floor,
Most gracious singer of high poems! where
The dancers will break footing, from the care
Of watching up thy pregnant lips for more.
And dost thou lift this house's latch too poor
For hand of thine? and canst thou think and bear
To let thy music drop here unaware
In folds of golden fulness at my door?
Look up and see the casement broken in,
The bats and owlets builders in the roof!
My cricket chirps against thy mandolin.
Hush, call no echo up in further proof
Of desolation! there's a voice within
That weeps . . . as thou must sing . . . alone, aloof.

V

I lift my heavy heart up solemnly,
As once Electra her sepulchral urn,
And, looking in thine eyes, I overturn
The ashes at thy feet. Behold and see
What a great heap of grief lay hid in me,
And how the red wild sparkles dimly burn
Through the ashen greyness. If thy foot in scorn
Could tread them out to darkness utterly,
It might be well perhaps. But if instead
Thou wait beside me for the wind to blow
The grey dust up, ... those laurels on thine head,
O my Belovèd, will not shield thee so,
That none of all the fires shall scorch and shred
The hair beneath. Stand farther off then! go.

VI

Go from me. Yet I feel that I shall stand
Henceforward in thy shadow. Nevermore
Alone upon the threshold of my door
Of individual life, I shall command
The uses of my soul, nor lift my hand
Serenely in the sunshine as before,
Without the sense of that which I forbore —
Thy touch upon the palm. The widest land
Doom takes to part us, leaves thy heart in mine
With pulses that beat double. What I do
And what I dream include thee, as the wine
Must taste of its own grapes. And when I sue
God for myself, He hears that name of thine,
And sees within my eyes the tears of two.

VII

The face of all the world is changed, I think,
Since first I heard the footsteps of thy soul
Move still, oh, still, beside me, as they stole
Betwixt me and the dreadful outer brink
Of obvious death, where I, who thought to sink,
Was caught up into love, and taught the whole
Of life in a new rhythm. The cup of dole
God gave for baptism, I am fain to drink,
And praise its sweetness, Sweet, with thee anear.
The names of country, heaven, are changed away
For where thou art or shalt be, there or here;
And this ... this lute and song ... loved yesterday,
(The singing angels know) are only dear
Because thy name moves right in what they say.

VIII

What can I give thee back, O liberal
And princely giver, who hast brought the gold
And purple of thine heart, unstained, untold,
And laid them on the outside of the wall
For such as I to take or leave withal,
In unexpected largesse? am I cold,
Ungrateful, that for these most manifold
High gifts, I render nothing back at all?
Not so; not cold, — but very poor instead.
Ask God who knows. For frequent tears have run
The colours from my life, and left so dead
And pale a stuff, it were not fitly done
To give the same as pillow to thy head.
Go farther! let it serve to trample on.

IX

Can it be right to give what I can give?
To let thee sit beneath the fall of tears
As salt as mine, and hear the sighing years
Re-sighing on my lips renunciative
Through those infrequent smiles which fail to live
For all thy adjurations? O my fears,
That this can scarce be right! We are not peers,
So to be lovers; and I own, and grieve,
That givers of such gifts as mine are, must
Be counted with the ungenerous. Out, alas!
I will not soil thy purple with my dust,
Nor breathe my poison on thy Venice-glass,
Nor give thee any love – which were unjust.
Beloved, I only love thee! let it pass.

X

Yet, love, mere love, is beautiful indeed
And worthy of acceptation. Fire is bright,
Let temple burn, or flax; an equal light
Leaps in the flame from cedar-plank or weed:
And love is fire. And when I say at need
I love thee ... mark! ... *I love thee* – in thy sight
I stand transfigured, glorified aright,
With conscience of the new rays that proceed
Out of my face toward thine. There's nothing low
In love, when love the lowest: meanest creatures
Who love God, God accepts while loving so.
And what I *feel*, across the inferior features
Of what I *am*, doth flash itself, and show
How that great work of Love enhances Nature's.

XI

And therefore if to love can be desert,
I am not all unworthy. Cheeks as pale
As these you see, and trembling knees that fail
To bear the burden of a heavy heart, –
This weary minstrel-life that once was girt
To climb Aornus, and can scarce avail
To pipe now 'gainst the valley nightingale
A melancholy music – why advert
To these things? O Belovèd, it is plain
I am not of thy worth nor for thy place!
And yet, because I love thee, I obtain
From that same love this vindicating grace,
To live on still in love, and yet in vain, –
To bless thee, yet renounce thee to thy face.

XII

Indeed this very love which is my boast,
And which, when rising up from breast to brow,
Doth crown me with a ruby large enow
To draw men's eyes and prove the inner cost, –
This love even, all my worth, to the uttermost,
I should not love withal, unless that thou
Hadst set me an example, shown me how,
When first thine earnest eyes with mine were crossed,
And love called love. And thus, I cannot speak
Of love even, as a good thing of my own:
Thy soul hath snatched up mine all faint and weak,
And placed it by thee on a golden throne, –
And that I love (O soul, we must be meek!)
Is by thee only, whom I love alone.

XIII

And wilt thou have me fashion into speech
The love I bear thee, finding words enough,
And hold the torch out, while the winds are rough,
Between our faces, to cast light on each? –
I drop it at thy feet. I cannot teach
My hand to hold my spirit so far off
From myself – me – that I should bring thee proof
In words, of love hid in me out of reach.
Nay, let the silence of my womanhood
Commend my woman-love to thy belief, –
Seeing that I stand unwon, however wooed,
And rend the garment of my life, in brief,
By a most dauntless, voiceless fortitude,
Lest one touch of this heart convey its grief.

XIV

If thou must love me, let it be for nought
Except for love's sake only. Do not say
'I love her for her smile – her look – her way
Of speaking gently, – for a trick of thought
That falls in well with mine, and certes brought
A sense of pleasant ease on such a day' –
For these things in themselves, Belovèd, may
Be changed, or change for thee, – and love, so wrought,
May be unwrought so. Neither love me for
Thine own dear pity's wiping my cheeks dry, –
A creature might forget to weep, who bore
Thy comfort long, and lose thy love thereby!
But love me for love's sake, that evermore
Thou mayst love on, through love's eternity.

XV

Accuse me not, beseech thee, that I wear
Too calm and sad a face in front of thine;
For we two look two ways, and cannot shine
With the same sunlight on our brow and hair.
On me thou lookest with no doubting care,
As on a bee shut in a crystalline;
Since sorrow hath shut me safe in love's divine,
And to spread wing and fly in the outer air
Were most impossible failure, if I strove
To fail so. But I look on thee – on thee –
Beholding, besides love, the end of love,
Hearing oblivion beyond memory;
As one who sits and gazes from above,
Over the rivers to the bitter sea.

XVI

And yet, because thou overcomest so,
Because thou art more noble and like a king,
Thou canst prevail against my fears and fling
Thy purple round me, till my heart shall grow
Too close against thine heart henceforth to know
How it shook when alone. Why, conquering
May prove as lordly and complete a thing
In lifting upward, as in crushing low!
And as a vanquished soldier yields his sword
To one who lifts him from the bloody earth,
Even so, Belovèd, I at last record,
Here ends my strife. If *thou* invite me forth,
I rise above abasement at the word.
Make thy love larger to enlarge my worth.

XVII

My poet, thou canst touch on all the notes
God set between His After and Before,
And strike up and strike off the general roar
Of the rushing worlds a melody that floats
In a serene air purely. Antidotes
Of medicated music, answering for
Mankind's forlornest uses, thou canst pour
From thence into their ears. God's will devotes
Thine to such ends, and mine to wait on thine.
How, Dearest, wilt thou have me for most use?
A hope, to sing by gladly? or a fine
Sad memory, with thy songs to interfuse?
A shade, in which to sing – of palm or pine?
A grave, on which to rest from singing? Choose.

XVIII

I never gave a lock of hair away
To a man, Dearest, except this to thee,
Which now upon my fingers thoughtfully,
I ring out to the full brown length and say
'Take it'. My day of youth went yesterday;
My hair no longer bounds to my foot's glee,
Nor plant I it from rose or myrtle-tree,
As girls do, any more: it only may
Now shade on two pale cheeks the mark of tears,
Taught drooping from the head that hangs aside
Through sorrow's trick. I thought the funeral-shears
Would take this first, but Love is justified –
Take it thou, – finding pure, from all those years,
The kiss my mother left here when she died.

XIX

The soul's Rialto hath its merchandise;
I barter curl for curl upon that mart,
And from my poet's forehead to my heart
Receive this lock which outweighs argosies, –
As purply black, as erst to Pindar's eyes
The dim purpureal tresses gloomed athwart
The nine white Muse-brows. For this counterpart, . . .
The bay-crown's shade, Belovèd, I surmise,
Still lingers on thy curl, it is so black!
Thus, with a fillet of smooth-kissing breath,
I tie the shadows safe from gliding back,
And lay the gift where nothing hindereth;
Here on my heart, as on thy brow, to lack
No natural heat till mine grows cold in death.

XX

Belovèd, my Belovèd, when I think
That thou wast in the world a year ago,
What time I sat alone here in the snow
And saw no footprint, heard the silence sink
No moment at thy voice, but, link by link,
Went counting all my chains as if that so
They never could fall off at any blow
Struck by thy possible hand, – why, thus I drink
Of life's great cup of wonder! Wonderful,
Never to feel thee thrill the day or night
With personal act or speech, – nor ever cull
Some prescience of thee with the blossoms white
Thou sawest growing! Atheists are as dull,
Who cannot guess God's presence out of sight.

XXI

Say over again, and yet once over again,
That thou dost love me. Though the word repeated
Should seem 'a cuckoo-song', as thou dost treat it,
Remember, never to the hill or plain,
Valley and wood, without her cuckoo-strain
Comes the fresh Spring in all her green completed.
Belovèd, I, amid the darkness greeted
By a doubtful spirit-voice, in that doubt's pain
Cry, 'Speak once more — thou lovest!' Who can fear
Too many stars, though each in heaven shall roll,
Too many flowers, though each shall crown the year?
Say thou dost love me, love me, love me — toll
The silver iterance! — only minding, Dear,
To love me also in silence with thy soul.

XXII

When our two souls stand up erect and strong,
Face to face, silent, drawing nigh and nigher,
Until the lengthening wings break into fire
At either curvèd point, — what bitter wrong
Can the earth do to us, that we should not long
Be here contented? Think. In mounting higher,
The angels would press on us and aspire
To drop some golden orb of perfect song
Into our deep, dear silence. Let us stay
Rather on earth, Belovèd, — where the unfit
Contrarious moods of men recoil away
And isolate pure spirits, and permit
A place to stand and love in for a day,
With darkness and the death-hour rounding it.

XXIII

Is it indeed so? If I lay here dead,
Wouldst thou miss any life in losing mine?
And would the sun for thee more coldly shine
Because of grave-damps falling round my head?
I marvelled, my Belovèd, when I read
Thy thought so in the letter. I am thine –
But . . . *so* much to thee? Can I pour thy wine
While my hands tremble? Then my soul, instead
Of dreams of death, resumes life's lower range.
Then, love me, Love! look on me – breathe on me!
As brighter ladies do not count it strange,
For love, to give up acres and degree,
I yield the grave for thy sake, and exchange
My near sweet view of Heaven, for earth with thee!

XXIV

Let the world's sharpness, like a clasping knife,
Shut in upon itself and do no harm
In this close hand of Love, now soft and warm,
And let us hear no sound of human strife
After the click of the shutting. Life to life –
I lean upon thee, Dear, without alarm,
And feel as safe as guarded by a charm
Against the stab of worldlings, who if rife
Are weak to injure. Very whitely still
The lilies of our lives may reassure
Their blossoms from their roots, accessible
Alone to heavenly dews that drop not fewer,
Growing straight, out of man's reach, on the hill.
God only, who made us rich, can make us poor.

XXV

A heavy heart, Belovèd, have I borne
From year to year until I saw thy face,
And sorrow after sorrow took the place
Of all those natural joys as lightly worn
As the stringed pearls, each lifted in its turn
By a beating heart at dance-time. Hopes apace
Were changed to long despairs, till God's own grace
Could scarcely lift above the world forlorn
My heavy heart. Then *thou* didst bid me bring
And let it drop adown thy calmly great
Deep being! Fast it sinketh, as a thing
Which its own nature doth precipitate,
While thine doth close above it, mediating
Betwixt the stars and the unaccomplished fate.

XXVI

I lived with visions for my company
Instead of men and women, years ago,
And found them gentle mates, nor thought to know
A sweeter music than they played to me.
But soon their trailing purple was not free
Of this world's dust, their lutes did silent grow,
And I myself grew faint and blind below
Their vanishing eyes. Then THOU didst come – to be,
Belovèd, what they seemed. Their shining fronts,
Their songs, their splendours (better, yet the same,
As river-water hallowed into fonts),
Met in thee, and from out thee overcame
My soul with satisfaction of all wants:
Because God's gifts put man's best dreams to shame.

XXVII

My own Belovèd, who hast lifted me
From this drear flat of earth where I was thrown,
And, in betwixt the languid ringlets, blown
A life-breath, till the forehead hopefully
Shines out again, as all the angels see,
Before thy saving kiss! My own, my own,
Who camest to me when the world was gone,
And I who looked for only God, found *thee*!
I find thee; I am safe, and strong, and glad.
As one who stands in dewless asphodel,
Looks backward on the tedious time he had
In the upper life, – so I, with bosom-swell,
Make witness, here, between the good and bad,
That Love, as strong as Death, retrieves as well.

XXVIII

My letters! all dead paper, mute and white!
And yet they seem alive and quivering
Against my tremulous hands which loose the string
And let them drop down on my knee tonight.
This said, – he wished to have me in his sight
Once, as a friend: this fixed a day in spring
To come and touch my hand ... a simple thing,
Yet I wept for it! – this, ... the paper's light ...
Said, *Dear, I love thee*; and I sank and quailed
As if God's future thundered on my past.
This said, *I am thine* – and so its ink has paled
With lying at my heart that beat too fast.
And this ... O love, thy words have ill availed
If, what this said, I dared repeat at last!

XXIX

I think of thee! – my thoughts do twine and bud
About thee, as wild vines, about a tree,
Put out broad leaves, and soon there's nought to see
Except the straggling green which hides the wood.
Yet, O my palm-tree, be it understood
I will not have my thoughts instead of thee
Who art dearer, better! Rather, instantly
Renew thy presence; as a strong tree should,
Rustle thy boughs and set thy trunk all bare,
And let these bands of greenery which insphere thee
Drop heavily down, – burst, shattered, everywhere!
Because, in this deep joy to see and hear thee
And breathe within thy shadow a new air,
I do not think of thee – I am too near thee.

XXX

I see thine image through my tears tonight,
And yet today I saw thee smiling. How
Refer the cause? – Beloved, is it thou
Or I, who makes me sad? The acolyte
Amid the chanted joy and thankful rite
May so fall flat, with pale insensate brow,
On the altar-stair. I hear thy voice and vow,
Perplexed, uncertain, since thou art out of sight,
As he, in his swooning ears, the choir's Amen.
Belovèd, dost thou love? or did I see all
The glory as I dreamed, and fainted when
Too vehement light dilated my ideal,
For my soul's eyes? Will that light come again,
As now these tears come – falling hot and real?

XXXI

Thou comest! all is said without a word.
I sit beneath thy looks, as children do
In the noon-sun, with souls that tremble through
Their happy eyelids from an unaverred
Yet prodigal inward joy. Behold, I erred
In that last doubt! and yet I cannot rue
The sin most, but the occasion – that we two
Should for a moment stand unministered
By a mutual presence. Ah, keep near and close,
Thou dovelike help! and, when my fears would rise,
With thy broad heart serenely interpose:
Brood down with thy divine sufficiencies
These thoughts which tremble when bereft of those,
Like callow birds left desert to the skies.

XXXII

The first time that the sun rose on thine oath
To love me, I looked forward to the moon
To slacken all those bonds which seemed too soon
And quickly tied to make a lasting troth.
Quick-loving hearts, I thought, may quickly loathe;
And, looking on myself, I seemed not one
For such man's love! – more like an out-of-tune
Worn viol, a good singer would be wroth
To spoil his song with, and which, snatched in haste,
Is laid down at the first ill-sounding note.
I did not wrong myself so, but I placed
A wrong on *thee*. For perfect strains may float
'Neath master-hands, from instruments defaced, –
And great souls, at one stroke, may do and doat.

XXXIII

Yes, call me by my pet-name! let me hear
The name I used to run at, when a child,
From innocent play, and leave the cowslips piled,
To glance up in some face that proved me dear
With the look of its eyes. I miss the clear
Fond voices which, being drawn and reconciled
Into the music of Heaven's undefiled,
Call me no longer. Silence on the bier,
While I call God – call God! – So let thy mouth
Be heir to those who are now exanimate.
Gather the north flowers to complete the south,
And catch the early love up in the late.
Yes, call me by that name, – and I, in truth,
With the same heart, will answer and not wait.

XXXIV

With the same heart, I said, I'll answer thee
As those, when thou shalt call me by my name –
Lo, the vain promise! is the same, the same,
Perplexed and ruffled by life's strategy?
When called before, I told how hastily
I dropped my flowers or brake off from a game,
To run and answer with the smile that came
At play last moment, and went on with me
Through my obedience. When I answer now,
I drop a grave thought, break from solitude;
Yet still my heart goes to thee – ponder how –
Not as to a single good, but all my good!
Lay thy hand on it, best one, and allow
That no child's foot could run fast as this blood.

XXXXV

If I leave all for thee, wilt thou exchange
And be all to me? Shall I never miss
Home-talk and blessing and the common kiss
That comes to each in turn, nor count it strange,
When I look up, to drop on a new range
Of walls and floors, another home than this?
Nay, wilt thou fill that place by me which is
Filled by dead eyes too tender to know change?
That's hardest. If to conquer love, has tried,
To conquer grief, tries more, as all things prove;
For grief indeed is love and grief beside.
Alas, I have grieved so I am hard to love.
Yet love me – wilt thou? Open thine heart wide,
And fold within the wet wings of thy dove.

XXXVI

When we met first and loved, I did not build
Upon the event with marble. Could it mean
To last, a love set pendulous between
Sorrow and sorrow? Nay, I rather thrilled,
Distrusting every light that seemed to gild
The onward path, and feared to overlean
A finger even. And, though I have grown serene
And strong since then, I think that God has willed
A still renewable fear ... O love, O troth ...
Lest these enclaspèd hands should never hold,
This mutual kiss drop down between us both
As an unowned thing, once the lips being cold.
And Love, be false! if *he*, to keep one oath,
Must lose one joy, by his life's star foretold.

XXXVII

Pardon, oh, pardon, that my soul should make,
Of all that strong divineness which I know
For thine and thee, an image only so
Formed of the sand, and fit to shift and break.
It is that distant years which did not take
Thy sovranty, recoiling with a blow,
Have forced my swimming brain to undergo
Their doubt and dread, and blindly to forsake
Thy purity of likeness and distort
Thy worthiest love to a worthless counterfeit:
As if a shipwrecked Pagan, safe in port,
His guardian sea-god to commemorate,
Should set a sculptured porpoise, gills a-snort
And vibrant tail, within the temple-gate.

XXXVIII

First time he kissed me, he but only kissed
The fingers of this hand wherewith I write;
And ever since, it grew more clean and white,
Slow to world-greetings, quick with its 'Oh, list',
When the angels speak. A ring of amethyst
I could not wear here, plainer to my sight,
Than that first kiss. The second, passed in height
The first, and sought the forehead, and half missed,
Half falling on the hair. O beyond meed!
That was the chrism of love, which love's own crown,
With sanctifying sweetness, did precede.
The third upon my lips was folded down
In perfect, purple state; since when, indeed,
I have been proud and said, 'My love, my own'.

XXXIX

Because thou hast the power and own'st the grace
To look through and behind this mask of me
(Against which years have beat thus blanchingly
With their rains), and behold my soul's true face,
The dim and weary witness of life's race, —
Because thou hast the faith and love to see,
Through that same soul's distracting lethargy,
The patient angel waiting for a place
In the new Heavens, — because nor sin nor woe,
Nor God's infliction, nor death's neighbourhood,
Nor all which others viewing, turn to go,
Nor all which makes me tired of all, self-viewed, —
Nothing repels thee, . . . Dearest, teach me so
To pour out gratitude, as thou dost, good!

XL

Oh, yes! they love through all this world of ours!
I will not gainsay love, called love forsooth.
I have heard love talked in my early youth,
And since, not so long back but that the flowers
Then gathered, smell still. Mussulmans and Giaours
Throw kerchiefs at a smile, and have no ruth
For any weeping. Polypheme's white tooth
Slips on the nut if, after frequent showers,
The shell is over-smooth, — and not so much
Will turn the thing called love, aside to hate
Or else to oblivion. But thou art not such
A lover, my Belovèd! thou canst wait
Through sorrow and sickness, to bring souls to touch,
And think it soon when others cry 'Too late'.

XLI

I thank all who have loved me in their hearts,
With thanks and love from mine. Deep thanks to all
Who paused a little near the prison-wall
To hear my music in its louder parts
Ere they went onward, each one to the mart's
Or temple's occupation, beyond call.
But thou, who, in my voice's sink and fall
When the sob took it, thy divinest Art's
Own instrument didst drop down at thy foot
To hearken what I said between my tears, . . .
Instruct me how to thank thee! Oh, to shoot
My soul's full meaning into future years,
That *they* should lend it utterance, and salute
Love that endures, from Life that disappears!

XLII

'*My future will not copy fair my past*' –
I wrote that once; and thinking at my side
My ministering life-angel justified
The word by his appealing look upcast
To the white throne of God, I turned at last,
And there, instead, saw thee, not unallied
To angels in thy soul! Then I, long tried
By natural ills, received the comfort fast,
While budding, at thy sight, my pilgrim's staff
Gave out green leaves with morning dews impearled.
I seek no copy now of life's first half:
Leave here the pages with long musing curled,
And write me new my future's epigraph,
New angel mine, unhoped for in the world!

XLIII

How do I love thee? Let me count the ways.
I love thee to the depth and breadth and height
My soul can reach, when feeling out of sight
For the ends of Being and ideal Grace.
I love thee to the level of everyday's
Most quiet need, by sun and candle-light.
I love thee freely, as men strive for Right;
I love thee purely, as they turn from Praise.
I love thee with the passion put to use
In my old griefs, and with my childhood's faith.
I love thee with a love I seemed to lose
With my lost saints, – I love thee with the breath,
Smiles, tears, of all my life! – and, if God choose,
I shall but love thee better after death.

XLIV

Belovèd, thou has brought me many flowers
Plucked in the garden, all the summer through
And winter, and it seemed as if they grew
In this close room, nor missed the sun and showers.
So, in the like name of that love of ours,
Take back these thoughts which here unfolded too,
And which on warm and cold days I withdrew
From my heart's ground. Indeed, those beds and bowers
Be overgrown with bitter weeds and rue,
And wait thy weeding; yet here's eglantine,
Here's ivy! – take them, as I used to do
Thy flowers, and keep them where they shall not pine.
Instruct thine eyes to keep their colours true,
And tell thy soul their roots are left in mine.

Two poems by Robert Browning

LIFE IN A LOVE

Escape me?
Never –
Beloved!
While I am I, and you are you,
So long as the world contains us both,
Me the loving and you the loth,
While the one eludes, must the other pursue.
My life is a fault at last, I fear:
It seems too much like a fate, indeed!
Though I do my best I shall scarce succeed.
But what if I fail of my purpose here?
It is but to keep the nerves at strain,
To dry one's eyes and laugh at a fall,
And, baffled, get up and begin again, –
So the chace takes up one's life, that's all.
While, look but once from your farthest bound
At me so deep in the dust and dark,
No sooner the old hope goes to ground
Than a new one, straight to the self-same mark,
I shape me –
Ever
Removed!

IN THREE DAYS

I

So, I shall see her in three days
And just one night, but nights are short,
Then two long hours, and that is morn.
See how I come, unchanged, unworn!
Feel, where my life broke off from thine,
How fresh the splinters keep and fine, –
Only a touch and we combine!

II

Too long, this time of year, the days!
But nights, at least the nights are short.
As night shows where her one moon is,
A hand's-breadth of pure light and bliss,
So life's night gives my lady birth
And my eyes hold her! What is worth
The rest of heaven, the rest of earth?

III

O loaded curls, release your store
Of warmth and scent, as once before
The tingling hair did, lights and darks
Outbreaking into fairy sparks,
When under curl and curl I pried
After the warmth and scent inside,
Thro' lights and darks how manifold –
The dark inspired, the light controlled!
As early Art embrowns the gold.

IV

What great fear, should one say, 'Three days
'That change the world might change as well
'Your fortune; and if joy delays,
'Be happy that no worse befell!'
What small fear, if another says,
'Three days and one short night beside
'May throw no shadow on your ways;
'But years must teem with change untried,
'With chance not easily defied,
'With an end somewhere undescried'.
No fear! – or if a fear be born
This minute, it dies out in scorn.
Fear? I shall see her in three days
And one night, now the nights are short,
Then just two hours, and that is morn.

Index of names

Abelard, Peter, 65

Barrett, Alfred (brother of E.B.B.), 186

Barrett, Arabel (sister of E.B.B.), 53, 69, 84–5, 116, 141, 143, 149, 157, 164–5, 178–9, 186, 192

Barrett, Charles John (Stormie) (brother of E.B.B.), 53, 87, 144, 168

Barrett, Edward Moulton (father of E.B.B.), 25, 29, 32–4, 46, 52–5, 58–9, 61, 69, 84, 87–90, 96, 100–3, 107, 110, 118, 135, 143–6, 153, 155, 158, 173–4, 184, 187, 190, 196–8

Barrett, Edward (brother of E.B.B.), 33–4, 89

Barrett, Elizabeth Barrett, works: Aurora Leigh, 98; Bertha in the Lane, 64; Catarina to Camoens, 118; The Cry of the Children, 100; *An Essay on Mind*, 98; Lady Geraldine's Courtship, 64; *Sonnets from the Portuguese*, 64 n., 65 n., 67 n., 70 n., 73 n., 98 n., 115 n., 120 n., 150 n.

Barrett, George (brother of E.B.B.), 53, 58–9, 90, 169, 187, 190

Barrett, Henrietta (sister of E.B.B.), 70, 84–5, 87–8, 143, 153, 168–9, 188, 194

Barrett, Henry (brother of E.B.B.), 179, 181–2

Barrett, Septimus (brother of E.B.B.), 186.

Bayley, Sarah, 115, 124, 127, 165

Bevan, Mr., 144

Blessington, Lady, 31

Boyd, Hugh Stuart, 192

Browning, Robert, works: *Bells and Pomegranates*, 6, 60 n., 62 n., 86 n., 97 n.; The Bishop Orders his Tomb at St. Praxed's Church, 28, 60; The Boy and the Angel, 28; Claret and Tokay, 28 n.; *Dramatic Romances and Lyrics*, 60 n.; England in Italy, 61; The Flight of the Duchess, 28 n., 60; Garden Fancies, 28; Gismond, 34; Home Thoughts from the Sea, 60; How they brought the Good News from Ghent to Aix, 60; The Laboratory, 28; Life in a Love, 121 n.; The Lost Leader, 60; The Lost Mistress, 61, 62; Luria, 10, 97; Paracelsus, 50, 138; Pauline, 82; Pictor Ignotus, 60; Saul, 36; Sibrandus Schafnaburgensis, 28 n.; Sordello, 28, 86; A Soul's Tragedy, 97

Browning, Robert (father of R.B.), 26, 110, 148, 194–5, 203

Browning, Mrs. (mother of R.B.), 179, 189, 192, 194–5, 203

Browning, Sarianna (sister of R.B.), 194–5, 202–3

Buffon, 3, 94

Byron, George Gordon, Lord, 26

Carlyle, Jane Welsh, 8

Carlyle, Thomas, 8, 10, 93–4

Chambers, Dr., 25, 32, 33

Chorley, Henry Fothergill, 86, 124, 128

Colburn, Henry, 44

Cromwell, Oliver, 93–4

229

For Gran and Grandpa

First published 1984 by
Walker Books Ltd,
184-192 Drummond Street,
London NW1 3HP

© 1984 Helen Oxenbury

First printed 1984
Printed and bound by
L.E.G.O., Vicenza, Italy

British Library Cataloguing in Publication Data
Oxenbury, Helen
Gran and grandpa.–(First picture books)
I. Title II. Series
823'.914[J] PZ7

ISBN 0-7445-0181-4

Gran and Grandpa

Helen Oxenbury

WALKER BOOKS
LONDON

I love visiting my Gran and Grandpa.
I go every week.

'Tell us what you've been doing
all week,' they say.
I tell them everything.
Then sometimes I teach them a new
song I learnt at school. But they
never get the tune quite right.

'Come on, Gran! Let's go and look
at all your things,' I say.
Gran has such interesting drawers
and boxes.

'How are your tomatoes, Grandpa?'
'I've saved you the first ripe one
   to pick,' he says.

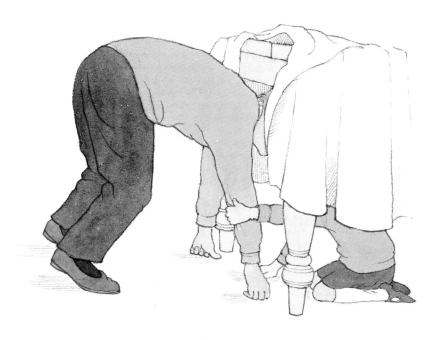

'I'll get the lunch now,' says Gran.
'Come and make a house with me,
 Grandpa,' I say.

'Lunch is ready!' calls Gran.
Grandpa can't get up.
'You shouldn't play these games
at your age,' Gran tells him.

'We could play hospitals now,'
I say after lunch.
Gran and Grandpa let me do
anything to them.

'I'll just get more bandages,' I say.
When I get back they're both asleep.
So I watch television quietly
until Dad comes.